ARKTIKA

ARKTIKA

*Through the North East Passage
by Icebreaker*

OLIVER WALSTON

SINCLAIR-STEVENSON

First published in Great Britain in 1994
by Sinclair-Stevenson
an imprint of Reed Consumer Books Ltd
Michelin House, 81 Fulham Road, London SW3 6RB
and Auckland, Melbourne, Singapore and Toronto

A CIP catalogue record for this book
is available at the British Library

ISBN 1 85619 253 9

Typeset by CentraCet Limited, Cambridge
Printed and bound in Great Britain by
Mackays of Chatham PLC, Chatham, Kent

Contents

List of Illustrations

Acknowledgements

Looking backwards, which is an occupation I have always found easy, it is obvious that the person I should thank first is a nameless man who probably worked in the Lubyanka. Quite why the KGB decided it was time for a foreigner to go through the North East Passage I shall never know. But I salute him, whoever he is.

Then there was Vladimir Yevseyev of the Murmansk Shipping Company. Not only was he my first contact with *Arktika*, but he and his wife Lucy gave me shelter, a memorable fiftieth birthday party and, best of all, friendship.

The crew of *Arktika* numbered 157 people. I thank them all. They are the finest and most generous bunch of people I have ever met. Among them Grigorii Ulitin, Alexander Barinof, Sergei Sidorenko, Maxim Shumilov and Valerii Losef were splendid seamen who became good comrades in the pre-1917 sense of the word.

Back in England I was lucky to have a neighbour who happened to know more about the Soviet Arctic than any human being outside Russia. Dr Terence Armstrong read the manuscript and made lots of valuable comments. So also did two improbably literate farmers, Simon Gourlay and Marie Skinner. None of them is in any way responsible for the errors and infelicities which remain.

While I was wandering through the eight seas between Murmansk and Vladivostock the farm back at Thriplow kept going. For this I must thank Dave Gould, Ted King, Dick Arbon, Lindsay Anderson and Gillett *père et fils*, Stan and Brian.

But most of all I thank my wife, Anne, to whom this book is dedicated. As a business partner, sleeping partner, drinking partner, deflater, reflater and friend she is beyond compare.

Thriplow Farm
November 1993

For it is also in man's nature
to wish to see and experience
the things that he has heard about
and thus to learn
whether the facts are as told or not.

From 'The King's Mirror',
a thirteenth-century Norwegian
seafaring chronicle

For Anna (*as the Russians call her*)
Lowell Walston

Introduction

A Cambridgeshire farmer standing alone on an ice floe in the East Siberian Sea is even more improbable than an Eskimo on a traffic island in Oxford Street. Some explanation is required.

It all started a few years earlier on a soft East Anglian autumn afternoon. The tractor turned at the headland, lowered the plough into the ground and burbled slowly back down the field. The last strip of stubble was being converted into brown earth. The plough had reached the hedge which marked the boundary of my farm.

A few months later I found myself in Prince Albert, Saskatchewan, where I was lecturing the local farmers on the delights of European agriculture and, even more enticing, European subsidies. After the meeting a man approached me with a question about fertiliser rates or pesticides and we started talking about his farm. He lived in a place called Carrot River on the edge of the prairies, north of which there was only bush.

That night in my motel I found myself wondering what it would be like to be the man beyond whose farm there was no farming. Somebody somewhere must be the man who farmed further north in Canada than anyone else. If I could find him I would have found the last farmer in Canada.

As it happened, this was not a particularly difficult task. The most northerly cultivated area in Canada is around the small town of High Level, about 600 kilometres north of Edmonton. Since there are fewer than a dozen farmers in High Level, it was a simple job finding out which of them farmed furthest north.

The view from downtown High Level might not have been as majestic as that peak in Darien, but as I looked along the main street to where a few scraggly birch trees marked the beginning of the bush, I knew just how Cortez must have felt.

Gene Dextrase was a quiet, shy man who combined farming with school teaching. He wasn't impressed by visitors who asked stupid questions.

'Are you aware,' I enquired in a voice which I intended to be portentous but succeeded only in being pretentious, 'that you are the most northerly farmer in Canada?'

'Well,' said Gene, 'I can't pretend I've ever thought about it, but if you say so, I guess you're right.'

It was time for me to see the last field on the last farm in Canada. We bumped down a rutted track in Gene's pick-up truck before stopping beside an open space of maybe fifteen hectares which was surrounded on two sides by low, scrubby birch trees.

'Here we are,' said Gene, with as much enthusiasm as he would have displayed had he been showing me his septic tank.

I had one more question.

'Why,' I wondered, 'did you stop ploughing here,' pointing to where the scrub began, 'and not a yard or a mile in that direction?'

'Gee,' said Gene, 'I don't really know. Maybe it was because the land was getting a little too wet and boggy.' He paused. 'Or maybe it was lunchtime.'

*

High Level, which had felt like a suburb of the North Pole, is in fact south of Oslo. Gene Dextrase might have been the last farmer in Canada but he certainly wasn't the last farmer in the world.

Thanks to the Gulf Stream, the most northerly farmer in the world must, I figured, be somewhere along the coast of Norway. The solution was simple. I would fly to Tromsø in northern Norway and, having rented a car, would drive to the North Cape, at which point I would turn round and drive back to Tromsø. The first farmer I saw on my return journey would have to be the last farmer in the world.

I reached the North Cape with no problems, waited with a sweating swarm of Dutch cyclists for the midnight sun to appear from behind the clouds (it never did), and headed south again.

After breakfast the next morning I saw a man forking hay in a small meadow beside the road. I was lucky because, unlike most Norwegians in the northern part of the country, Karl Karlsen spoke some English. He kept six cows and thirty sheep and was definitely a professional farmer, even if he did do some fishing too. But he was adamant that he was not the most northerly farmer in Norway. Somewhere over to the east, he said, were other farmers to the north of him. This was extremely frustrating, as it had instantly invalidated my entire thesis.

When I came to the next farm my luck began to change. There in the farmyard was the local vet who, together with the artificial inseminator, was making a house call. They found my request all too simple.

'No problem,' said the inseminator, with his arm hidden inside a patient (in both senses) cow, 'I cover the whole of Finnmark and I know all the herds in the region. The man you're looking for is called Jenssen. He lives on Bekkarfjord, nearly a day's drive from here.'

Steinar Jenssen was milking his eleven Norwegian Red cows, some of whom were wearing bovine brassières to support their very large udders. His wife, wearing a red woolly hat, was helping him in the cow stalls which occupied the ground floor of the barn. In the loft above was stored the fodder so it could be forked down to the cattle through a hole in the floor.

Like Gene Dextrase, Steinar Jenssen had never even considered the possibility of being the last farmer in Norway, let alone the world. When I suggested this to him he grinned.

'I suppose it's possible,' he admitted. 'I certainly don't know of anyone who milks cows north of me, but perhaps there is someone.' He rubbed his chin and continued, 'Mind you, I don't envy them, because it wouldn't be an easy life. Up here we have so little time in the summer. We have to do all our work in three months instead of the six months they have in the south of Norway where the growing season is longer and the winter shorter.'

It was nearly nine in the evening, but the sun was still high in the sky.

'It may seem pleasant for you southerners to see the sun at midnight,' said Jenssen 'but it makes farming difficult. Don't forget that from the middle of November until late January I never see the sun at all. At around lunchtime there's a faint glow in the sky and that's the nearest to daylight we ever get.' Mrs Jenssen nodded wearily.

As I left, Steinar Jenssen was getting into his overalls and his wife had again put on her red woollen cap. I turned to look back across the fjord. There was still snow on the distant mountains and the wind had whipped the water into whitecaps. In the distance I could just make out a small figure walking towards the barn with a bucket in each hand.

xvi

Steinar Jenssen certainly looked like the last farmer in the world.

A few months later I was talking to a man who knew all about reindeer, particularly the special reindeer which live on Svalbard, the islands lying between Norway and the North Pole.

'It's a strange part of the world,' he told me. 'Do you know, for example, that the Russian coalminers on Svalbard keep their own cows and pigs so they can have fresh milk and meat?'

This was appalling news; Svalbard was at least 600 kilometres further north than Steinar Jenssen.

Eventually I made the long flight up to Svalbard, landed at Longyearbyen and took a small fishing boat down the coast to the Russian town of Barentsburg. There I met Galina, a buxom lady from the Ukraine whose job was to look after twelve black and white cows. They were housed throughout the year in a well-insulated barn and ate hay which had been shipped in from Leningrad. Galina then showed me the pigs, who also lived indoors but managed to survive on the household scraps which were collected each day from the miners' houses.

On my way home from Svalbard I had to spend the night in Tromsø, which is never a hardship. Home of the most northern university in the world (and just about the most northern everything else as well), Tromsø is on an island connected to the mainland by two ethereal bridges. The houses, built on the steep hillside which runs down to the waterfront, are wooden, painted in pale blues, greens and yellows. My only problem was that I had, by accident, booked myself into the only temperance hotel in town. As a result I spent the evening in one of the bars along the waterfront and drank lots of excellent Mack Beer, brewed (inevitably) by the most northerly brewery in the world.

As I was drinking my second litre, accompanied by desiccated strips of cod which smelled bad and tasted worse, I realised that the two men sitting opposite were speaking English. They turned out to be the British and American naval attachés from Oslo and were in town for an event which was taking place the next day.

The new Russian nuclear icebreaker, *Vaygach*, was due to call in at Tromsø on her maiden voyage from Leningrad, where her reactor had been installed, to Murmansk where she was to be based. This information excited me greatly. Ever since I had started wandering round the Canadian north country I had become increasingly interested – obsessed even – in the Arctic. I had travelled through Alaska, from Nome on the Bering Straits to Prudhoe Bay on the north slope where the Trans Alaska Pipeline begins. I had spent two weeks in Arctic Canada, starting at Inuvik on the Beaufort Sea and making my way up to the country's most northerly settlement, Grise Fiord on the southern coast of Ellesmere Island. The one part of the Arctic which had remained unattainable was the Siberian coastline.

The next day I found myself sitting with fifty Norwegian businessmen in the large and airy lecture theatre aboard *Vaygach*. The Murmansk Shipping Company, owners of the icebreaker, were not simply showing off their new ship, they were trying to make money. Lots of money.

Their message was simple. The North East Passage along the top of Siberia was the shortest route from Europe to the Far East. It would cut ten days off the journey from Hamburg through the Suez Canal to Tokyo. So not only would it be quicker, it would also be cheaper. And now, thanks to perestroika and the fleet of nuclear icebreakers, the North East Passage was definitely open for business.

xviii

The President of the Murmansk Shipping Company looked like Central Casting's idea of a Politburo member. As wide as he was tall, he wore a dark blue suit and a deep-brimmed hat. He stood behind the lectern and read a tedious prepared speech about the economic advantage of the North East Passage, or Northern Sea Route as he called it. The lecture over, he took questions from the audience. At least in theory he took questions. In practice the man who answered was the same man who had translated the President's speech, a good-looking, slender, grey-haired Russian who spoke English with a faint American accent.

After the questions were over I went up to the translator, congratulated him on his English and exchanged visiting cards. His name was Vladimir Yevseyev. When I returned to England I wrote Vladimir a letter. Would it, I asked, be possible for me to travel through the North East Passage on a nuclear icebreaker?

Nine months and a fistful of telexes later, the answer came back.

Da.

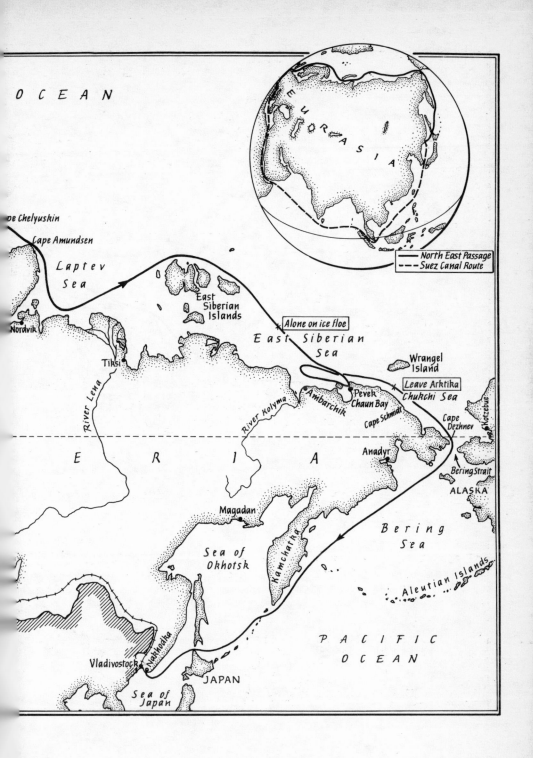

O C E A N

Cape Chelyuskin
Cape Amundsen

Laptev
Sea

Nordvik

Tiksi

River Lena

East
Siberian
Islands

Alone on ice floe

East Siberian
Sea

Wrangel
Island

Leave Arktika

River Kolyma

Ambarchik

Pevek
Chaun Bay

Chukchi Sea

Cape Schmidt

Kotzebue

Cape
Dezhnev

S B E R I A

Anadyr

Bering Strait

ALASKA

Magadan

Kamchatka

Bering
Sea

Sea of
Okhotsk

Aleutian Islands

P A C I F I C

O C E A N

Vladivostock

Nakhodka

JAPAN

Sea of
Japan

EURASIA

North East Passage
Suez Canal Route

1 Boris Gleb

The customs officer picked his nose, examined the findings
and glanced at the Norwegian who put his duffle bag on to
the conveyor belt. I waited until it had disappeared into
the X-ray machine before doing the same. The nose-picker
sat upright in his chair, wiped his finger on his trousers
and pushed a button which reversed the belt. There was a
pause while he stared at the screen.

'No good,' he said, 'You must open.'

A younger man with pianist's fingers and bad teeth
joined him in front of the screen and together they studied
the two rows of five ovoids which appeared next to the
electric razor in the corner of my suitcase. He pointed to
the shapes and, as he did so, pulled an imaginary pin from
an imaginary hand grenade, lobbed it into the corner of the
shed and covered his ears.

'Bombs,' he announced. 'Very bad.'

By this time my fellow travellers, a group of Norwegians
on their way to a Russian language course in Murmansk,
were pushing forward for a better view of the hidden hand
grenades. As I dug through layers of clothes and paperback
books I thanked Thor and the other Viking gods that my laundry was clean. A cardboard box tied with string appeared
from under the pyjamas. I presented it to the older Russian.

1

'No,' he said. 'You open.'

Inside were ten shapes wrapped in Kleenex. I removed the paper and handed one of them to my inquisitor. It was an egg. A very big egg. It was almost four inches tall and, just like a hand grenade, coloured pale khaki.

Earlier that morning I had been doing some last-minute shopping in the best fishmonger's in Tromsø.

'You're in luck,' said Mr Dragoy, 'we still have a few gulls' eggs left, but it's the end of the season so there won't be any more.' Norwegian food is usually boring, but there are a few things which excite me and Mr Dragoy sells them all. I had bought prawns fresh from the waters around Svalbard, gravad lax which Dragoy makes himself and, best of all, the ten Arctic gulls' eggs. Every year, for a few weeks in early summer, the most foolhardy boys in northern Norway scramble down the cliffs to liberate these eggs from the gulls' nests. Most seem to find their way to Mr Dragoy's shop, where they are treated like caviar and sold at a similar price.

The reason for my shopping binge was not simply gluttony. It happened to be my fiftieth birthday and I was looking forward to a small party in Murmansk that night.

Like Checkpoint Charlie and the bridge at Lo Wu, the border crossing at Boris Gleb is an icon of the Cold War. Deep in a lake-bespattered pine forest, it is the only point at which a European NATO country actually touched the Soviet Union. Nevertheless, its significance was more theoretical than actual. For three decades the red and green striped barrier was rarely lifted. The only regular activity was the monthly meeting of the Norwegian-Russian Border Commission, when medalled officers with polished shoes would meet around a green baize table either in Boris Gleb or on the Norwegian side at Storskoog, to discuss such important matters as where the reindeer had damaged the

2

fence. The business over, they would, depending on which side of the border they met, toast each other in aquavit or vodka before saluting and marching back under the barrier to their barracks.

That morning Boris Gleb had all the outward and visible signs of a real border post. Even at 4 a.m., under an Arctic summer sun, the KGB border guards with green bands round their hats looked almost amicable as they herded the Norwegians into an orderly queue. Inside the wooden hut were posters of the Kremlin after dark, a Siberian snowscape and Tamerlaine's tomb in Samarkand.

Eventually my hand grenades were accepted as eggs and I clambered up into a battered brown bus with steamed-up windows which was waiting to take us to the nearby town of Nikel, where the Murmansk train was due to leave at 6 a.m.

We bumped along the forest track while the Norwegians sang songs and I looked at the iron curtain. My neighbour, a red-faced blond man, offered me a swig from his hip flask.

'I am Olaf,' he announced. 'I have made this from berries. It is good.' I didn't doubt it for a moment, but at 5 a.m. on an empty stomach the thought made me retch. 'You'll be sorry,' said Olaf. 'You won't be able to buy vodka in Murmansk. Gorbachev's rationed the stuff.'

We passed a watchtower and Olaf's friend from across the aisle interrupted the homily on alcohol. 'If I were a Russian I'd get drunk all day. For a start it keeps the bloody cold out, and in these parts that's no bad thing.' Since it was a soft summer morning I found it hard to imagine the scene he described. 'I did my military service up here,' he continued, 'and I couldn't wait to get back to Trondheim where I come from. Mind you, the Russians have it far worse. For example, they don't have any heating in their watchtowers. One day we were watching their post

3

through binoculars and we saw them throw something out. It looked like a large piece of timber until we realised it was a soldier who'd died the night before. He'd frozen stiff and they couldn't carry him down the ladder so they simply chucked him out.'

On the Russian side the border consisted of three separate fences two hundred metres apart. Between them were raked strips of earth which would show any footprints to the patrols. The outer two fences were of wire mesh three metres high, while the innermost one was made of both electrified and barbed wire. Along its eastern side pairs of soldiers patrolled with dogs.

The bus tottered up a gentle slope from which I could see in all directions. Ahead of us, spewing dark grey smoke, were the chimneys of Nikel. On the far side of the town it appeared as if a forest fire had just been put out. The landscape was uniformly black and the trees had been reduced to stumps. As we approached, it became clear that the damage had been caused not by fire but by the pollution from Nikel, blown eastward by the wind. It looked like a set from *All Quiet on the Western Front*. The fumes had killed every living thing. The forest had died and nothing had grown. Blackened tree stumps stood on black hills through which black streams ran down to a black river.

Nikel was the dirtiest place I have ever seen. Filthier by far than the worst of the coalmining towns in Polish Silesia, it also appeared to be dead. Tattered curtains flapped through broken windows. A single lorry was parked on the main street; both its front tyres had been removed and the windscreen was cracked. The lights were on in the local *gastronom* (food shop) and the window display consisted of a pyramid of tinned cabbage from Bulgaria. There was no sign of a customer. The bus shelter had been destroyed – maybe because there were no buses. Only the

4

curling plumes of smoke from the nickel smelter's chimneys showed that something was moving in Nikel that day.

Eventually our bus stopped beside a railway line on the edge of town. On the other side was a gully in which black, slimy water oozed past cigarette packets and old lorry tyres. No platform and no buildings marked the spot from which the Moscow train departed. This, nonetheless, was Nikel's *vauxhall*.[1]

Six grimy green carriages were waiting. Their lace curtains were grey flecked with brown and the windows were so smeared that from inside the train it was hard to see more than a blurred outline of the surrounding countryside. Looking at the landscape I knew what it would be like to have cataracts.

Two filthy blue diesel engines approached the train. Like Thomas the Tank Engine's friend Gordon, they were clearly in a bad mood, because they backed on to the carriages with a bump which knocked my neighbour's rucksack out of the luggage rack on to his head. A few minutes later the driver repeated this trick by starting off with an even more ferocious jerk.

One slight consolation was the presence of a dining car in which a platoon of soldiers were eating borscht and black bread. A florid waiter, whose shirt was open to the navel (not as a sartorial statement but simply because it had no buttons), placed a plate of cucumber, sour cream and half a boiled egg in front of me. The main course consisted of fatty strips of meat, carrots, beetroot and spuds. It was hot and good. One of the Norwegians asked

[1] A Russian delegation came to England in the early nineteenth century to study the railway system. For some reason they arrived at Vauxhall station in south London and, as a result, this has become the Russian word for station.

for bread and, after a long interval, the waiter reappeared with slices of both white and grey loaves wrapped delicately in tissue paper. He then rather spoilt the hygienic illusion by picking up two slices, inspecting both sides and dropping them abruptly on to the table.

From the outside, our train may have looked like any other in the Soviet Union, but when we came to pay the bill it was evident that we were on board a sophisticated international express. Or so the waiter insisted when he refused to accept roubles and demanded dollars. To the fury of my friends, he also refused Norwegian kroner.

The waiter wasn't the only businessman on board. A series of men, all dressed in black tracksuits and Adidas trainers, wandered up and down the wide corridor hawking vodka, Georgian champagne and what they claimed was caviar. Their headquarters appeared to be the small compartment next to the samovar where the female attendant supposedly brewed tea for the passengers. In practice she did nothing of the sort; her time was fully occupied entertaining her entrepreneurial accomplices.

We arrived in Murmansk eight hours after leaving Nikel. For a 200-kilometre trip this meant we averaged 25 kph, which should get us an entry in *The Guinness Book of Records* for the slowest scheduled train ride in the world.

The station in Murmansk, pale green with a large dome surmounted by the inevitable red star, occupies a footnote in Russian history. It was here in May 1918, after the final consolidation of Soviet power, that Alexander Kerensky arrived from Moscow, travelling in disguise on an 'extraterritorial' train carrying Serbian officers who were being repatriated. Arriving in what he described as a 'drab, deserted town', which was under the control of the Soviets even though it was still occupied by the last remnants of the allied armies, he made his way to the French cruiser

General Hobe, where he refused the offer of a rest and instead had the ship's barber shave off his beard. A few days later, the man who had been the first – and so far only – democratic Prime Minister of Russia went on board a British trawler which took him to Thurso. Kerensky lived for another forty-seven years, but never returned to Russia.

Vladimir Yevseyev, wearing a leather jacket and looking like one of Marlon Brando's mates in *The Wild Ones*, recognised me – which was just as well since I had forgotten what he looked like since I had last seen him in Tromsø a year before. Ten minutes later the Murmansk Shipping Company's Volkswagen minibus dropped us in a courtyard surrounded by tall apartment blocks. As he entered the front door, Vladimir turned and said, 'Please be careful where you step. We have trouble with the drains.' A dark and foul-smelling puddle stood where a doormat might have been.

The Yevseyevs lived on the top floor with views out over Murmansk. In front lay the docks and the railway lines and behind, far off in the distance, a shallow hill surmounted by a 25-metre slab-sided statue of a helmeted Russian soldier.

'It is our war memorial,' said Vladimir, as he poured me a vodka. 'We are good at war memorials in this country.'

At that moment the front door burst open and a torrent of Russian preceded the speaker. 'This is Lucy,' explained Vladimir. A plumpish woman with dark red hair and a beauty spot on her right cheek looked me up and down as she removed her coat. 'Lucy speaks no English,' said Vladimir, 'but she would like you to stay with us and not in a hotel.' I was about to accept this offer when Lucy took the initiative by enfolding me in a warm, long and, unless she was an exceptional actress, heartfelt hug.

When Lucy hugs you, you stayed hugged. I liked her.

I liked Vladimir, too, although he had a reserve which seemed more than just shyness. There was an element of mystery about him which I found puzzling. He had travelled prodigiously. After he had told me about the years he and Lucy had spent in Hyderabad where they were manufacturing MiG aircraft for the Indian government, I suggested that he was probably a member of the KGB.

'Who me?' replied Vladimir, his eyebrows raised. 'They wouldn't stand a guy like me for more than a moment.'[2]

Murmansk, like the rest of Russia, was in ferment. The next day was the first election ever to be held in the USSR, and if you looked hard you could even see signs of it. On the glass doors of the public library a colour poster for Boris Yeltsin had been stuck up with sellotape. Why, I wondered, did nobody take it down from what was, after all, a public building?

'Because,' replied Vladimir, 'the people who work in the library must like Yeltsin.'

The four-storey House of Political Education, which had been used occasionally as a VIP hotel, was being prepared as a polling station. Here the posters were for the politically correct candidate, the former Prime Minister, Nikolai Ryzhkov.

'We call him the blubbing Bolshevik,' said Vladimir, referring to a recent incident in which he had been reported as having wept.

We walked up a wide staircase to the second floor to where a peroxide blonde with vermilion lipstick sat silently behind a long, empty table. I asked Vladimir if I could take a Ryzhkov poster as a souvenir. After a brief

2 Some months later a friend who is experienced in such matters explained the position to me. 'There's really only one answer to the question "Are you a member of the KGB?" It has to be "No". But as a general rule the intelligent Russians you meet in London are probably KGB and the charming ones are the spies.'

8

exchange, the blonde led me up two more floors to where the Murmansk version of *Citizens for Ryzhkov* had its offices.

'Take whatever you want,' she said grandly, gesturing to a horseshoe table full of primitive political propaganda. I scooped up a selection and, as I left, asked her if she happened to know where the Yeltsin headquarters was. 'No,' was the brisk reply. It had, I realised, been a stupid question.

Fiftieth birthday parties are usually memorable, but this one was unforgettable. Alexander, the Yevseyevs' son-in-law, joined us and apologised because his wife, Anna, was out of town. We sat on the sofa and Lucy put Julio Iglesias on the tape deck while we drank our first vodka. Then came the gulls' eggs, cooked according to Dragoy's instructions: place in cold water and remove twelve minutes after the water boils. Their whites were ethereal and softer than any hen's egg. I wished I had brought celery salt. Then gravad lax with Dragoy's delicate dill sauce. Lucy had also bought some Russian salmon, which was very salty and went well with white bread and lashings of Norwegian butter. More vodka and back to serious eating. This time pickled cabbage with dill and cranberries, tomatoes, spring onions and whole cloves of garlic. And all washed down by *kompot*, a fruit juice which Lucy had made from their own garden in the Ukraine. Served from an earthenware bottle, it was made by boiling dried apples and cherries.

After many toasts we reached the present-giving stage. Vladimir went to the bedroom and returned with three paintings Alexander had done of Murmansk. Two were scenes of the harbour and one a close-up of the waterfront. I was particularly touched because that afternoon I had seen some paintings of Murmansk in a book shop and had casually said that I would like one. I also received a book

9

of Russian poems and a chunk of amethyst on which was mounted a pen.

It was almost midnight when Vladimir and I decided to go for a brief walk before bed. Murmansk looked the way ports ought to look, but rarely do these days. No nonsense with containers. Rows and rows of tall cranes like storks standing on one leg lined the shore just as they once did in London, Liverpool or Hamburg. The occasional ship's hooter sounded. Off in the distance, bathed in midnight sunlight, was a low range of snow-covered hills on the far side of the Kola River.

The next morning, without a trace of a hangover, the Yevseyevs walked the 100 metres across the park to the polling station. On the door somebody had put up a poster which showed a young woman (representing Russia) knocking on the outside of a window. Indoors was a pyjama-clad man lying in bed. The caption read, 'Wake up. Go and vote. Your country's future is in your hands.'

We climbed one flight of stairs to a row of tables where the supervisors were sitting. Vladimir and Lucy showed their passports and were issued with ballot papers containing the names of the six presidential candidates. Instead of placing a cross beside your preferred candidate, Vladimir explained that you had to cross out the names of the five you did not want to vote for. A small queue had gathered in front of the polling booths and we waited in line. When his turn came Vladimir took both ballot papers, drew the curtain behind him and emerged a few seconds later. He put one of the ballot papers into a box and, instead of giving the other to Lucy, presented it to me.

'Here,' he said, 'Lucy would like you to have it as a souvenir of this, the first election in Russia.'

I stammered a *spaseba*. To have a validated but unused

10

ballot paper is rare in any election. This one, I reflected, might even be unique.

After all this democracy it was time for business and Vladimir took me to his office at the Murmansk Shipping Company to find out the latest news about my icebreaker. *Arktika*, it seemed, was nearing the end of her annual refit and was due to sail within forty-eight hours.

As I sat at a long conference table in a room full of modern Finnish furniture, Vladimir suddenly became very serious. 'Please do not be offended,' he began. 'You must remember that you are the first foreigner to be permitted through the North East Passage for over fifty years and the authorities are, I suppose, a little bit nervous. The last non-Russians to do what you are about to do were the crew of the German armed raider, *Komet*. It was in the summer of 1940, during the time of the Hitler-Stalin pact and we helped the ship go from Norway through into the Pacific.'

The story of *Komet* was the stuff of Hornblower adventures. Built just before the war, she was one of a small group of ships which outwardly looked like a tramp steamer. Yet below her hatches were enough guns and torpedoes to threaten a cruiser.

Komet sailed from Bergen on 9 July 1940, under the command of Robert Eyssen. Her orders were to go through the North East Passage to the Bering Straits and into the Pacific, where she should wander through the shipping lanes looking for unarmed allied freighters. If approached by an allied warship she would disguise herself and pretend to be a neutral vessel.

After waiting in the Barents Sea for a month while ice conditions improved, *Komet* eventually met up with the two Soviet icebreakers, *Stalin* and *Lenin*, on 13 August. Poor Captain Eyssen, whose ship was running on Central European Time, was invited to a party by the Russian

11

captains, whose ships were on local time. The result was that the German officer found that he was expected to drink vodka at what for him was six o'clock in the morning. After this hiccup, the voyage went smoothly until 31 August. They had passed Cape Chelyuskin and had been met by the icebreaker *Kaganovich* when the Russians received orders to turn around and bring *Komet* back with them to Europe. It appeared that the Soviet admiralty had received reports that the Americans were keeping a close watch on the Bering Straits and that they even had warships patrolling off Wrangel Island.

Eyssen refused to turn back and, accepting all liability for whatever might befall him, pressed on eastwards without any icebreaker assistance. He made excellent progress and eventually reached the Bering Straits on 10 September. In completing the voyage in twenty-three days, *Komet* broke the record for the North East Passage.

'Since then,' explained Vladimir, 'the Northern Sea Route, as we always call the North East Passage, has been a closed military area.[3] That's why we had to get permission from the Ministry of Defence in Moscow before you were allowed to come here.'

Vladimir seemed to be telling me all this by way of explanation for what he was about to say. 'You won't be surprised, therefore, to hear that there are a few conditions which the KGB insist you accept before you are allowed on board *Arktika*.' Another pause. I was beginning to think I would have to describe the sexual preferences of all the cabinet ministers with whom I had been at school, or promise to take photographs of a North Sea oil rig. 'You

---

[3] The last time foreign surface ships attempted to go through at least part of the North East Passage was in 1967 when the American icebreakers *Edisto* and *Eastwind* were refused permission to pass through the Vilkitsky Straits.

12

must first write your objectives down on a piece of paper. Then you must agree to let the KGB process any photographs which you take during the voyage. This will be done in Vladivostock.'

I agreed enthusiastically, relieved at having been let off so lightly.

'And now,' continued Vladimir, 'I must ask you some questions.' I braced myself. 'Do you have a Geiger counter?' I did not. 'Good,' replied Vladimir, visibly relieved. 'The KGB expected that you would bring one.' Another pause. He was clearly building up to something difficult. 'Do you have a video camera?' No, I replied. Only a still camera. 'Good,' repeated Vladimir. 'That is all.'

On our way back to the flat for lunch, Vladimir suggested that we take a slightly roundabout route as there was something he felt I should see. We drove up the steep hill, at the summit of which towered the granite soldier war memorial, and then down into a shallow valley where a neatly trimmed hedge and wrought iron gates showed the boundary of the British Naval Cemetery. Rows of white crosses marked the graves of the men who had died on the awful convoys to Murmansk during the last war. The first grave I saw was commemorating Petty Officer Williams. The date of his death was 11 June 1941. It just happened to be the day I had been born.

The afternoon was spent wandering aimlessly around town. I watched queues line up outside the Neptune fish shop, then checked out the contents of the bookstore, which included Ian Fleming's *From Russia with Love* and reproductions of Salvador Dali's *Crucifixion*. The Communist Party headquarters, a white marble modern building, would have looked almost elegant had somebody not written THE BEATLES FOR EVER in red paint along one wall.

That evening in the Murmansk Shipping Company's

restaurant on the quay, we were served by a pretty Ukrainian girl with white teeth and black eyes. When she heard I was a foreigner she became even more animated. 'Do you love Real Madrid?' she kept asking. I replied that I only loved one football club and that was Sunderland, which was a port not entirely unlike Murmansk. 'Murmansk not good. Murmansk dirty, Murmansk cold, Murmansk dark.' I could see her point, but Sunderland doesn't win many prizes for neatness or charm either.

As we came to the end of our half litre of vodka, the man on the neighbouring table, who had been sitting alone all evening, vomited quietly all over the floor. Vladimir, embarrassed that this ancient Russian ritual had taken place in front of a foreigner, hurried me away back to the flat.

After climbing six flights of stairs I slumped down in an armchair. 'How about a vodka?' suggested Vladimir brightly. 'It's the last boat to Istanbul.' I must have looked puzzled. 'Originally,' he explained, 'it referred to the last boat on which the Whites fled from Odessa after the revolution. Today it just means the last chance.'

2 On board

Arktika, together with all the other nuclear-powered ships in Murmansk harbour, was moored in a special area about a kilometre and a half away from the main docks. Our minibus bumped and bounced over potholes which would discomfort even a New Yorker. We passed piles of rusting scrap, discarded wooden reels around which electric cable had once been wound and electricity poles against which old paper had accumulated like tumbleweed on a Montana barbed wire fence. Eventually we reached a corrugated tin shack above which was a notice which said simply 'Atom Fleet'. A rope had been hung across the road to discourage, but certainly not prevent, unauthorised traffic. As I tried to imagine what the entrance to the nuclear base at Norfolk, Virginia must look like, Vladimir knocked on the warped wooden door which was eventually opened by a stout lady in what had once been a white overall.

Inside was another woman wearing one of those white surgical-type caps usually seen in the chocolate factories of Bourneville or Basel. She looked at Vladimir's pass and spoke into the receiver of an ancient telephone. All seemed to be in order and after a few minutes the first woman dropped the rope into a puddle and we drove into the nuclear dockyard.

Arktika was not moored to the quay but instead was attached to another ship called the *Imandra*,[1] across which we had to scramble with my luggage. To do this we had to walk around the hatch covers which had been removed by a large derrick. Into the holds was being lowered a series of stainless steel tubes which had been hoisted out of the bowels of *Arktika*. The crew handling this cargo were all dressed in white like the woman who had just allowed us into the dockyard.

Eventually, after struggling up and down various companionways, we reached *Arktika*, which was instantly recognisable by its dark orange superstructure. As we walked beneath the bows, I noticed that the word *ARKTIKA* had been painted over another name. Vladimir explained. 'For a few years she was called the *Leonid Brezhnev*, but it didn't last long.' It seemed to have lasted long enough for the letters to be welded to the hull.

Arktika was the second atomic icebreaker ever built. Launched in 1975, sixteen years after the *Lenin* had pioneered the technology, her two reactors produce 75,000 horsepower, making her almost twice as powerful as her predecessor. Her dimensions are equally impressive: 148 metres long, 30 metres wide and weighing 21,000 tonnes, *Arktika* was comfortably the biggest and strongest icebreaker in the world when she was built. Since then, she has been joined by her sister ships, *Sibir*, *Rossiya* and *Sovietsky Soyuz*.

I had been allocated cabin No. 13, which was normally

[1] This was the ship which took much of the nuclear waste from Murmansk and dumped it into the ocean off Novaya Zemlya where it lies today, unprotected, on the seabed. *The Economist* has estimated that between 1964 and 1986 7000 tonnes of solid radioactive waste and 1600 cubic metres of liquid waste were taken from the atom base in Murmansk and dumped into the Barents and Kara Seas.

occupied by the first mate: Vladimir assured me he had been re-housed in another cabin. First mates on nuclear icebreakers were clearly well looked after. My suite of three rooms on the starboard corner of the Bridge Deck No. 2 consisted of a living room, bedroom and bathroom. The living room was long and narrow, with three portholes. In it was a fridge big enough to house a pubescent polar bear, a black and white TV set of similar proportions, a sofa and a desk. Along the walls and around the portholes was a jungle of pot plants which the previous occupant had trained to climb along a cat's cradle of string. The carpet was red and striped, the walls pale brown and the curtains orange. There were also lace curtains. *Arktika* was, after all, a Russian ship.

I checked out the drawers and discovered a box of Christmas tree decorations and some sanitary towels. On the wall was a Siberian scene of a stream trickling through a snowy forest.

Adjoining the living room was a small bedroom whose porthole faced forward. It was just large enough for a decent-sized bunk and a built-in wardrobe which contained wire coat hangers and a set of barbells.

My bathroom was particularly interesting. There was a full-sized bath on legs, the sort you see in Edwardian English country houses. More unusual still was the fact that there was a bath plug, an item which in Russia was rarer than caviar and twice as useful. On the bath there was a huge wooden bath rack, not to keep shaving gear, loofahs and flannels but on which to rest an even more enormous plastic bowl. This, I assumed, was for my laundry, because nearby was a packet of detergent called *BIO-C*. Tucked away in a corner was an old-fashioned washboard, the kind on which laundry women once scrubbed

17

clothes and which Lonnie Donegan later adapted as a musical instrument.

There were also various rubber gloves and plastic sponges lying about and looking rather sinister. My feverish imagination assumed that they were for washing radiation off protective clothing. It was odd (and stupid) how one's fears became more lurid on a nuclear-powered ship. For example, every time I went on deck I had to pass two vents which blew warm air out from the bowels of the ship. These, I decided, were coming straight from the hottest part of the reactor room and thus were loaded with radioactivity.

The basin was conventional – but without a plug. The lavatory lowered the tone (and raised the smell) considerably. It was a particularly rancid affair built on German lines with a tray which might have been useful for a medical inspection of motions, but could have had no other possible use. The plumbing surrounding the lavatory looked like something out of the reactor room below decks, except for the fact that it leaked fitfully. The whole contraption was flushed with a pedal which either released a tiny dribble of water or – if I applied all my weight – sent a jet powerful enough to strip paint from the hull.

I had just unpacked my coffee-making equipment when there was a knock at the door. I opened it to find a tall, bearded man wearing a denim jacket and tracksuit bottoms.

'Hello,' he said in that thick way which only Russians can manage. 'My name is Maxim and I am the second mate. Please come with me. The captain wishes to see you.' I followed him up two companionways and entered the captain's cabin, which was directly below the bridge.

Captain Grigorii Alexeivich Ulitin stuck out his hand and beamed. A small, compact, white-haired man of fifty-seven, he was wearing uniform with four gold stripes on his sleeves, a white shirt and black tie. After all the normal pleasantries, he invited me for dinner that evening. 'If you would like,' he began, 'we shall go and visit a friend of mine who is the captain of another nuclear ship in port today.' I agreed enthusiastically.

Two hours later Captain Ulitin and I were seated in the master's cabin of the atomic freighter *Sevmorput*, which was moored a few hundred metres away from *Arktika*. Painted a vivid orange, it stretched for 260 metres and made *Arktika* look small. It was, I learned, the biggest nuclear-powered merchant ship in the world. Built in 1989, it was specifically designed for Arctic work with its ice-breaking bow and strengthened hull. Rather than containers, *Sevmorput*'s cargo consisted of rectangular steel barges, known as lighters, which it was able to drop off and pick up by means of a complicated system of winches over the stern. These barges, having been lowered into the water, would then be towed to one of the many settlements which line the coast and rivers of Arctic Siberia.

Back on board *Arktika*, Ulitin invited me up to his cabin for a quick snack of salami, spam, cucumber and a glass or two of Siberian vodka which was five per cent stronger than the normal Stolichnaya. As we ate we watched the television news. Mrs Thatcher had arrived in Moscow and was talking to Gorbachev, and the British astronaut, Helen Sharman, had returned to earth.

I asked the captain what *Arktika*'s mission would be. He grinned.

'I know what I have been told today, but that may not be the same as I am told tomorrow.' Seeing that I was puzzled, he explained, 'Ice conditions change so fast and so often that we sometimes don't know what we are going to be doing until a day or two before.' For the time being, his orders were to take *Arktika* east to the port of Pevek near where some cargo ships from Vladivostock would be waiting to be escorted westwards again through the ice to various ports along the Siberian coast.

What, I wondered, would happen to me when we reached Pevek?

'Oh, don't worry about that. We'll find you a ship which will be going back east and I'm sure they will have a bunk for you. But don't ask me what will happen after that. I'm only an icebreaker captain and not a travel agent.'

I had never heard of Pevek, so when I returned to my cabin I looked at the map. Lying between the Kolyma River and the Bering Straits, it appeared to be the last major port in eastern Siberia. I shut my eyes and tried to imagine what it looked like, but all I could see were polar bears. Not surprisingly, I slept well that night.

Sometime that evening a handwritten document went up on the ship's notice board, announcing the election results on *Arktika*. Not every crew member voted.

The votes were cast for the following candidates:

Yeltsin	117
Gerinovsky	11
Ryzhkov	6
Toleyev	5
Bakatin	3
Markashov	1

The next day I went out in the early morning sunshine. The glossy dark green hatch covers over the nuclear reactors were being swept by two crewmen using bunches of birch twigs. It seemed to sum up the Soviet Union.

Arktika was not a beautiful ship in the conventional sense. Her bows were the normal icebreaker shape, falling almost vertically at first before raking steeply backwards just above the waterline. It was this section which acted as the blade to cut through the ice. The hull had a pronounced curve which meant that the middle decks were wider than either the upper or the lower ones. This is a characteristic of all ships designed to withstand heavy ice. A curve is, of course, much stronger than a flat side, as anyone who has tried to squeeze an egg will know.

At first glance, the stern did not look exceptional. Only when I got close to it did I notice that it had been cut into a deeply indented notch. This was for a practical reason: it enabled *Arktika* to tow a ship through the ice by lashing its bows tightly and securely into the notch on our stern.

Above the stern was a helicopter deck, on which sat an orange and blue MI-2 helicopter with the word *Aeroflot* painted in big black letters. At the forward end of the deck was a hangar with large sliding doors.

I was having my first coffee of the morning when a tall, good-looking officer appeared. He had soft mousy hair, a slightly weak chin and a shy smile.

'You are Oliver,' he said in a passable English. I agreed. 'This is your key.' I must have looked puzzled, as indeed I was. 'I am Sergei Sidorenko. This was my cabin,' he explained, 'but now it is your cabin.' It was my cue to offer a cup of coffee. Sergei refused. 'No,' he said, 'I have a better idea. Come with me to the cabin of the second captain. He is making coffee now.'

Alexander Barinov looked far too young to be second captain of *Arktika*. He had a black bushy beard, even bushier black hair, twinkling eyes and a beer belly which would have done credit to a Bavarian.

'There's an old Russian naval saying,' said Alexander, pointing to his waistline. 'A sailor without a gut is like a barge without a cargo.'

Both officers wanted to know what I was doing on *Arktika*. With the exception of a Japanese television crew which had spent three days on the ship some years ago, they had never seen a foreigner on board. I explained that I was a farmer who happened to like the Arctic.

'A peasant?' asked Alexander. 'Like a man who plants crops and keeps animals?'

As I was trying to explain how large my farm was, it occurred to me that they would understand if I told them I was a *kulak* (a prosperous farmer who employed labourers) and not a peasant.

'No, you are not a *kulak*,' said Sergei. 'They were not good men. They used to exploit other people. We don't like *kulaks*.'

I persisted. I was a *kulak*. I did employ – though I hoped I didn't exploit – other people. I farmed 1200 hectares of land, which was rather more than most peasants. There was a long silence while both officers pondered this information.

'OK,' said Alexander eventually, 'you're a *kulak*.'

Henceforth, throughout the ship I was known as the Kulak.

It was time for lunch, and Alexander led me down one deck to the officers' dining room. At the top of the curving flight of stairs was a vast bronze frieze commemorating the building of *Arktika* in the Baltic Shipyard of Leningrad in 1974. Five metres wide and more than a metre high, the bas-relief was in the finest traditions of Brezhnev Portentous Style, depicting heroic shipyard workers, belching blast furnaces, cranes and all other outward and very visible signs of heavy industrial might and glory. I wondered if the crew found it as embarrassing as they should, then decided they probably didn't even notice it any more.

The captain and his senior officers sat at a table for eight in the centre of the dining room and around them on smaller tables were clustered the navigators, radio officers, electrical and nuclear officers. On the forward wall were two large bronze bas-reliefs of bearded figures who turned out to be Otto Schmidt, a pioneer of Arctic exploration, and Professor Kurchatov, the Father of Soviet Nuclear Power.

Tatiana, Raisa and Oxana were, I discovered, the names of the three ladies who were serving in the officers' dining room. I decided to try out my new-found charm in the shape of goodies from the Cash and Carry in Cambridge and so, without any more foreplay, gave them each a pair of tights. Tatiana, a slightly scrawny, horse-like lady with big teeth and short hair, at first refused, but accepted shyly when I insisted. Raisa had instantly gone to the top of my hit parade by returning my smile the moment I walked into the dining room. A cheerful brunette with thick arms and thin legs, she was overjoyed and went running off to her quarters to stow the booty. Oxana, who was somewhat stockier and required (or so I calculated) the larger size of tights, was not present when I returned with a selection of different merchandise. So I left hers with Tatiana. However, returning to my cabin I passed her on the stairs and went back with her to the pantry where she worked. She was so overwhelmed that she gave me a vast and wet kiss on the cheek.

The food, at least while we were in port, was adequate, consisting of good soup and a main course of meat (very occasionally fish) with either pasta or potatoes. But the quantities were invariably small and no second helpings were ever offered.

For reasons which I never quite understood, I had somehow assumed that *Arktika* would be a dry ship on which no alcohol was permitted. I was, in a perverse sort of way, looking forward to a few weeks without the stuff. My illusions were, however, threatened first by the captain's supply of vodka and then, on my first night aboard, by the sight of one of the female crew collecting bottles in a large plastic bag. Only when Sergei, the first mate, invited me to his cabin for a beer did I realise that *Arktika* was a Russian ship in every sense of the word.

'I only have beer,' he said apologetically. 'As you know, vodka is rationed and since it is near the end of the month I don't have any left.' So we drank beer out of teacups and talked politics. 'Gorbachev is good for the West,' he told me. 'He likes Margaret Thatcher. He likes her very much. You can see that when they are on television together like they were last night. Did you notice his eyes? They were like those of a man in love.' I wondered who would be good for the USSR if Gorbachev was good for the West. 'I think Yeltsin,' was the reply. And then a pause. 'At least, I hope Yeltsin.'

I was getting ready for bed when there was yet another knock at the door.

'You are English,' said a small man with straight hair and soft eyes. 'My name is Sergei Tomilin. May I come in?' He looked at my laptop computer and his eyes lit up. 'We have a computer on board. Maybe you would like to see it. There are many games for it. You would like it very much.' We discussed the relative merits of various computers and I wondered if Sergei would like a coffee. 'Yes, please. But wait.' And so saying, he disappeared down the corridor at a brisk trot. A few minutes later he re-appeared with a large chocolate cake. 'I bought this today in town. We have rations but I will not need them during the trip, so I bought a cake instead.'

Sergei was twenty-eight and had worked on *Arktika* as a nuclear engineer for the past six years.

24

'I have many friends on the other icebreakers,' he told me, 'but they all consider *Arktika* to be the mother ship because this is where most of them were trained.'

Only later in the evening, after he had established how much money I earned, did the conversation switch to his own ambitions.

'My bride and I want to leave the Soviet Union,' he told me conspiratorially, 'and we would like to go to South Africa.' Surprised by this choice of destination, I asked him why.

'It is warm,' replied Sergei, and then paused. 'We know that the black people are fighting,' he said. 'Is this true?'

How had he voted on 12 June, I asked.

'I voted for Yeltsin, but none of them are any good. Gorbachev has done his job and he should go now.' Who should take his place? 'I don't know. There isn't anybody really.'

The next morning there was a lot of activity on the bridge. The captain was walking back and forth impatiently. He was, as usual, wearing his uniform, as were the other officers. Sergei was talking to the shore through a walkie-talkie, and all around the port of Murmansk seemed to have come to life. Every few minutes I could hear a ship's hooter blowing short blasts. Astern of us a diesel submarine was reversing out of the naval base into the channel, leaving a cloud of black smoke behind it.

On our port side a new ship had appeared overnight, a freighter with an icebreaker bow; she was called *Navarin*. Sergei explained that she had returned that night from Antarctica where she had recently become famous in the Soviet Merchant Marine through rescuing two other ships from being trapped in the ice. This heroic aura was slightly spoilt by the fact that her decks were loaded with second-hand Fords, Toyotas and Opels which her crew must have bought at some northern European port. The used car dealers in Hamburg, Bremen or Copenhagen must celebrate when they see a Russian ship on the horizon these days.

The pilot cutter came alongside at 11.30 and deposited two extra people on the bridge. Out on the deck astern of the bridge a seaman hoisted the white and red flag denoting 'We have a Pilot on Board'. There was time for a quick lunch of soup, rissole, spaghetti and yoghurt. Sergei, who sat next to me, was in a sombre mood and I asked him why. He remained silent for a bit, staring into his soup, and then looked me straight in the face.

'I shall miss my wife very much. She is called Galina.' He looked as if he was about to cry, so I clucked sympathetically and tried not to show my embarrassment. 'And Katya too. She is only five. They are very beautiful and I won't see them again until October.'

Half an hour later, up on the bridge, Sergei had pulled himself together. As the ship's chronometer showed exactly midday, Captain Ulitin nodded to him and he pushed the centre of the three throttle levers gently forward. *Arktika*'s bow began to move imperceptibly round towards the western shore. The captain grinned and shrugged his shoulders and Maxim smiled the smile of a man whose long wait was over. We turned 180 degrees to face downstream before increasing speed. Passing pens of what looked like obsolete submarines, and two guided missile carriers, we approached two black and streamlined submarines and the aircraft carrier *Kiev* with its sloping deck and forest of radar.

Behind us all except one of the Soviet nuclear icebreaker fleet was visible. *Lenin*, the world's first atomic icebreaker, was tied up alongside the quay. Built in 1959, she had been taken out of service less than a year earlier and was being converted into a floating museum. *Rossiya*, the newest of

26

Arktika's sister ships, was now alongside the tender, *Iman-dra*. *Sovietsky Soyuz*, another of the *Arktika* class, was still in her dry dock a kilometre or so away up the inlet, while *Taymyr* and *Vygach*, the two new Finnish-built icebreakers with their shallow drafts and slab-like super-structures, were anchored out in the roads. The only nuclear icebreaker missing was the fourth member of the *Arktika* class, *Sibir*.

Sergei pushed the outer two throttles forward and we began to move slowly down the channel between low, olive green, scrubby hills on which the snow still remained in a few sheltered hollows. Off to starboard was the vast war memorial which guards Murmansk. Its triumphant and glorious effect was lessened by the detritus below it on the banks of the inlet. Littering the shore, between the Atom Base and the naval yard, were the carcasses of old warships, rusting and semi-submerged where they had been abandoned.

3 The Barents Sea

Snow flurries were gusting from the north as we approached Severomorsk, the great naval base and headquarters of the Northern Fleet. In the distance I saw a vast floating dock carrying two cruisers, one destroyer and a very streamlined submarine. Still further away, coming up the inlet from the open sea, was another aircraft carrier of the *Kiev* class. Through the binoculars I could see a white-painted number 092 on the funnel.

'That means it's the *Baku*,' announced Maxim.

On the starboard shore was a pale blue hangar with a sloping concrete pad going down to the water on which stood a row of tiny hovercraft. In front of the base itself, as if awaiting inspection by a general from Moscow, were lines of tanks and artillery. And above them all, mounted on a rocky promontory, was an ancient twin-engined flying boat which looked like a World War II Catalina.

To the port side on the slope of a hill was the town of Polyarni. Only the location was picturesque. Grey apartment blocks and squat brown offices were interspersed with factories and warehouses. Ahead was the open sea which appeared just as the cutter came alongside to take off the pilots.

Maxim picked up a microphone and made a brisk

announcement which echoed throughout the ship. I asked him for a translation.

'I told the crew,' he said with a grin, 'that there would be gales soon and they should lash everything down tightly.'

Ahead of us on the horizon was a low grey shape.

'It is one of our warships which places mines,' explained Maxim. 'Our naval forces will exercise here for three days.'

Minutes later I rushed to the porthole to see where a loud noise was coming from. Outside, a four-engined aircraft was flying past us at deck height. Khaki-coloured with a red star on the fuselage, it had a long tail which I assumed was for Anti Submarine radar. This was just the sort of subject which the KGB would appreciate when they processed my film in Vladivostock.

My little short-wave radio was unable to pick up the BBC from inside the cabin, so I went up to the bridge in the hope that someone would help me rig up an antenna. The steersman, with a goatee beard and a mermaid tattooed on his forearm, could not have been more cheerful. The problem was that he had only one word of English, 'Owdo-youdo', which he repeated ceaselessly – happy that at least I understood what he said. I was hardly in a position to be critical, even though by then my Russian vocabulary had expanded to a dozen words. Eventually a combination of sign language and the radio itself prompted him to point me towards a door aft of the bridge. It turned out to be the radio room, in which a lugubrious young man sat in front of an ashtray full of cigarette ends.

'Hello,' he said in English. 'I know who you are and have been waiting for you to visit me. My name is Leonid.'

I explained that I could not receive the BBC on my radio.

'That,' said Leonid gravely, 'is no problem. We can receive the BBC on the ship's radio if you wish to hear the news from your country.'

Would it, I wondered, be possible for me to erect an aerial for my own radio?

'That,' repeated Leonid, 'is no problem either.' He rummaged through a drawer and produced a roll of copper wire. Ten minutes later he had stretched the wire from a rail high above the bridge down to one of the portholes in my cabin three decks below. The reception was almost perfect.

When I came down for lunch the next day, I brought with me the news that I had just heard on the BBC. Their Moscow correspondent reported that Boris Yeltsin had received 55 per cent of the vote and was, as a result, President of the Russian Federation.

Sergei, who had just come off watch, was particularly happy.

'The big mistake,' he told me, 'was made in 1917.' I thought he said 1970 and asked if he blamed Brezhnev. 'No,' he repeated, 'Lenin in 1917. I think it was bad to start the collective farms. No wonder the peasants did not want to join them.' But it wasn't the plight of the peasants which worried him. His wife was living in Rostov on Don and life was becoming very difficult.

'It is terrible, terrible. Her mother stands in a queue for three hours every day and sometimes does not buy any food at all.'

I wondered if things were becoming worse. He thought for a second.

'Yes. Each week they are worse than before. And I can see no stop to it either. I don't know where it will all end.' Another pause. 'It is hard for my wife, much harder than it is for me on *Arktika*. Here we are given our food and everything is done for us.' He smiled to himself. 'My wife would like it here.'

I had brought with me photostats of three documents which I hoped would interest some of the people I met on board. The first two of these were letters to my grandfather and were dated 1879. Charles Waldstein had been born into a German-American family in New York and, after graduating from Columbia University, went to Europe and did his PhD at Heidelberg. He then moved to London where he met an old German man with whom he became close friends. Close enough, anyway, for the old man to use a nickname and, when writing in German, the familiar second person singular. The first of the two letters was the more interesting. It read:

13 Dec '79

Lieber Waldhörnlein

You will, I hope, be so good as to come and dine with me tomorrow (Sunday) at 2 o'clock. There will be a young Russian who is well worth studying, being something of a 'type'. Don't be frightened! He carries neither dagger nor revolver nor explosive 'chemicals' about him. Besides, your name does not yet figure on the 'black' list.

And now vale faveque

Karl Marx

The other document, the title page of a book entitled *Russia and History's Turning Point*, dated from the period when I was living in New York. A party had been given to celebrate the publication of this book and I had taken along a copy for the author to autograph. The inscription, written in a very shaky hand with a felt-tipped pen, read

To Oliver Walston.
Alexander Kerensky.
Nov. 3 1965.

Later that evening I knocked on the door of the second master's cabin. We talked first about the election result, which had made him very excited, and then I produced my photostats. At first Alexander could not read the signature on the letters, but suddenly the kopeck dropped.

'It's not possible,' he said. Then, after pondering the implications, asked, 'Where are the originals of these letters?' I told him that they were at home. 'But,' said Alexander, 'they should be in a museum.' He summoned Sergei and together they re-read the letters. It was like watching two lapsed Catholics nervously touching a holy relic with a mixture of excitement and revulsion.

The Kerensky inscription had less impact.

'What was he like?' asked Sergei. I explained that I had met him for a few seconds only when he was an extremely old man.

'Never mind,' said Alexander. 'You have met the man who ruled Russia before Lenin. Incredible.'

We were just beginning to talk about the similarity between Gorbachev and Kerensky when the door opened and the captain stuck his head round the corner.

'Party this evening,' he announced. 'My cabin at eight o'clock.'

There were seven of us seated under a benign Lenin wearing a blue polka-dot tie. At the other end of the captain's room, which ran half the width of the bridge, was a mural showing Kirov standing beside his horse in the Caucasus, addressing a group of appreciative peasants. On the forward wall a row of portholes looked towards the bows, while opposite was a huge polar map with the North Pole in the centre. A low bookcase contained mementoes from a delegation of coalminers from the Donbas and steelworkers from Leningrad. At the centre of the display cabinet was an illuminated volume commemorating one of the great moments in modern maritime history. In 1977, with Captain Ulitin then second in command, *Arktika* became the first surface ship ever to reach the North Pole.[1]

In addition to the captain and Alexander Barinov (who, I was surprised to see, did not drink alcohol) there was the chief first mate, Vladimir Kulikov, a taciturn man with greasy dark hair and a perpetual scowl; the senior chief engineer, Sergei Markin, who looked like a larger version of Lech Walesa with his bushy moustache and twinkling eyes. Acting as interpreter was Sergei, who was replaced by Maxim half way through the dinner when he had to go on watch. The table was served by Raisa, whose scarlet dress clashed dreadfully with her orange hair.

The meal began with cucumber and tomatoes in sour cream, together with salami. This was accompanied by a bottle of Georgian champagne and a short speech by the captain which turned out to be an elaborate toast to my fiftieth birthday. He reached under his chair and produced a cut glass bowl which had been engraved to commemorate the event.

'You must understand,' he said, 'that we have never had a foreigner on board *Arktika* before and certainly never a foreigner who celebrated his birthday with us. That is why we are taking the matter very seriously.' There was another reason which he did not mention. Among a spectrum of splendid characteristics, the Russians have a total inability to resist any form of party.

I replied to the toast in a stilted and stupidly formal manner by saying how grateful, happy and honoured I was to be with them. Producing a bottle of whisky, I suggested a toast to *Arktika* and its crew. This was the cue for everyone else to leap to their feet with their own toasts,

[1] This was almost certainly the only Arctic expedition ever to include a serving cabinet minister. T.G.Guzhenko, the Minister of Merchant Marine, went along for the ride.

and within a few minutes the empty whisky bottle had been replaced by a full bottle of vodka. I looked at the birthday cards which my family had embargoed until a suitable moment. The most popular of these was a picture of the Mona Lisa who, when the card was opened, was shown to be wearing a bra.

Raisa cleared the *zakuski* (hors d'oeuvres, which are invariably the best part of a Russian meal) and gave us each half a roast chicken with fresh cranberries. Moist and well cooked, it was washed down by beer or salty Narzan mineral water.

After the meal ended, Raisa cleared the table and we sat around on the sofa under the picture of Kirov. The captain asked me if I liked music. I nodded and tried to convey with body language that I liked music a lot. This was what he had been hoping, because he immediately opened a large cupboard and pulled out an accordion which he strapped round his shoulders. As he tuned up – or perhaps he was just getting into the mood – he began to hum softly. Maxim acted as impresario, announcing, 'The captain is going to play you a song about the sailors from Liverpool who brought the convoys to Murmansk during the war.' I remembered the man who had died on my birthday and tried to look cheerful.

What Grigorii Alexeivich lacked in musical skill, he more than compensated for with energy and enthusiasm. Half an hour later he had exhausted both his repertoire and himself. But the best was still to come. Raisa, who had been waiting in the passageway outside the captain's cabin, pounced as I came through the door. An enormous wet kiss landed smack on my mouth as she thrust a small package into my hand.

'*Semyachki*,' she said as I disentangled myself as gracefully as possible; then she simpered prettily and fled. Only when I had reached the safety of my cabin did I dare look inside the package. It was a paper bag full of sunflower seeds.

The next morning I went up to the bridge, clutching a mug of coffee. Sergei was on watch. Why, he wondered, was the Union Jack such a peculiar pattern? I tried to explain about the Scottish cross of St Andrew and the English cross of St George. Where was the cross of Wales, he asked. And of Ireland, too? It was not the time for a lesson in British history, and I doubted if I was even competent to recount it. Somewhat disappointed, Sergei tried another approach. Why were they killing each other in Northern Ireland? Once again my grasp of history, and his of the English language, made the topic difficult to pursue in any detail.

From the shelter of the bridge it looked like a warm day, so I went outside to watch two sailors hosing down the deck. The scale on the thermometer fixed to the rail showed the conditions for which *Arktika* had been designed. It began at a maximum of ten degrees Celsius and went down to seventy degrees below zero. At the stern two young men, one tall and thin and the other like a Russian Billy Bunter, were polishing the helicopter, while above them the hammer and sickle fluttered yellow and scarlet in the sunshine.

On my return I found that Sergei's interest in British history had waned a bit. He looked up from the chart table where he had been studying a weather map and said, 'You will be happy tonight. We shall meet ice at around midnight.' He was right. I was happy. Very happy indeed. Until then we might have been sailing in the Caribbean. A flat sea, a bright sun and the occasional gull. It was not what I had expected of the North East Passage.

Far over the horizon to starboard, the Kola Peninsula turned south to form the western shore of the White Sea.

It was there in 1553 that the first Englishman to look for the North East Passage had died. Sir Hugh Willoughby, after failing to meet up with his second in command, Chancellor, wintered on this miserable coast with the crews from the *Bona Esperanza* and *Bona Confidentia*. None of them survived; it is usually assumed that they suffocated in the fumes from their stoves. Chancellor was luckier. He sailed south into the White Sea, eventually landing at Colmagro, which later became Archangel. From there he travelled 800 kilometres overland to Moscow. Unlike most foreigners, he must have made a good impression on Ivan the Terrible, because he emerged from Russia with a treaty which granted trading rights to British ships and which, as a direct result, led to the founding of the Muscovy Company. The North East Passage, however, remained unconquered for another 325 years.

In 1750 a London cartographer called Emanuel Bowen published 'A new and accurate map of the North Pole'. He felt it necessary to give an explanation of his efforts in a footnote which reads as follows:

> By the view which this polar map exhibits of the compass and the extent of sea and land lying east and west of the meridian of London, may be estimated the Importance of the many attempts which have been formerly made, and is at present making, to discover a Passage to China and the East Indies. For could this desirable Discovery be made, either by a North East Passage, as has been hitherto in vain attempted, or by a North West Passage, as is now again attempting, it would greatly shorten the length and lessen the expenses of East India voyages, and consequently be of considerable advantage to our British Trade and Navigation.

The moment seemed ripe for an expedition of my own, so I set off towards the area where I assumed the nuclear reactor control room was located. It wasn't difficult to find since it sat in the centre of the ship, where it occupied a lot of space above the engine room.

My first impression was that I had stumbled into a power station – which, I suppose, is precisely what it was. Because it was Russian – and designed in the early 1970s – it looked much more like Battersea than Sizewell B. The control centre was simply a large, low-ceilinged room with banks of dials on every wall. On the far right was the console controlling the twin reactors at which sat two men staring at coloured lights, representing the important processes which were taking place. Elsewhere were the controls for the steam generators, the electrical motors and umpteen other functions.

I had entered through the double steel doors rather nervously, as I had not actually been invited. For a moment I stood silently in the doorway, hoping that someone would notice me. They didn't. I had either to withdraw or to make an impression. I chose the latter.

'Does anyone here speak English?' I said in what I hoped was a cheerful manner.

A slight young man with prematurely grey hair looked up from the control panel at which he was sitting and said, 'I shall try.'

The speaker's name was Dimitri Nikitin, and he was the third electrical officer. A few minutes later, when I was just beginning to learn about his wife and daughter back home in Leningrad, Sergei, the cake and computer enthusiast, turned up. This seemed like a good moment to ask to see the reactors. Dimitri consulted Sergei, who looked for the officer of the watch to whom he could pass the buck. He was in luck.

A phone call to the bridge had the desired effect.

'I think they like you,' said Dimitri. 'In former times we

were not permitted to show the reactor to people who were not members of the crew.'

We left the control room, went down two decks and walked down a long passage before turning left towards the centre of the ship. A large cream-coloured steel door had a skull and crossbones painted crudely under the international symbol for radioactivity.

'First you've got to put on special clothes,' said Dimitri as he slid back the bolt and led the way into a small room illuminated by a single naked light bulb. From an old wooden desk he extracted a dull aluminium tube the size of a pen.

'It's a dosimeter,' he explained.

I followed him into a changing room where a pile of fresh white laundry was stacked in a corner. From it Dimitri gathered a pair of cotton trousers, a coat which made me look like a cricket umpire and a tall cap which gave me the appearance of a chef who had fallen on hard times. I stripped down to my underpants and put on the uniform. The gear was completed by cotton overshoes and white gloves.

We passed down two more decks and went through another set of thick steel doors to where a row of felt slippers was lined up under a bench. The smell reminded me of the changing room at my prep school.

'You must put on these shoes,' explained Dimitri. 'We will leave them here when we return.'

Finally we passed through two more doors and found ourselves in the reactor room itself. It was like being in a cathedral, with the roof fifteen metres above my head. I realised that I was looking at the underside of the hatch which the crew had been working on a few days earlier. Beneath the catwalk were the two nuclear reactors which looked like stainless steel cabinets from which ran a maze of stainless steel pipes.

Everything was very clean, without a speck of dust visible even in the nooks and crannies where pipes joined or steel ladders were attached to the walls.

'Go ahead,' said Dimitri. 'Go wherever you want.'

I tried to look serious yet nonchalant, but was ashamed to realise that my imagination was in danger of tumbling out of control. Words, the meaning of which I did not remotely understand, rumbled through my brain. Alpha, beta and gamma particles, radionuclides, roentgens, rems and rads must all have been whizzing through me, around me or inside me. Even if they weren't, their existence was making me feel uneasy.

'You would not be allowed to be here if we were running at maximum power,' said Dimitri. 'The radiation would be too great. But now we are in the open sea with no ice we have shut down the reactors to less than half their permitted output.'

I felt a bit better.

The procedure for getting out of the reactor room was even more elaborate than it had been to get in. The first obstacle came in the shape of a confined space into which one squeezed to be 'sniffed' all over like a bitch on heat. Then, having removed my felt slippers, I was again checked by a man with a Geiger counter who ran it over my body much as a security man looks for hidden weapons at Heathrow. The only problem seemed to be my camera which, having had an inspection all of its own, appeared to have a speck of radioactivity somewhere. It turned out to have been a false reading and, having dressed again, I was eventually allowed to take it back to the outside world.

On the bridge Maxim had come on watch and was dressed like a gas station attendant from small-town Oklahoma. Wearing a denim jacket and a baseball cap, he was staring at the satellite navigation console which told him that we were at 69.56N and 48.36E. An ice report had just been placed on the table by the radio officer. It confirmed that we were due to meet our first ice that evening at 20.00. By then we would be just east of the southern tip of Novaya Zemlya.[2]

Earlier that day I had asked the captain if there were any restrictions on what I could photograph. He thought for a moment.

'Only one,' he replied. 'The KGB have informed me that you must not photograph a panorama.'

I was puzzled by this embargo and asked Sergei to make sure that he had translated correctly.

'Yes,' said Sergei with a touch of irritation. 'A panorama is a series of pictures.' He mimed a photograph panning round the horizon. 'But,' he added, 'it will only apply if you photograph the shoreline.'

I pondered this instruction for a while before deciding to ignore it. Photographs of the shore, as anyone who has tried to capture Calais from a retreating ferry will know, are a waste of time. Besides, since the KGB were going to process all my photographs, I had no doubt they would throw out any which displeased them.

In one important respect security restrictions had been lifted for me. I had noticed that some of the navigation charts on the bridge had a small orange mark on the bottom right-hand corner. Maxim explained the significance.

'These charts are the secret ones,' he told me. 'The orange lines mean that they are, how do you say, classified?

[2] Literally, New Land, these two long thin islands are a continuation of the Urals. They must be some of the most radioactive real estate on earth. The islands were the site of the Russian nuclear tests and the surrounding sea is where most of Murmansk's nuclear wastes have been tipped over the past two decades.

In former times it was a definite rule that if anybody came on to the bridge who was not a crew member, these charts had to be hidden immediately. Now we do not bother about such things.'

It wasn't difficult to see why the Russians felt so strongly about their charts. The waters off the entire Siberian coastline are over a continental shelf and so are extremely shallow. Information concerning precise depths would have been – and probably still was – of great interest to anyone wishing to navigate in this region.

Only when I had returned to England did I realise quite how much the restrictions had been loosened for me. Previously, all foreign ships sailing to Siberian ports had first to call in at Murmansk to be 'controlled'. This meant that not only did two Russian pilots come aboard, but also that all binoculars and cameras were sealed. The binoculars were permitted to be unsealed after the ship cleared Murmansk, but the cameras remained sealed until the ship left Murmansk on the homeward passage.

I was lying on my bunk trying to get to grips with *Crime and Punishment* when the phone rang. It was Maxim from the bridge, in a state of some excitement.

'Oliver. Look out of your window. We have ice.'

As he spoke I was, in fact, looking out of the porthole forward to the bows where, through the driving snow, I could see ice floes dotting the dark sea like dandruff on velvet. To begin with the floes were small, averaging maybe three metres across, but after a few minutes they grew larger so that some of them were twenty metres wide.

Maxim suggested I went out on to the bows, where both the view and the sound would be better. I had only just arrived at the bow when the ship's whistle sounded twice. Like a trespassing and nervous schoolboy, it occurred to me that maybe someone on the bridge was trying to tell me that I was not allowed out on the bow deck. There was hardly time to consider this problem when a voice came booming out over the tannoy.

'Oliver,' it said, 'can you see the seals? Look to your left.' And sure enough, there on a small ice floe was a solitary seal slithering into the water only a few metres from our bow. Up ahead I could see more seals, some of them directly in the path of the ship. They appeared totally unconcerned that a nuclear icebreaker was bearing down on top of them. On every ice floe there were seals. The bigger ones contained up to one hundred seals each, and the smaller ones had solitary animals.

For the first time since leaving Murmansk I began to feel that I was really in the Arctic.

4 The Kara Sea

'Blue water ends at Trinidad,' wrote Evelyn Waugh. Travelling, as he then was, towards British Guiana, it was probably true. But for me, on the eastern edge of the Barents Sea, the blue water *started* at Trinidad. And with it started the Gulf Stream which then swooshed diagonally across the Atlantic, past Ireland, the Hebrides, the Orkneys, across the North Sea and up along the Norwegian coast before rounding the North Cape. By then it was only just warm enough to keep the ice out of Murmansk, and by the time it reached the western shores of Novaya Zemlya it wasn't just exhausted, it was actually beginning to freeze.

Yet whatever the temperature of the water outside the hull, everything was warm and cosy inside. And nowhere was it warmer than in the dining room where we ate four times a day, half an hour before the watches changed. Breakfast at 7.30 would usually be bread and butter with maybe a slice of salami and a glass of tea. Lunch at 11.30 would start with soup before a small portion of mashed potatoes, meat and perhaps half a tomato. Pudding was normally an apple. Also on the table were slices of raw onion and a jar of vitamin tablets. The remaining two meals at 3.30 and 7.30 were similar to breakfast and lunch.

On that particular day tea consisted of grey bread and

43

thick, brown, tasteless jam with biscuits which combined the appearence of macaroons with the texture of a tractor tyre. They had been designed for their long shelf life rather than their gastronomic properties. As a special surprise we were occasionally each given four caramels wrapped in paper. I treated these with caution since they had enough stickiness to remove every filling in my mouth. Having once met the ship's dentist socially, I had no wish to get to know him better.

Alexander, the second captain, was definitely a good egg. So when he invited me for coffee that evening I accepted happily. Not only did it enable me to get to know him better, it also gave me the opportunity of watching a TV quiz game called *Roulette*. Russian television had already realised that it was difficult to insult the intelligence of the average viewer. The contest was quite as inane as any of its Western equivalents, and the audience was similarly hysterical when a participant won a prize. Which was strange in view of the fact that the biggest award of the evening was not a holiday in Sochi or a living-room suite in brown dralon, but a jumbo packet of detergent. We were, I was proudly informed by Maxim, able to pick up TV programmes from a satellite until we reached the New Siberian Islands. East of them we would be without television. It was an attractive prospect.

The open water of that morning did not last and by early evening we were once again surrounded by ice floes – bigger than the first lot and a great deal more frequent, too. Sergei, the officer of the watch, gave Owdoyoudo permission to steer his own course between the floes. I went out again on to the bows to watch the ice. The small pieces made a barely audible thump as they struck the hull. I remembered the day I was walking along Burlington Gardens behind the Royal Academy in London. I heard the

44

same soft thump and looked up to see that a taxi had just hit an old lady as she tried to cross the road. It is not a generally known fact that the sound of small ice floes hitting a large ship is similar to that of small human beings hitting a large car.

The big floes produced a completely different sound. They clanged as they hit the hull, as a funeral bell would sound if you were standing in the belfry. And the biggest floes of all, which Owdoyoudo was trying to avoid, did more than make a noise; they actually moved the entire ship, sending a shiver which could be felt way back on the helicopter deck.

It was time for my evening visit to Leonid in the radio room. As usual, he was rolling a cigarette and nursing a glass of tea. We talked for a bit about football before our conversation was interrupted by the sound of Morse code coming through one of the speakers. Leonid instinctively grabbed paper and pencil as he concentrated on the sounds. He scribbled for a minute or so and then looked up at me with a grin.

'You will be interested by this,' he said. 'The icebreaker *Captain Sorokin* is fifty nautical miles east of us with a ship she is escorting to Dikson. But she has found very heavy ice and has stopped, so that we must go and help her.'

I relayed this information to Sergei, who took the news calmly.

'This is not surprising,' he said. 'The *Sorokin* is a small ship, about quarter of our power, and it is still early in the season so the ice could well be very thick.'

At that point the captain, who had also been told the news, came on deck. For the first time I noticed that he was not wearing his uniform but instead was dressed, like all Russians when they want to relax, in a tracksuit.

45

He was in a philosophical mood as he looked out across a level sea which was becoming increasingly white.

'I've been sailing for thirty-nine years, so I don't suppose I'll see anything these days which will surprise me. I reckon I've seen just about all there is to see in these waters. Mind you, it hasn't all been easy.'

Had he, I wondered, ever been frightened?

'No. Never.' He paused. 'Yes, come to think of it, I was once. I remember now. I was aged twenty-six and we were on an icebreaker making for Tixi. It was September and we'd just passed the Taymyr Peninsula and were in the Laptev Sea when we became completely stuck in the ice. At first I thought this was rather good fun. Most of the young officers on board blamed the captain and said that if they'd been in charge they'd have done things differently. But after a few days we all changed our tunes. After a week the ice had closed in so tightly that we thought it might even crush the ship – or "nip it" as we say. It eventually took us three months to reach Tixi, and we did so by drifting with the ice rather than under our own power. By the time we arrived I'd revised my opinions about our captain – and an awful lot of other things too.'

Was there enough food?

'Oh yes, that was the least of our problems. Planes came and parachuted supplies to us. You might even say they bombed us with food.' He grinned, and the lines in his face multiplied threefold.

Gradually over the next twelve hours the ice floes grew bigger and closer together until the next morning I woke up, looked out of my porthole and noticed that ice was now covering at least three quarters of the surface of the sea. The noise of floes hitting the hull had become a continuous but muted roar which I soon got used to. The movement was a lot harder to stand.

46

On board a normal ship at sea the motions are approximately rhythmical; you have a good idea of what to expect next and how to brace yourself. On an icebreaker, however, the movement is completely random. Suddenly the ship will come to a complete halt as it hits a particularly thick piece of ice. When that happens, cups fly from tables and typing becomes impossible.

Down in the control room Dimitri told me that we had increased our power from 30 per cent to 50 per cent, although we were still managing to make a respectable fifteen knots. It appeared that the *Captain Sorokin* was now twenty nautical miles east of us and had heaved to with its escort, the cargo ship *Captain Danilkin*.

I sensed a certain glee on the bridge at the idea that a 22,000 horsepower icebreaker could not manage the ice conditions and was now waiting to be rescued by *Arktika*. Sergei grinned hugely when he told me about the *Captain Sorokin*'s predicament.

'Is this interesting?' he enquired. When I replied that I found it fascinating, he said, 'It is always like that for the first month. Afterwards . . .' and he shrugged his shoulders.'

At around midday the sun came out, shining weakly through the fog which had covered the sea. The ice continued to get thicker and, according to Sergei, was between one and 2.5 metres. At least it was still loose and floating, so we were keeping up a steady twelve knots. With only two nautical miles to go before we reached the two immobile ships, it was time to return to the bridge.

The tension was tangible. The captain, striding back and forth, was clearly agitated. Alexander was at the port side with his hand on the throttles, Maxim was looking into the radar screen, Leonid the radio operator had come out to wait for the action, and three or four others, including the helmsman and his assistant, all added to the crowd.

Although we could see the two ships on the radar, the fog had cut visibility to less than one hundred metres. And then, suddenly out of the swirling fog appeared the enormous orange hull[1] of the *Captain Danilkin*. At exactly the moment we were abeam, the sun broke through and we could see not only the freighter but also, a few hundred metres ahead, the icebreaker with its yellow superstructure and black hull.

When we eventually passed the *Captain Sorokin* I noticed that she had an oddly serrated bow, unlike any icebreaker I had seen. This, I later learned, was an experimental design which had been fitted the year before in Germany. It was intended to make her more effective in the smooth river ice at the mouth of the Ob, Lena or Yenisei where conditions are very different from out in the ocean. Perhaps it also explained why the *Captain Sorokin* had been so unsuccessful in sea ice which should not normally have given an icebreaker much trouble.

The radio crackled back and forth between the three vessels, with Sergei acting as our voice. *Captain Danilkin* had been instructed to take up position in the middle of the convoy with *Captain Sorokin* at the rear. While I was looking at the big chart on the back wall of the bridge there was another hurried radio conversation. The captain came up to me and said, in his jerky English, '*Sibir* will come tomorrow.' It appeared that the ice conditions in the Kara Straits were very bad and the only remaining nuclear icebreaker on station had also been summoned to help us. This meant there would be three icebreakers looking after a single ship. I was beginning to understand why the Northern Sea Route was so expensive.

Alexander pushed the throttles forward to produce 70

[1] This class of ship, an SA-15, was nicknamed 'carrot' because of the colour of its hull.

per cent power, but as he did so our speed dropped to eight knots. The ice was getting thicker. Maxim consulted a reference book, looked at the ice again and announced in episcopal tones, 'Medium first year ice with hummocks.'

The hummocks were sticking up two metres above the surface, and when I looked astern to see the chunks which we had broken, they were at least that deep below the surface. If this was medium ice I wondered what heavy ice would look like.

I remembered an old patois proverb from the Caribbean island of St Lucia which was used by workers in the banana fields. 'The blade of a cutlass in the water leaves no mark.' It did not apply to icebreakers. The mark we were making through the ice could have been seen from space.

The Tungus, one of the native Arctic peoples of Siberia, knew all about ships in the ice. Their language makes great use of riddles, and one in particular refers to a ship: 'I go and go but leave no trace; I cut and cut but leave no blood.'

After midnight I went up the ladder to the flying bridge, the roof above the enclosed bridge from which one could get a view out over the entire ship. Although the temperature was −4 degrees and I was wearing a thin sweater, the lack of wind meant it did not feel cold. The noise of the ship crashing through the ice sounded like distant thunder and the whole vessel moved jerkily in a way which was more agricultural than nautical. A weak sun shone faintly through the wisps of fog, lighting up the ice floes and reflecting off the smooth sea. Behind us the other two ships were hidden in the murk.

It had not been a good night. Sleeping on an icebreaker in heavy ice is a knack which can only be learned by experience. Every time I managed to drift off we seemed to hit a particularly heavy piece and the entire ship would shudder to an abrupt stop. Since my bunk was long-wise down the length of the ship this meant that in extreme cases I would hit my head, like the load on a lorry sliding forwards after a heavy braking. It was both uncomfortable when it happened and disconcerting when I found myself tensed and waiting for the next impact.

I eventually woke at ten o'clock to find that my cabin was saturated with the sort of light that would have made even Matisse wince. *Arktika* had apparently come to a complete halt some time during the night and the sunshine poured through the portholes, bouncing off the level white ice around us. Half-blinded by the incandescence, I tottered over to the coffee machine and ground the beans I had brought with me. From somewhere deep in the ship I could hear the faint noise of engines starting up again and by the time I had boiled the water and poured it into the filter paper, we were under way. A minute or two later, as I was in the bathroom brushing my teeth, *Arktika* did what she had been designed to do: she came into violent contact with a large piece of ice. By the time I had rushed naked into the cabin it was too late. The mug was smashed and a black lake was spreading across the counter top and making a tiny coffee-fall on to the carpet.

One of the odd things about the Arctic is that the weather changes frequently and without warning. The sunshine which had almost ruptured my retina was replaced an hour later by a wall of fog which swirled around the ship so densely that I could not see the bows from the bridge. On other days I would look out across the ice and see five or six distinct and different fog banks drifting aimlessly around like opaque mirages in an icy desert. Every so often there was a small crash as a chunk of ice, which had frozen on the mast during the night, thawed and fell on to the deck from a great height.

On the bridge the tension of the previous night had

disappeared. The captain was in his usual position on the port side, Sergei was hunched over the charts and the helmsman had his eyes on the horizon. I said a cheerful *Dobry Ootra* to him but he didn't reply.

'He is a very serious man,' explained Sergei. 'He does not talk much.' The captain also looked rather serious. 'He has a problem,' said Sergei, 'which is why our *ptichka*[2] is flying this morning for the first time. Come. I will show you.' And he unfolded a large chart which more than covered the table on the bridge.

There are two possible routes from the Barents Sea into the Kara Sea. The shorter of these is through the Kara Straits, a wide channel which separates Novaya Zemlya from Vaygach Island; the alternative is by way of the narrow Yugorsky Straits between Vaygach Island and the Siberian mainland.

'The problem is,' explained Sergei patiently, 'that the ice is bad, very bad indeed, in the Kara Straits. It may be necessary for us to pass through the Yugorsky Straits instead, but this is not usual and will only be done if there is no alternative.'

I looked at the chart and saw that this channel was not just narrow; it contained a ninety-degree bend which meant that we would enter in an easterly direction and emerge into the Kara Sea pointing due north.

The *ptichka* eventually returned, landing with a clatter on the helicopter deck at the stern. Before the rotor had finished turning a short man with a large belly and deep-set eyes emerged from the right-hand door and, ducking as he ran, disappeared into a nearby hatchway on his way to report to the captain. A veteran of thirty-six years in the Arctic, Valerii Mikhailovich Losef was the hydrologist, the

[2] Literally, little bird. Slang for the ship's helicopter.

second most important man on the ship. The title was a bit misleading since his real function was to be the ship's scout. It was Valerii Mikhailovich's job to go up in the *ptichka* and search out the best route for us to take through the ice.

That afternoon his advice was clear. Both the Yugorsky and Kara Straits were choked with ice, but the latter was closer and, much more significant, also contained fault lines. Captain Ulitin retained the final responsibility for where the ship should steer, but throughout my time on *Arktika* I never saw him disagree with Valerii Mikhailovich. They had known each other for over two decades and had evolved a close professional relationship.

After the *ptichka* had returned, been serviced and finally lashed down, the helicopter deck reverted to its usual function – exercise track. I put on my thick parka and a woolly cap and clambered down the three companionways between the bridge and the stern. On one of the intervening decks I passed two sailors and stopped to see what they were doing. One was carrying a Geiger counter which looked like one of those metal detectors you can buy in electrical shops. The other was making chalk marks on the dark green deck. On anything other than a nuclear-powered ship, I would have ignored the activity, but here it suddenly seemed to be deeply significant. I made signs to show that I was curious and the Geiger man put his earphones on my head. I could hear nothing, even when he pointed to an oscillating needle on the dial, which I assumed meant that he had detected some slight radiation.

After my brisk walk round the helicopter deck I returned to the bridge. On its flat roof was an open area from which one could get a view of the entire ship. In a fresh and very cold wind I watched black, jagged cracks spurt out across the white surface in front of the ship as our bows split the

52

ice. When I turned to look at the stern, *Arktika*'s wake seemed to be made of chunks of frozen Aqua-velva after-shave. Some of them were bigger than a Ford Cortina.

Off our port bow I saw a ship which appeared to have stopped and was waiting motionless in the ice. My source of information was, as usual, down on the bridge.

'It's the *Sibir*,' explained Maxim. 'She is on her way back to Murmansk, but is waiting to take on supplies from the *Danilkin*.' He paused, grinned, and added, ' I also think she has some problems with her navigation equipment.' I wondered if there was a Russian word for *schadenfreude*.

As I stared through the binoculars at *Arktika*'s sister ship, I found myself whistling the tune of 'Moscow Nights'. I felt a tap on the shoulder. It was Maxim again.

'What is English for?' and he pursed his lips and blew.

'Whistle,' I said.

'Oh yes, of course. Please, Oliver, do not whistle on the bridge. It is unlucky for sailors because you will summon up the wind and make a storm. You should know,' he continued. 'It is a tradition which British sailors began, I believe. It is from the days of sailing ships but we still believe it today, even on atomic icebreakers.'

Suitably chastened, I made a mental note never to whistle on *Arktika*. Maxim must have read my mind.

'You can whistle if you wish, but please not on the bridge. Oh yes, two other things while I remember. You should not step on the bulkheads and when in port you should not sit on the bollards.'

The Russian Merchant Marine was obviously riddled with superstition. Was there anything else, I wondered.

'No. It is, as you say, Liberty Hall.' Maxim loved his idiomatic flourishes.

The gang which had been using the Geiger counter was by then chipping away at the green paint below the chalk marks. Another man was sweeping the flakes of paint with a bundle of twigs, while two other seamen were trying to unscrew a hatch cover which had been painted orange so many times they were having a job locating the bolts.

5 Mangazheya

We spent the best part of the day waiting while *Sibir* loaded stores from the *Danilkin*. Around us the ice had become jagged, uneven and very messy. Instead of being white and level like the icing on a cake, it looked like a derelict monumental mason's yard with ancient offcuts of Carrera marble littering the landscape. In spite of the fact that the ice was solid and covered the total surface of the sea, there were still great gashes of pale blue to show where the water had recently melted and then frozen again.

After dinner that evening I was out walking on the deck when a porthole opened and a head emerged. It belonged to one of the many Sergeis on board. This one was an electrical engineer whom I had met for the first time that afternoon.

'Come and see us,' he suggested.

I entered a small cabin to find Sergei, Maxim, Leonid the radio operator and Sasha, another radio operator, listening to country and western tapes, drinking vodka and eating smoked mackerel. Maxim was feeling particularly mellow having just emerged from a sauna. My contribution to the party was some coffee and a Buddy Holly tape.

After less than half an hour we had finished the vodka and I began to gather up my detritus. At this point a beer bottle containing what looked like water appeared on the table.

'One for the road, as you say in England,' suggested Sergei. He noticed my puzzlement and added proudly, 'It's vodka. We make it here in this cabin.' I looked for a still but could see nothing. The reason, it turned out, was that the 'vodka' was simply watered down industrial alcohol which was used on board for cleaning purposes. 'We need it for maintaining electrical apparatus,' Sergei explained. 'It is much purer than Russian vodka – and stronger too.' It seemed that even after it had been diluted it was still 55 per cent alcohol.

Whatever the octane rating, it was sufficient to inebriate Sergei, who was in danger of becoming a bore. He sat on the bed with his arm round Sasha (who didn't seem to mind) and his English became ever less perfect. Maxim, sensibly, had long since left us for more important duties.

The party was interrupted by a crew member who burst in and announced that *Sibir* was coming alongside within the next half hour and would take our mail back to Murmansk. Sergei, by now unable to stand up, let alone write a letter, sat on the bunk grinning happily. I doubt if he noticed my departure.

I made my way astern to the helicopter deck where a group had gathered to wait for *Sibir*, which was somewhere out in the swirling fog. Eventually she emerged from the encircling gloom, a vast and sinister shape, backing slowly towards us. It was like looking into a mirror. An identical ship, different only because her superstructure was painted cream and not orange, was inching towards us. Like *Arktika*, her helicopter deck was also full of spectators, laughing and shouting insults across the narrowing gap of crushed ice. Eventually our sterns touched and a hawser was thrown across to lash the two ships together.

Leonid appeared and asked me if I would like to come and visit his opposite number in the *Sibir*'s radio room. This seemed like a wonderful idea, and we clambered down to the deck below from where it would be possible to cross to the other ship. As we were waiting in what seemed like a queue, Alexander came bustling past, carrying a plastic package.

'These are letters to our wives,' he explained. 'I must hurry.'

There was a babble of voices from the front of the queue and Leonid's face fell.

'We cannot go on board *Sibir*,' he said. 'She is leaving now. It is too late.' And sure enough, the hawser had already been untied. The gap between the ships widened as *Sibir*'s three propellers began to unleash a controlled submarine explosion which crunched up the ice floes into gin-and-tonic-sized cubes.

It had been a surreal and strangely moving experience to see two nuclear icebreakers stern to stern in the middle of the Kara Straits, with their crews behaving like Liverpool and Everton supporters on different sides of Wembley Stadium. Half an hour later the ice was quiet again. As I passed Sergei's cabin I noticed the light was on. I looked through the porthole and saw him asleep on his chair with a mug of cold coffee still in his hand.

Lucky Sergei. I still had not learned how to sleep well on board, and it wasn't simply because of the motion of the ship in ice. There was another even more insoluble problem – temperature. There was no such thing as a thermostat and the only way to regulate the heat in my quarters was to open the portholes. This worked well for the living room where the portholes were on the side of the ship and admitted a gentle breeze. In my bedroom, however, the portholes faced forward, so if they were opened even a crack, a gale of cold air would rip through the room. I experimented with every possible permutation and was unable to find a satisfactory method. Eventually I asked Sergei, the cabin's usual occupant, what he did about the problem. His answer was uncomplicated.

'When I come off watch I just go to sleep. Maybe you should be given some work to do on board. You wouldn't worry about such matters then.'

I felt like an effete *kulak*.

By then we were hugging the Siberian coast to avoid the worst of the ice. Far off in the distance I could just make out low brown hills with a dusting of snow. Looking at the map I had put up on the wall of my cabin, I saw that these were the end of the Urals, which petered out on the Yamal Peninsula before turning north west to continue as Novaya Zemlya. Beyond the shore lay the tundra with its treeless plain serrated by bogs, lakes and streams, all of which eventually fed into the great Siberian rivers. As a schoolboy poring over an atlas and tracing the course of the river Ob, I had always found the tundra an exciting part of the world. Forty years later, from the comfort of my cabin, it still excited me.

Of course, the reality was rather different. Just beyond the horizon lay the city of Vorkuta, one of the landmarks of the Gulag Archipelago, where some of Stalin's earliest and most savage labour camps had been constructed. Vorkuta's original citizens, and probably today's too, would not have shared my pathetic thrills. I was living in an unreal world and I knew it.

A day or two later I was brushing my teeth in the morning when I realised something was wrong. We were still moving, the engines were still running, but something was different. And then I realised: the motion of the ship had ceased. There was no bucking, no grinding. Through the porthole there was only black, smooth, water. It might have been Lake Windermere. A kilometre or so astern I could see where the ice had stopped in a clear, sharp line.

It was a polynya. I had read about these mysterious stretches of open water surrounded by ice, but had never realised how dramatic they would be. The actual cause of polynyas has never been satisfactorily explained. Some are probably the result of upwellings of warmer water from deep below the sea's surface, others could be caused by currents or wind. Some, like the North Water, on the western coast of Greenland, are hundreds of kilometres across, while others are smaller than an urban reservoir. Anyway, there I was, toothpaste dribbling down my chin, staring out at my first polynya.

Maxim was supremely unmoved by my excitement. He had more important things on his mind.

'Come quickly, Oliver,' he shouted. 'I think she will be naked soon.' I walked through to the chartroom where I found him hunched over *Arktika*'s only personal computer. The screen consisted of a grainy picture of a girl in underpants and bra which was superimposed over five playing cards.

'See,' said Maxim triumphantly, 'I have beaten her again and now she will have to take off her brazier.'

A brazier, I explained, was something you light fires in. The word he was looking for was brassière.

'It does not matter how you say it,' replied Maxim. 'Only what you do to them,' and he gave a schoolboy cackle. The picture disappeared from the screen, to be replaced by a bra-less female.

Eventually Maxim won his game and turned triumphantly away from the computer. 'Do you know Lounge Lizard Larry?'

I did not.

'Or F-19 Stealth Fighter? It's very good except your job is to bomb Russian bases and we don't like doing that. The best of all is Grand Prix because you can drive Formula One cars. This is good fun. Particularly for Russians. We only drive Zaporozhets,[1] and they're worse than wheelbarrows.'

He took a swig from his glass of tea and decided it was time to be a Merchant Marine officer again.

'We bought the computer to help us organise the ship,' he explained. 'Look, I will show you the crew list if you like.'

A minute later the printer burst into life and started to spew out a long list of names. *Arktika*, it appeared, had a complement of 157, excluding me. There were eighteen women.

I was studying the list when Maxim interrupted again.

'Do you see anything strange?' I did not. 'Look at the officers,' he suggested. 'What do you see?' I saw the following:

GRIGORII ALEXEIVICH ULITIN, CAPTAIN. 58
ALEXANDER NIKOLAIVICH BARINOF, 2ND CAPTAIN. 36
VLADIMIR SEMONOVICH KULIKOV, 1ST CHIEF MATE. 43
SERGEI VLADIMIROVICH SIDORENKO, 2ND CHIEF MATE. 30
MAXIM BENJAMINOVICH SHUMILOV, 2ND MATE. 30
ANDREI IVANOVICH CHEREPUKHIN, 4TH MATE. 27
VALERII MIKHAILOVICH LOSEF, HYDROLOGIST. 56

Nothing seemed amiss. Maxim was becoming impatient.

'Look,' he said, 'where is the first mate?' He was right, there was no first mate. 'That,' said Maxim, 'is perestroika.

[1] A rear-engined air-cooled car which makes a Trabant seem exotic.

60

Until January this year there had always been a first mate who was the political commissar, but this position was abolished.'

I was digesting this fact when Leonid, who had been standing silently in the doorway, said with some vehemence, 'We are very happy.'

Out on deck I looked astern at the now familiar shapes of the *Sorokin* and *Danilkin*. The day before they had changed places so that the cargo ship was at the rear of our small convoy.

'This manoeuvre is called perestroika,' explained Sergei at lunch. 'You think that Mikhail Sergeivich Gorbachev invented perestroika, don't you? Well, we've been using the word in Arctic convoys for ages.'

That afternoon on the bridge Sergei was staring out at the ice. The polynya had lasted for only a couple hours. After a long silence he turned to me and said, 'You know the other night at dinner you asked me what my dream was?'

I remembered. It had been during my birthday party in the captain's cabin and I was surprised that nobody appeared to have an ambition he was able to talk about.

'Well,' continued Sergei, 'I do have a dream but I didn't want to tell you because the captain was there.' Another pause as he looked astern to where the *Captain Danilkin* had taken up position where the *Captain Sorokin* had previously been. 'My dream is to sail under the flag of Russia and not under that red flag you see on the stern.'

He pointed at my lapel, where a few days earlier someone had pinned the old flag of Russia which had recently become the emblem of Boris Yeltsin's movement.

'It has three stripes, white, blue and red,' continued Segei, who was by now becoming animated. 'My colleagues in the navy would perfer to sail under the old Russian fleet

61

flag which is blue with a white diagonal St Andrew's cross. But for me in the merchant fleet, the Russian flag is the one I would like to fly from my ship.'

I was very moved.[2]

Out on deck a cluster of men were walking briskly round and round the helicopter deck. They looked like prisoners in an exercise yard, hunched up against the Arctic wind. One of them beckoned to me to join them and I did so. It was the best possible exercise. No hawsers to trip over, no companionways to climb up and down, just a track surrounding the helicopter. Each circuit took approximately thirty-five seconds, or a bit more if I stuck deliberately to the outside of the deck and didn't cut any corners. Above me the hammer and sickle was fluttering on a new scarlet flag. The old one had blown down that morning and had been replaced by the quartermaster.

Astern lay the *Captains Danilkin* and *Sorokin* and far off to port the first of a new herd of ice floes was just visible, brilliant white on the dark blue sea. From time to time snowbows (rainbows made from snow) would appear as small and well-defined snowstorms hurried across the water. On one occasion *Arktika* went under a snowbow, like a magical triumphal arch.

I had intended to put in fifteen minutes of brisk walking, but when I next looked at my watch found that nearly half an hour had elapsed. By then the cold wind was beginning to penetrate my jacket. Besides, it was time for tea.

[2] Three months after I had returned home I received a letter from Sergei. It told me about the remainder of the voyage and how happy he was to be back at home in Murmansk. The final paragraph read as follows: 'You remember that I told you I wanted to sail under the flag of Russia? Perhaps you do not. Anyway, just after you had left *Arktika*, on August 22nd, we had a little ceremony. We all collected at the stern and Gregorii Alexeivich hauled down the red flag with the hammer. Instead he hauled up the flag of Russia which we talked about. We were all very happy and some of us cried.'

Somewhere over the southern horizon was the first of the great Siberian rivers we were going to pass. The Ob and the Irtysh together form Russia's equivalent of the Mississippi and Missouri. The Ob actually starts in China before tumbling down through the Altai Mountains past Semipalatinsk and Omsk and then flowing northwards along the eastern slopes of the Urals to where it is joined by the Irtysh some thousand kilometres from its mouth. The mouth of the Ob is unlike those of the other Siberian rivers. Instead of a wide delta like the Lena or the Kolyma, the Ob discharges into its own private gulf, which stretches another thousand kilometres until it reaches the Kara Sea.

It was on an inlet which leads from this gulf that Mangazheya, the most mysterious of Siberian cities, is said to have existed. Nothing visible remains of Mangazheya today, although the Russian historian Professor Belov[3] has found evidence of habitation on the banks of the Taz River. There are also various historical documents which throw some light on what happened to cause so large a settlement to disappear completely. One of these dates from 1601 and was written by a trader named Leontiy Ivanov Stubin. He described the route to Mangazheya as passing through the Yugorsky Straits into the Kara Sea and thence to the west coast of the Yamal Peninsula. Only light, shallow draft ships could possibly make the journey, since it involved sailing up the Mutnaya River and then being carried across a long portage until the ships were relaunched again on the Zeleya River, down which they sailed into the gulf of the Ob. From there the route turned east up the Taz River, eventually reaching Mangazheya, after what must have been an extraordinary journey.

Another contemporary account claimed that by the late

[3] A rare combination of a good historian and a devout communist. He also wrote the official history of the North East Passage.

sixteenth century Mangazheya rivalled Archangel as a trading centre. The Tsars, however, seem to have disliked the place precisely because trade and revenues were being taken from Archangel. On 6 February 1616, a Dutch ship reached Mangazheya and the Governor of Tobolsk complained to the Tsar. As a result, an Imperial Decree was issued which forbade the fur trade from taking place except in designated places (i.e. not Mangazheya). Eventually these rules were tightened to the extent that in 1619 the Tsar actually decreed the death penalty for any Russian guiding a foreigner to Mangazheya.

Yet whatever the reason, logistics or politics or both, Mangazheya seems to have disappeared with extraordinary suddenness, thereby giving rise to the theory that, like Atlantis and Troy, it may never have existed at all.

It was on an evening when we were a mere 150 kilometres or so from the Yamal Peninsula that I found myself sitting in the officers' dining room with that most taciturn and mysterious of men, Valerii Mikhailovich Losef. He had spent thirty-six years in the Arctic and was by then a legend among the hydrologists back in Murmansk. I wondered if he believed in Mangazheya.

His answer dispelled any doubts I might have had.

'Oh yes, of course I do.' He scratched his neck and continued, 'I gather it's hard to see any remains now, in fact the exact location is not even certain. But Professor Belov has found coins and human remains at a location near where the city was supposed to be. They say that from an aeroplane, if the weather conditions are good, you can still see the outline of where a city was located.'

It was also on the Yamal Peninsula that sailors from Western Europe first came in contact with the Samoyed[4]

____

[4] Now usually known by the politically correct name of Nentsy.

people. These were sort of Arctic dervishes whose life revolved around their reindeer and their shamans. The former moseyed across the tundra grazing lichen, moss and the occasional grass, while the latter maintained their religious and political leadership with the help of mystical trances in which they performed weird – and scarcely believable – feats. As early as 1556 the English sailor Richard Johnson reported seeing 'devilish rites'. Richard Hakluyt, the sixteenth-century Archdeacon of Westminster who collected stories of exploration and published them in his three-volume *Principall Navigations, Voiages and Discoveries of the English Nation*, tells of a shaman who had clearly solved the problem of how to keep his congregation's attention from wandering during the service. It seems that he got hold of a sword 'and put it into his bellie halfeway and something lesse, but no wound was to be seen (they continuing in their sweet song still). Then he put the sworde into the fire till it was warme, and so thrust it into the slitte of his shirt, and thrust it through his bodie, as I thought, in at his navill and out at his fundament; the poynt being out of his shirt behind, I layde my finger upon it, then he pulled out the sworde and sate downe.'

The next morning I was lying in my bath lost in a world half way between sleep and contemplation when all of a sudden *Arktika* stopped dead, as if it had hit a wall of ice. Which is precisely what had happened. The effect on my bath was seismic. A miniature tsunami roared down from the taps and broke like surf when it reached my face before swooshing out over the end of the bath on to the floor. The second wave was less powerful, but also ended up on the floor.

Putting thoughts of the *Titanic* aside, I jumped out, dressed and ran up to the bridge. As I was standing by the window so soon after my bath, condensation began to form on the glass. Owdoyoudo, who was at the helm, pointed at me and said something in Russian to Sergei, who grinned and nodded. It was clear that I was the subject of their private joke, so I asked what they were laughing at.

'Well,' said Sergei, 'we have a saying, "If the window steams up then one of us was drunk yesterday."'

The piece of floating ice which had almost emptied my bath was only a hint of what was still to come. Although there was still clear water visible, the floes were by then so large that the captain himself had come on to the bridge and, displacing the officer of the watch, was giving instructions to Owdoyoudo, who was steering a zig-zag course. How the two ships behind managed to follow us remained a mystery.

'They won't have to much longer,' said Sergei. 'We should be at Dikson within four hours and then they'll leave us.'

Dikson,[5] or Dikson Island to be precise, is a tiny settlement on the western shore of the mouth of the Yenisei. This river, which rises over five thousand kilometres away in the Mongolian steppes, flows almost due north before it reaches the Kara Sea. It is the most important artery leading off the Northern Sea Route. More traffic goes from Murmansk to Dudinka than to any other Siberian port. It was for Dudinka that the *Captain Danilkin* was destined. She was carrying general cargo which would be trans-shipped from Dudinka to Norilsk, a copper-mining city with a population of over a quarter of a million which had been entirely built by Stalin's slave labourers in the nearby Gulag. On her return the *Danilkin* would probably be

[5] Named after Baron Oskar Dikson, a Swedish merchant who, with the Russian Sibirikov, financed the first successful passage of the North East Passage by Nordenskiöld in 1878–9.

carrying nickel ore which would retrace my footsteps and end up in that filthy smelter at Nikel on the Norwegian border.

It wasn't necessary to be an oceanographer to notice that there was something very different about the sea. As we neared the mouth of the Yenisei the ice floes disappeared and the colour of the water changed from black-blue to dark brown.

That afternoon, while I was drinking tea and eating *baraka* (tiny doughnut-shaped biscuits with the consistency of granite), the radio burst into life. It was Dikson trying to contact us. The captain picked up his radio-telephone mouthpiece and replied. By then reception had faded.

'Damned radio,' he said, looking at me. 'It's easier speaking to London than to Dikson. Typical.' And he grinned.

Outside on deck there was a flurry of activity as a seaman hoisted two flags. I assumed this was a Nelsonian attempt to communicate with Dikson radio station, but there appeared to be no answering display.

As usual, Maxim came to my rescue.

'We are talking to the *Danilkin* and *Sorokin*. The flags represent the letters W and O. If you want to know what this means, go and look on the bridge in front of the smaller radar screen.'

I did as he suggested. There, up on the bulkhead, was a series of signal flags and, very conveniently, their messages were written in both Russian and English. The letters WO meant 'Icebreaker escort complete. Proceed to your destination.'

6 Looking for polar bears

I went out on deck to watch the *ptichka* land on its return from Dikson, where it had taken two men from the *Captain Danilkin* and had collected the mail for *Arktika*. The chief helicopter pilot, Valentin Albansky, a scrawny, handsome man with dark, slicked-back hair, was sitting in the left-hand seat waiting for the rotor to stop when he saw me and gave the thumbs up sign. Puzzled by this gesture, I waited until he had unstrapped himself and had talked to the two boys from the ground crew who were about to refuel the machine.

'You should have been with us,' said Valentin. 'We saw a bear. He was yellow, which means that he was very old.' By now every member of the crew must have known that the English *kulak*'s only ambition was to see a polar bear. I had talked about little else since leaving Murmansk, and everyone I spoke to told me that I just had to be patient. It was, they assured me, absolutely inevitable that we would see bears.

I interrogated Valentin as if he were being debriefed after a reconnaissance mission. Where had the bear been? What was it doing? Would we be able to see it from the ship? The details he gave me were only sketchy.

'We were about ten kilometres from the shore, flying at

our normal fifty metres,' he explained. 'He was eating a seal he'd just caught and so didn't mind the noise of the helicopter because he was too busy, or too hungry.'

I reported this conversation to Maxim when I met him on his way to play netball in the gym.

'You shouldn't get so excited about bears,' he told me. 'On the other hand if you were to see one of those pink seagulls, now that would be really something.' Maxim's sense of humour often left a bit to be desired.

That afternoon I decided to use some good old-fashioned capitalist incentive as part of my campaign to see a polar bear. The deal was that the first person to sight one would receive a packet of Marlboros.

'Count me out,' said the captain. 'I don't smoke.'

But at least Owdoyoudo found the offer attractive. And since his job involved standing behind the wheel staring into the distance for most of the day, he was a good person to have on my side.

When Owdoyoudo was not on duty behind the wheel, he appeared to have another occupation which I found puzzling. He would sit for hours weaving old pieces of plastic string into something which looked like a doormat. This slightly arcane activity took place in the dark room behind the bridge which was called the *chaikana* (tea room) because a samovar was permanently boiling there. It was a strange room, full of cream-coloured equipment with black plastic knobs which reminded me of Mr Briault's dentist's surgery in Upper Wimpole Street back in the 1950s. Everybody was surprisingly vague about what the machinery was for, and to make the *chaikana* even more sinister, the walls were hung with coloured posters of NATO warships.

Only towards the end of my time on *Arktika* did I discover the true purpose of the *chaikana*. Russian icebreakers were merchant ships, officered by the Merchant

69

Marine. However, contingency plans had been made under which, in time of war, the icebreakers would immediately be transferred to the navy and refitted as warships. The *chaikana* was, it seemed, *Arktika's* weapons control centre and the dentist's equipment was all the hardware needed to run a warship and fire its artillery.

Only after I had learned this did the large circles on the fore and after decks make sense. These were the mountings for the guns which would be controlled from the *chaikana*. *Arktika*, designed in the late 1960s and launched in 1975, was a child of the Cold War.

I was back on my bunk crashing through Dostoyevsky when the phone rang. It was Maxim to say that Valerii Mikhailovich, the hydrologist, had just radioed in from the helicopter to say that there was a polar bear on an ice floe dead ahead of us at a range of six kilometres.

Looking for polar bears is very much like looking for mushrooms. At first you don't quite know what features your eyes should be searching for. All I knew was that polar bears were white, had a leg at each corner and a black nose sticking out the front of their face. Faced with a 360-degree panorama of snow and ice, with hummocks, shadows, patterns and shapes, I kept imagining that I was seeing polar bears in the distance. And then the first mate pointed one out to me.

'Two babies,' he said, using the full range of his English vocabulary. And sure enough, off in the distance, about a kilometre and a half away, I could see the ambling yellow-ish shape of a mother, followed by two very white blobs. It was one of the more exciting moments of my life.

Far to the starboard a colony of ringed seals, like enormous slugs, were lying on the ice, unconcerned by our presence or – still more intrusive – the sound of the *ptichka* which was up looking for leads through the ice. It seemed that at any moment the bears would meet the seals and lunch would be consummated.

I was surprised by how badly camouflaged polar bears really were. Ever since I was taken as a child to see Brumas, the first polar bear to be born at London Zoo, I had always assumed that their white fur would make them impossible to see against the ice; but in reality they weren't white at all. Instead they were covered with yellowy, creamy, rather scruffy fur which made them stand out against the grey-white background.

An hour or so later we hit fast ice, so called because it is attached to the land and not just floating on the surface of the sea. It was by a long way the toughest ice we had yet met, and after a few hundred metres we came to a complete stop. Behind us the *Captain Danilkin* was also working hard, puffing out clouds of diesel smoke which wafted black across the whiteness. Whenever she struck a particularly hard bit of ice her square bows rose up and made her look like an ugly Mississippi tugboat. Her lines might have been functional, but they certainly weren't beautiful.

Throughout the afternoon conditions became worse, with the *Captain Danilkin* sometimes falling so far behind that we were forced to go round in large circles to free her from the ice. Eventually the captain decided that enough was enough, and he gave the signal for the *Danilkin* to move up into our stern. I had known in theory why Russian icebreakers had notches cut in their sterns, but I had yet to see it being put into practice.

One man stood on our stern gesturing with the sort of hand signals that you see at airports when a jumbo is being parked at the ramp. Eventually, after a lot of semaphore, the *Danilkin* put her bow tight up against the notch in *Arktika*'s stern which was padded with thick chunks of matting. I had assumed that we were going to tow her, but

71

the vast hawsers which lined the stern were not actually used. Instead we moved forward in tandem for a few minutes until – without any visible warning – we parted company and turned north, leaving the *Danilkin* and *Sorokin* to head south up the Yenisei estuary towards Dudinka.

The Yenisei had for centuries appeared on the maps as one of the great Siberian rivers, but no ship had ever been able to reach it from the sea. This all changed in 1874 when a cargo vessel managed to sail as far as the mouth of the river. As so often happened in the history of the North East Passage, it was not a Russian ship. In fact it hailed from Hull and was captained by a man called Joseph Wiggins, thanks to whom for a brief period it looked as if the much dreamed-about Northern Sea Route would actually become a reality. The shipping line Wiggins later founded to exploit the Siberian river trade did enjoy a few years of prosperity. Its greatest and most improbable achievement was to carry British railway tracks 1800 kilometres up the Yenisei to Krasnoyarsk, where they were used for the Trans-Siberian Railway. But by the end of the century the company was in trouble. A combination of high insurance rates and the fact that Wiggins's ships always returned empty meant that the economics simply did not make sense.

No sooner had the *Captain Danilkin* detached itself from our stern than the helicopter, whose engine had been running throughout the whole manoeuvre, took off and headed east. I later learned that the maritime minuet we had been executing had simply been so that a crew member could come aboard *Arktika* and be flown to Dikson.

Helicopters are not very friendly things. Not only do they make a lot of noise, but they are also dangerous. Sergei told me that in April that year the second mate on *Sibir* had been killed by the tail rotor. He had gone out on deck to meet it and for some reason had forgotten about the propeller at the tail.

'Be careful of helicopters,' Sergei warned. '*Kulaks* are not used to them.'

Dikson Island looked almost pretty. Low, flat hills rose gently from the sea, which was itself covered with ice. On the more exposed spots the snow had been blown away, leaving brown patches. Through a sporadic blizzard, I could catch glimpses of the settlement. There was a pale brick-red lighthouse, looking a bit like a silo on a Pennsylvania Dutch farm, which dominated the cluster of blue and red bungalows. On the mainland I saw what I assumed was an airfield. There was also a large turquoise hangar, masses of radio masts and things which could have been either radar or missiles, or both.

At Dikson we turned the corner and started to sail north east along the Taymyr Peninsula towards our next objective, Cape Chelyuskin.

The discovery of Cape Chelyuskin was one of the more exciting moments in the history of the Siberian Arctic. In 1733 Catherine the Great, worried by the fact that nobody quite knew where the northern shore of her empire was located, put together the largest single Arctic expedition that has ever been launched. Called the Great Northern Expedition, it was actually five separate expeditions, each of which had been allocated a different section of the coast to explore. The project was under the overall command of a Dane, Vitus Bering, who himself concentrated on the easternmost end of the empire. Another party, led by the Laptev brothers, had been given the job of surveying the coast westward from the Lena. It began successfully and managed to sail as far as the Yenisei before it was stopped by ice. The expedition's pilot, a man named Semyon

Chelyuskin, volunteered to continue along the shore, taking two soldiers and three sledges. Eventually, in 1641, he found himself at the most northerly point on the mainland of the Old World. Two hundred and thirty-seven years later the Swedish explorer and scientist Adolf Erik Nordenskiöld became the first man to sail past the cape, which he generously named after Chelyuskin.

That evening, on my usual walk round the helicopter deck, I felt that something was different. As I looked out astern over the smashed-up wake to the horizon, I realised that for the first time in 1500 kilometres we did not have two ships following behind us. There had been something oddly comforting about seeing the black and orange hulls coming in and out of the fog banks and following our wake precisely even when we were twisting and turning. Now we were on our own.

The conversation that night at dinner was, as usual, sparse. The soup was good, the meat tough and in microscopic quantities and the apple was so bruised that I left it uneaten.

'Don't you like apples?' asked the captain, who clearly coveted mine. I lied, saying that I had already eaten quite enough, thank you.

I remembered the joke Maxim had made that afternoon about the pink seagull. Had Captain Ulitin ever seen one? He pondered for a while before answering.

'Yes, I've seen them. In fact, come to think of it, the winter we got stuck off Tixi I actually caught a gull and painted it pink. Is that pink enough for a *kulak*?' I was being gullible.

I didn't think about pink gulls again until one afternoon at home I was looking through an illustrated book on the natural history of Russia, called *Realms of the Russian Bear*. There I came across a magnificent picture of Captain

Ulitin's gull. It is apparently one of the most famous of all Arctic birds and had been named Ross's Gull (*Rhodostethia Rosea*) after the Scottish Arctic explorer, Sir James Clark Ross who, on his third trip searching for the North West Passage in 1823, shot a small gull with 'the most delicate rose colour on its breast'. For the remainder of the nineteeth century the breeding site of this gull remained a mystery, until a Russian High Court Judge, Sergei Alexandrovich Buturlin, found three colonies near the Kolyma River in north-eastern Siberia.[1]

The best thing about these gulls was the old Siberian legend of how they got their pink colour in the first place. It seems that the birds are the spirits of two attractive girls who died 'in their quest for even greater beauty'. An old spinster advised them to bathe in the depths of winter so their complexions would become pink and healthy. The girls did just as she suggested, but (and this will surprise no one who has put a finger into Arctic water) they immediately became numb and drowned. Their souls, however, return year after year in the shape of these pink birds.

It was always difficult to know what to do in the two hours before midnight. The sky was bright and I never felt remotely sleepy. I usually passed the time in the radio room, since this was Leonid's watch and he spoke reasonable English.

On one of these evenings I was examining an old radio set, marvelling at the valves, some of which were 25

[1] On 28 January 1993 *The Scotsman* reported that three Ross's gulls had been spotted at Fraserburgh in north-east Scotland. Birdwatchers from all over the UK fluttered into town in a state of great excitement, since there had only been five sightings of these gulls in the United Kingdom since 1846. An expert was quoted as saying, 'It's amazing. This is the largest sighting of these gulls there has ever been outside the Arctic.'

centimetres tall and glowed like electric toasters. I had not noticed Sergei, who had slipped in from the bridge to forage for biscuits, until a voice behind me said, 'It's Ilyich's bulb.' I gave a start and turned round to see Sergei grinning.

Who, I wondered, was Ilyich?

'Ilyich?' repeated Sergei. 'You don't know Ilyich? The founder of our country. Our great and revered leader, Vladimir Ilyich Lenin? He brought us electricity, which is why all over this country the electric light bulbs are called Ilyich's bulb.' He stopped to allow the significance to permeate through to my skull. 'If you want to be a *kulak* you will have to learn about Ilyich's bulb.'

When it was low in the sky, the sunlight played tricks with the scenery. As the shadows lengthened the icescape changed. Instead of being flat and featureless, the horizon sometimes resembled the heathland of south Cambridgeshire with spinneys, hedges and wide open fields. The humps, crevices and mounds had shadows I never saw at midday. It was all too simple, as I whiled away the time staring out across the ice, to see submarines, battleships and even cities off in the distance. The easiest thing to imagine at times like this was a polar bear lurking in every shadow.

With four days to go before the longest day of the year, everyone on the bridge was wearing sunglasses at two in the morning. The glittering dazzle off the ice could hurt your eyes if you looked directly at it.

I should not have gone to bed that night. At about two o'clock we hit the thickest ice we had yet encountered, and from then on *Arktika* rolled, bucked and ground its way through the solid Kara Sea. From time to time we found ourselves in open water and for a few brief moments the vibration stopped, the noise subsided and I drifted off to sleep again. Then, with a thundering crunch, we would hit a new wall of ice; the alarm clock would slide off the bedside table and I would sit bolt upright in bed. As if this weren't enough, the temperature in my cabin varied from subtropical to Arctic. My Russian equivalent of a duvet, a blanket folded double and wrapped in a sheet, would have been perfectly adequate if the room temperature had been around 20 degrees, but it could not cope with the extraordinary variations which happened depending on whether or not my porthole was ajar.

For the past ten days the *ptichka* had been flying at least once a day, and often as many as four times. From my cabin I could hear the twin jet engines warming up and then it would fly past at porthole height, making a horrendous clatter. From time to time I would loiter around the helicopter deck in the hope that I might be invited on board as a passenger. When this tactic appeared to be unsuccessful I took to dropping heavy hints on the bridge about how interesting it would be to accompany Valerii Mikhailovich on one of his scouting missions. These too were ignored, and I had just about given up hope of ever travelling on the helicopter when the captain asked me if I was free that morning.

This was a strange question, since nobody on the ship had more spare time than me. I smiled prettily and admitted that I might be able to postpone my activities if the alternative were attractive enough.

Two hours later, wearing pyjamas under my trousers and three sweaters on my top half, I was huddled in the back of the MI-2 helicopter. Beside me, sitting on the wooden floor was Valentin, the chief helicopter pilot. In the left-hand front seat his deputy, Oleg Varnavsky, was behind the controls and in his normal position on the right was Valerii Mikhailovich, hatless in a navy blue parka.

The two jet engines started with a whine and the rotors

began to turn very slowly. As the speed built up so did the noise. Valentin leant across and handed me a pair of earphones. None of us wore lifejackets or immersion suits, which meant that if we had ditched in the sea we wouldn't have lasted more than a couple of minutes. There was, however, a loaded rifle on a rack behind me, so at least we should have been safe from polar bears.

The revs mounted and, almost imperceptibly, we lifted away from the deck before pointing our nose down towards the sea and swooping out on the starboard side of the ship. It was magic. Within minutes *Arktika* was far away in the distance, looking like the decoration on a vast iced cake. I half expected to see it surrounded by a ring of candles with a sign in red saying 'Happy Christmas'.

The ice was a lot whiter than any I had seen, and the sea itself a dark emerald green. Along the pressure ridges, where the ice had been pushed up into miniature mountain ranges, there were jagged lines of turquoise. Channels of open water, for no reason that I could see, gave way to stretches of unbroken ice. In front of me Valerii Mikhailovich was constantly resetting the compass to show the pilot in which direction to fly. It seemed as if we were wandering at random across the landscape, but I knew that he was methodically looking for signs which would tell him where the ice was weakest. Occasionally he would make a note on a pad which rested on his knee, but most of the time he simply looked out across the ice like a man in a commuter train watching the level crossings go by.

After an hour of zig-zagging at never more than sixty metres above the ice, it was time to return to the ship. Before we did so Valerii Mikhailovich decided to have a bit of fun. Passing the chart back to me, he pointed out two islands on the map and then gesticulated to a spot on our port bow. A few minutes later we came swooping in low over a cluster of pale blue huts and did two wide circles before hovering over what looked like a radio mast. From the chart I could see that we were at Troynoy Island and the buildings were apparently Polar Station Osetrov (sturgeon). Valentin assured me that the base was manned, but nobody came out to wave.

On our way back to the ship we skirted the mainland, although it was impossible to see exactly where the shore-line was. In a few spots a line of driftwood showed that under the snow was a shingle beach, but usually the sea, shore and land were all covered by ice which just looked white from the helicopter.

The air was ludicrously clear. I felt as if I could see further than I had ever done before. Yet I saw only one animal that morning: a huge and flabby walrus lying asleep on the ice beside some water. On our third pass he woke up and slid off into the sea to escape the noise of the helicopter.

Arktika grew bigger and bigger, but even when we were hovering above her, the painted circle on the helicopter deck still looked frighteningly small. After we had landed, and before the rotors had stopped, Valentin asked me if I would like to take some photographs of the ship. I agreed excitedly. Strapping myself into the seat which Valerii Mikhailovich had just left, I was a mite disturbed to see that Valentin was removing the door.

'You make better pictures this way,' he shouted. And he was right. For the next half hour we zoomed and swooped, dived and rolled and did things which I never knew a helicopter could do.

It soon became obvious that I wasn't the only reason why Valentin was doing these aerobatics. Below us a small gleeful crowd was lining *Arktika*'s rails to watch what was happening to the *kulak* in the *ptichka*.

7 Stalinist saunas

The first fifty years of my life had been happy, and one of
the reasons was that I had never been near a sauna. In the
previous two weeks this policy had, however, been increasingly difficult to preserve. I had on various occasions
received casual invitations from members of the crew to
join them in the ship's sauna but had successfully deflected
them by pleading pressure of work, an appointment with
the captain or even an imminent and entirely fictional
flight on the *ptichka*.

This time there was no escape. Maxim, dressed in a T-
shirt and boxer shorts, stood in my doorway until I agreed
to join him. He had brought me not only a towel and a pair
of rubber flip-flops, but also a felt helmet which reminded
me of the headgear worn by the participants in the Eton
Wall Game.

We walked towards the stern before going down four
decks, far below the waterline. The passages seemed to be
darker and narrower, but this may just have been a symp-
tom of my increasing terror. Eventually we reached a heavy
door which Maxim opened to reveal a wood-lined changing
room with benches on which naked men were sprawled.
Some appeared to be sleeping, or at least in catatonic

trances, while others were drinking cups of hot liquid which they poured from thermos flasks.

'Do not worry,' said Maxim, sensing my fear. 'I have asked Yuri to be your guide. He is the sauna expert on board.'

I had met Yuri Sevostyanov, the officer in command of control systems, on a couple of occasions, but had never got to know him since his English was poor and he seemed particularly shy. Here in the sauna, however, he was Tsar.

A man of medium height with wavy brown hair, Yuri had the soft chubby cheeks of someone who spends most of his life indoors. He also seemed to have exceptionally pink skin, until I realised that everyone who had recently emerged from the sauna had pink skin. Indeed, many of them looked nearer scarlet than pink.

As I was undressing, Yuri began to deliver a lecture about the history of sauna in general and its importance to red-blooded Russians in particular. Sauna originated in Finland, he explained, where the population was genteel and more than a bit foppish. Proof of this could be seen from the fact that a Finnish sauna rarely exceeds 80 degrees Celsius. Russian saunas, said Yuri, were somewhat warmer.

Carrying a plastic bucket and a bunch of floppy green leaves, Yuri led me through another wooden door to a room in which there was a line of shower cubicles down one side and what looked like a miniature bowling alley, long and narrow, down the other.

'Put on your hat,' he suggested. 'You will need it to protect your hair.' At the same time he removed a flat piece of wood from a row which was hanging on the wall above us. 'You will need this to sit on. The seats are too hot.'

The moment had arrived. Yuri used both hands to tug

open a heavy wooden door. If you bend down to remove the Christmas turkey from the oven, your face occasionally gets a waft of unpleasantly hot air in the instant after the oven door is opened. The effect on my naked body was identical, but with Maxim behind me, there was no possibility of retreating.

I was in a dark chamber lit by a single dim light bulb. Around the wood-lined walls were three terraces of wooden benches and in the centre, occupying the position of the altar in one of those modern amphitheatrical churches, was what appeared to be a stove. Yuri put the wooden plate on the bench and motioned to me to sit down. For a moment I was so stupefied that I could neither move nor think.

The heat was unlike anything I had ever experienced. When I eventually opened my mouth to speak, my tongue, palate and tonsils felt as if they were cooking.

'What's the temperature in here?' I croaked.

'Let me see,' said Maxim in the same voice he used on the bridge, and he squinted at a thermometer on the wall. 'One hundred and thirteen degrees Celsius. Hot, eh?'

Somewhere along the production line of life, a worker whose mind must have been on other things fitted me with an Eskimo's thermostat. The result has been that I have always loathed hot climates and been happiest when there is frost on the ground. Hence my presence in the Kara Sea that day. Hence also my supreme discomfort at finding myself in a little dark hole with the temperature high enough to boil an egg.

I sat with my head in my hands, staring at my feet as sweat came out of every pore in my body and splashed audibly on to the concrete floor. The agony was only tolerable, I kept reassuring myself, because I knew I could walk through the door out into the real cool world any time I felt like it.

And then an extraordinary thing happened. I found I was enjoying it. The fear seemed to have been sweated out and I was feeling more relaxed than I had ever been in my life before.

After about ten minutes Yuri poked me in the ribs and gestured that it was time to go outside. As I emerged into the shower room, he pointed to the long narrow space along the far wall.

'Go and stand at the end,' he commanded. I did so, and turned round in time to see him pick up what looked like a watering-can rose connected to the plumbing by a long flexible pipe. This was, however, no ordinary rose. It was 30 centimetres across and had two handles attached, which Yuri was now gripping with both hands. I was dimly aware of being a target in a fairground shooting range.

Maxim turned on a large brass stopcock and threw a switch on the bulkhead. A loud roaring noise started and a jet of freezing water knocked me sideways so that I had to steady myself against the wall. Yuri was holding the bucking rose, which kept twisting out of his hands as the pressure built up. I let out a scream of shock and terror, but it had no effect on the naked man with the water jet. I tried to shout but could not. Then it stopped as suddenly as it had started.

My ordeal was not yet over. This time Yuri didn't take a wooden plate for me to sit on. Instead he brought two towels which he folded so that they covered the whole of the uppermost bench. I was instructed to lie down on my back, and did so nervously. The temperature on the highest bench seemed to be even greater than it had been for my previous session. And what made it still worse was the fact that Yuri started to flick water out of a plastic bucket on to the stove, creating clouds of steam. He then opened a small bottle of eucalyptus oil and put a few drops on to the hot rocks. The result took me back forty-five years to when, as a little boy with a cold, I sat under a towel inhaling something called Friars Balsam. If there's one thing worse than a hot climate, it's a hot and humid climate. I thought I'd died and gone to hell.

I lay on my back and wished that the stove would stop generating steam. My prayers were answered. Yuri ceased flicking water on to the hot surface and instead started to brush me with the leaves as if he was giving me a rough undercoat with a bad paintbrush. I remembered the photographs of Yves Klein painting his nude models bright blue before dragging them across a canvas. Occasionally Yuri would dip the bundle of leaves into a bucket and start again, working from my face down to my feet.

'Turn over now,' he said thickly. I turned over on to my stomach and the process was repeated. The brushstrokes gradually became brush slaps, not hard but certainly not soothing. The slaps grew stronger and the noise of wet leaves hitting flabby Englishman grew louder.

Out again into the shower room, I refused categorically to endure the shooting-gallery torture once more, and instead opted for the civilised (and warm) shower in one of the cubicles. Judging by the line of men soaping themselves, it appeared that the majority of my fellow sauna victims agreed with me. Alexander, who had arrived late, had no such reservations and submitted to the high-pressure treatment. As the water, which I later learned was sea water at ambient temperature, hit him he let out a series of big roars like a Russian bear having an orgasm.

'Now for massage,' said Yuri. 'Come.' And he led me back into the changing room where once again he spread two towels out on a bench and invited – even commanded – me to lie down.

A massage, like a sauna, was something I had hitherto managed to do without. But then I had never before met Yuri Sevostyanov. Starting on my toes, he worked slowly up the lengthy of my extremely pink body, rubbing in concentric circles with large and surprisingly hard hands. 'Turn over' came the command. I turned over on to my front. Then the serious stuff began, as Yuri decided that my spine needed his especial care.

As he reached my lower vertebrae he stopped.

'Have you ever had an injury here?' he asked. 'Because it feels tight here,' prodding just above my coccyx. And, so saying, he dug his thumbs into my spine and rested his hundred kilos on top of them. I wondered if anything in life was meant to hurt that much, but since Alexander and Maxim were watching, I said nothing.

Yuri was right. Thirty-two years previously I had injured my back while rowing. Not only did it put a stop to my athletic career, but a few years later it kept me from being called up into the United States Army to fight in Vietnam.

After the massage, we all went back for a third dose of sauna at which the wet leaf treatment was repeated. Finally a cool shower and into my T-shirt and underpants before returning to my cabin and collapsing on the bunk.

I had not been back for more than five minutes when the phone rang. It was the fourth mate, Andrei Cherepukhin. In an impossibly thick accent, he said 'Hurry. To the bridge please. Hurry.' I puffed up to the bridge to find the captain, first mate and fourth mate looking astern on the port side to where a big polar bear was standing no more than 150 metres away, at the edge of the channel we had just cut. By the time I had gone back to my cabin to fetch a telephoto lens, the bear had swum across the channel and was on our starboard side.

Arktika was going astern, which was odd since we hadn't hit any particularly hard ice. Out on the deck in my T-shirt, I took a series of photographs as we approached the puzzled and motionless bear. After a couple of minutes it sensibly decided that an approaching atomic icebreaker was not something it wanted to tolerate any longer, so it ambled off across the ice floes in long, lolloping strides – completely unhurried and evidently unafraid. Barry Lopez, in his book *Arctic Dreams*, wrote that the early whalers used to call the polar bear 'farmer' because of his 'very agricultural appearance as he stalks leisurely over the furrowed fields of ice'.

Behind me stood the captain, grinning hugely. It was a mark of how wonderful this man was that he would stop and reverse a nuclear icebreaker so an English *kulak* could have a better view of a polar farmer.

After all the excitement I returned to my cabin to find a note on the door. It read 'Supper with Yuri tonight. Please come.' Yuri's cabin was, like mine, one of the good ones, reserved for officers of some seniority. Although it was one deck below, it was of equal size and had the advantage of looking out forward to the bows.

As I entered, carrying a bar of Cadbury's milk chocolate, I noticed that it was going to be a reunion of the sauna team. Alexander was sitting on the sofa nursing a glass of tea while Maxim and Yuri had opened a bottle of beer. In front of them on a low coffee table was what Russians do best – *zakuski*. Someone had gone to a great deal of trouble, not simply to get hold of the grub, but also to lay it out prettily. There were tomatoes sliced thinly in semicircles, fatty pork sliced rather thicker and arranged in rectangles, a fish called stavrida, similar to mackerel, which had been cut across the backbone and lay in a heap, cucumber, arranged like the tomatoes and, best of all, a quart jar of cranberries. In the centre of the table stood a bottle of pepper vodka. I realised that, as a result of the sweat I'd lost in the sauna, I wasn't just thirsty, I was also stupendously hungry.

We began, inevitably, with the pepper vodka. As it slid down my throat I felt as if I were gulping liquid vindaloo. By the time the vodka had reached my stomach, my throat had already recovered and I was aware that my right arm was outstretched, holding a glass which was waiting to be refilled. It didn't have to wait long.

The fatty pork and black bread went well with the vodka, but I noticed that Yuri and Maxim were taking a spoonful of cranberries after every gulp. This, they explained, either delayed the onset of inebriation or increased the intake of vodka, which sounded like two sides of the same equation.

Yuri was an interesting chap. Aged forty-nine he was a few months younger than me. If he had been a Western European I would have suspected his wispy black fringe of being a toupee, but in Russia this seemed unlikely. On his cabin wall there was a photograph of Gorbachev and one of the arch-conservative Ligachev. I hoped this showed agnosticism and not timidity.

Yuri had been with *Arktika* ever since she had been launched in 1975, and so knew everything there was to be known about the automated systems on board.

'Of course,' he told me a bit sadly, 'we're not nearly as automated as nuclear-powered vessels are in the West. But you mustn't forget that this ship was designed nearly twenty-five years ago.'

What I wanted to know was how an Arctic merchant seaman had learned to be a masseur.

'Hah,' he grinned. 'That's a long story and you'd be bored

if I told you even part of it.' He took a swig of beer, munched some cucumber and began. 'Do you know what yoga is?'

I replied that I had a rough idea, though I wasn't a practitioner myself.

'In this country it isn't all that easy to find out about yoga. I suppose you could even say it's been discouraged.' Another swig of beer. 'Anyway, it all began with yoga heaven knows how long ago. But then I got interested in other things, too. I started studying the martial arts like kung fu and judo, and from there I became interested in alternative medicine. I used to read anything I could get my hands on, although this wasn't easy because these sort of things were also discouraged. From there I started to hear about extrasensory perception, and that's what really interests me these days. That and massage without contact.'

Massage without contact? I could have done with a bit less contact a few hours earlier when Yuri had been walking on my spine.

'Yes, well I don't actually practise any of that stuff. I don't know enough about it, but I'm studying whenever possible.' As he spoke he pulled open his desk drawer and removed a sheaf of photocopied paper. 'Look at these,' he said. 'I had to copy them because they're hard to find in bookshops. In fact they are impossible.'

From the illustrations and diagrams it was obvious that they were a textbook of massage. There in the middle of the frozen Kara Sea I was looking at a way-out flaky samizdat which had been passed round by true believers. Thank God for xerography.

As we emptied the pepper vodka and started on the beer, the conversation turned to our families.

Like all men his age, Yuri was dreading his fiftieth

birthday. Of his two children, the eldest was a fisherman who had once visited Scotland on a training mission. His daughter, of whom he was inordinately proud, was finishing her high school in Murmansk.

Maxim was married to a doctor who lived in Moscow with their small daughter.

'It's tough for her having me away for four months at a time,' he told me. 'But one of these days I'm going to stop working on an icebreaker and go into something commercial instead. To do this I want to take a course in business and I think I've already arranged this.'[1] I remembered a programme I had seen on television the previous night. It came on immediately after *Vremya*, the national news, and seemed to be about finance. Throughout the programme the word 'biznez' kept cropping up. It had clearly been adopted by the Russian language as its own.

Alexander remained silent throughout the conversation, preferring to listen while the rest of us gabbled increasingly incoherently.

We had started on the last bottle of beer when I described how the captain had reversed the ship to let me get a better view of a polar bear that afternoon.

'That's incredible,' said Maxim. 'Grigorii Alexeivich has a pretty tough reputation in the fleet. He's not the sort of man to stop a ship without a very good reason.'

Alexander woke from his stupor. 'No, Max,' he said. 'You've got him all wrong. I can quite see him doing that. He's got a very soft heart.'

The argument about Ulitin's character teetered on for a few minutes before Yuri interrupted. 'Do any of you

---

[1] And so he had. Maxim left *Arktika* only a few weeks after I did, and flew back to Moscow. A year later I received a fax from him. He had completed his course and had found a job with a shipping company in Sofia. He seemed very happy indeed.

remember Igor Sergeivich? He used to be the hydrologist on the *Lenin* for a long time.' Neither Maxim nor Alexander could recall him.

'Well, he once had a polar bear all of his own. He found this cub on an ice floe one day. Its mother must have died. The animal was still very small so he was able to trap it and take it back on board his ship. He called the bear Mashka and it used to live in a cage on the foredeck. The bear was very tame and spent much of the day with Igor. When he was transferred to the *Lenin*, he took Mashka with him, and for a while the bear became the unofficial ship's mascot. The snag was that when Mashka was about two years old, his shipmates decided that they weren't too keen on having a semi-mature polar bear on board. They really can be very vicious indeed.

'Eventually it was decided by the higher-ups in Moscow that the bear should be given to President Kekkonnen of Finland, so when the *Lenin* was next back in Murmansk, Mashka was crated up and flown to Helsinki, where she was put into the zoo.

'Years later, or so the story goes, Igor found himself in Helsinki. He went to the zoo and looked for the polar bears. Among the bears in the cage was one enormous female. Igor went up to the bars and whispered, very softly, "Mashka" and the big bear pricked its ears up. "Mashka," whispered Igor again, and the bear came over to the side of the cage and lay down beside her old master.

'Anyway,' said Yuri, 'that's the story. I can't guarantee it's true, but I do know that Igor existed.'

8 Flying the *Ptichka*

I woke later than usual next morning, probably because the clocks had gone back an hour. This was a fairly frequent event because at those northern latitudes you don't have to go very far east to reach a new time zone. The ship appeared to be moving normally and wasn't crashing around too much, so I didn't have to hold on to the basin while I scrubbed my teeth. But when I went to make coffee I realised that the view out of the porthole was different. In fact there wasn't a view at all; just a white blob of nothingness.

As usual, when bored or curious, I took my coffee up on to the bridge to see if the view from there was any different. It wasn't. It looked as if someone had glued sheets of white paper to all the windows.

My morning ritual on the bridge was unvarying. I went straight to the large table aft of the wheel. There, surmounted by satellite navigation aids with their digital read-outs, and beside the chart, lay the ship's log. Twice a day I would copy down the ship's position, which had been carefully recorded at the end of each watch. I would also make a note of the distance we had travelled the preceding four hours.

That morning it looked as if there had been a clerical

error. Between midnight and four o'clock we managed to cover 6.7 nautical miles, and on the following watch we did nine miles.

The captain was in conference with Valerii Mikhailovich, poring over the ice map which had resulted from yesterday's *ptichka* flight. Their body language transmitted the clear message that they would not welcome any trivial chit-chat from the *kulak*, so I left them in peace and went in search of other company. Owdoyoudo, perched on the tall stool behind the wheel, beamed energetically and said, 'Owdoyoudo.' I beamed with equal ferocity and confirmed that I did very well, thank you. Our lack of each other's language meant that this was the sum total of our social intercourse, so I continued on my search for an English-speaking human being.

Eventually I found one, in the shape of Sergei. He emerged from the small deck astern of the bridge blowing on his hands and shivering deeply.

'It is not warm,' he explained. 'I have been checking the temperature and it is minus seven degrees.'

But frigidity was not Sergei's problem that morning.

'It is the ice,' he muttered. 'Very bad. Very bad indeed.' This came as a surprise since I'd been unable to see any ice when I'd looked a few minutes earlier.

'It is worst we have found yet,' continued Sergei. 'There are hummocks, some of them five metres thick. No ship in the world can go through those. Even *Arktika*.' Listening to him describe what conditions had been like that night, I thanked God that alcohol had numbed most of my senses. 'It was very slow,' he told me. 'Sometimes we had to go back and forwards four or even five times. This takes a lot of time and it is not good for the ship. It's not good for the crew either, because it is a lot of hard work.'

It appeared that not only was the ice thick but, far more

serious, the pressure of the ice was very great. Pressure, Sergei explained, was often a lot more significant than simply the thickness of the ice.

'When there is not a lot of pressure the pieces of ice can always go beneath the ship when we break them. The broken ice can also go beneath the remaining ice. But when there is a lot of pressure there is nowhere for the ice to go. That gives us very great problems indeed.'

He went on to explain that on the most modern ice-breakers, but not on *Arktika*, there is a series of holes along the water line through which compressed air is pumped to produce a mass of bubbles. In conditions like those we were experiencing, the bubbles would act as a lubricant.

One of the strange things I noticed about that day's ice was that it was so strong and so thick that the fissures did not run ahead of the ship as they did in thinner ice. The ice on either side remained solid even when we eventually smashed our way through. As I looked towards the stern I could see that the channel we had carved had almost straight sides and not the normal jagged edges I had grown used to.

The captain and Valerii Mikhailovich eventually ended their discussion, with the latter going below for a glass of tea. I edged over towards the port side of the bridge where the captain was staring into whiteness.

'Very difficult,' he said. 'No helicopter today. You cannot fly if you cannot see.' As he completed the sentence he braced himself against the bulkhead, anticipating the crash which came a second later. Not having thirty-seven years of icebreaking experience, I didn't anticipate anything, which is why I landed on the floor.

Sergei, who was in command, standing on the far side of the bridge with a window open so he could see better, burst out laughing. His hand was on the three throttle levers, and whenever he saw that the ship was about to stop, he pushed them hard astern.

'I must do this immediately,' he told me, 'because there is about thirty centimetres of snow on top of the ice and that is what is causing the problem. *Arktika* can manage very well with fast ice like this, but the snow is very sticky and unless I go astern immediately, we can stick to the ice.'

I picked myself up, happy that I had emptied my coffee mug, and looked out of the aft windows of the bridge. The stern was rising rapidly, which meant that the bows had just begun their downward crunch. Sometimes they would rise as much as three metres into the air before falling back and slicing through the ice.

I was watching this irrregular but mesmeric movement of the bows when I felt someone tapping my shoulder. It was Yuri.

'Good morning,' he said cheerfully. 'I hope you did sleep well.' Like every other member of *Arktika*'s crew, Yuri displayed absolutely no signs of a hangover. My admiration for Russians in general, and icebreaker crews in particular, continued to grow.

Yuri had come to the bridge to check on some wiring which was concealed behind one of the panels. I looked into the small space where he was shining a torch and saw a labyrinth of coloured cables. No microprocessors or printed circuits. *Arktika* was a steam-age ship.

By lunchtime the horizon had returned and Valerii Mikhailovich suggested I might like to come with him in the *ptichka*. After almost two weeks, I had now been accepted by this most diffident of men. It made me very happy.

As usual, we spent an hour and a half flying over the ice looking for leads, during which time the hydrologist showed no emotion whatsoever as he stared out across the level ice. Eventually he put down the pad on which he had been making some notes and turned to me.

'Maybe,' he shouted above the noise of the engines, 'we will look for animals.'

We turned towards the shore, which was marked by a line of driftwood. Beyond was a range of low hills, the tops of which were dark brown from where the snow had been blown. The helicopter swooped in low over the beach and up a valley of dark grey rocks. As it did so Valerii Mikhailovich tapped me on the shoulder and pointed at some black dots in the distance. They were a small herd of reindeer, searching for moss and lichen in the snow-free patches.

As we approached they heard the sound of our engine and took off at a gallop. But a helicopter is a lot faster than a reindeer, and we soon overtook them. They stopped, terrified, then wheeled about, heading straight back towards the coast. We did the same, coming in very low at haunch height behind them. As we came past the leading animals in the herd I could see their mouths open and their white teeth as they gasped for breath. Not being a hunting man, I should have disapproved of chasing reindeer in a helicopter, but it was fun. It also enabled me to get an unusual view of a reindeer herd at full gallop. After a few minutes the pilot became bored and gave up the hunt, rising into the air before turning back towards *Arktika*. As we did so he shouted something to Valerii Mikhailovich and banked steeply to the left. Once again we pointed our nose at the ground and dropped steeply towards what looked like a snow bank. Only then did I see it. A large polar bear had been disturbed by our antics and was ambling along the valley bottom towards the sea.

We came lower and lower until we were only a few

metres away from the bear who then, obviously irritated by the noise and the down draft, broke into a trot.

Even at London Zoo I had never been closer to a polar bear. On its sharply pointed head I could see its nostrils dilated as it, like the reindeer, began to panic. It broke into a slow, rhythmical run, kicking up puffs of snow with its big paws. We dropped astern and I could see its stump of a tail and the brown patch of fur around its behind. This time, I felt sympathy for the animal and gestured to the pilot to stop the chase. He seemed to agree, and we swung up and away to leave the bear galloping onwards down the valley.

Excited by seeing these animals in the wild, and exhilarated by the chase, I lay on the floor of the helicopter for the flight back to the ship. Fifteen minutes later I was prodded by Valerii Mikhailovich and sat upright, expecting to see another bear, or maybe a walrus. Instead we were hovering over a lighthouse, pink and deserted. The lantern had blown down and the blue front door was flapping in the wind. To me it looked like an abandoned spot of nothingness, but to Russian merchant seamen it was Beluga Island, one of the most sacred spots in the Arctic.

At 8.30 that evening *Arktika*'s whistle sounded three long blasts while one of the seamen, hatless in the cold wind, dipped the hammer and sickle flag. Every Soviet icebreaker which passes Beluga Island goes through this ritual.

It all goes back to 1932 when the ice breaker *Sibiryakov* became the first ship ever to navigate the North East Passage in a single season. Never mind the fact that by the time she reached the Bering Straits she did not have a propeller and had to be towed through by a trawler, the North East Passage had been conquered after four hundred years of failure. Stalin was ecstatic and wrote to the

96

expedition's leader, Otto Schmidt (whose shaggy face watched over me every day at mealtimes), 'There are no fortresses which Bolshevik daring and organisation are not able to storm.'[1]

Ten years later the same ship was again an inspiration for the whole nation, although this time the story did not have a happy ending. On 25 August 1942 the *Sibiryakov*, which had been lightly armed at the beginning of the war, was patrolling the coastal waters off the Taymyr Peninsula when she met the German pocket battleship *Admiral Scheer*, which had been dispatched to the Arctic on a mission called Operation Wunderland.[2] Outgunned, outmanned and outclassed, the *Sibiryakov* stood no chance. She went down with all hands just off Beluga Island. Which is why *Arktika* dipped her flag and blew her whistle that white afternoon in June.

After the helicopter flight I slept for a bit on my bunk and so arrived in the dining room after the other eight officers on the captain's table had eaten. Only a few other people in the rest of the dining room were still finishing their meals; one of them was Valerii Mikhailovich. It seemed like a good time to find out more about this quiet man who said almost nothing but still managed to project greater authority than any other person on board.

How is it, I asked him, that during the entire flight that afternoon he had not taken a single note in an hour and a half? He looked a bit surprised by the question, studied his plate for a few seconds before running his fingers through his hair.

[1] This sentence later passed into the Stalinist catechism of meaningless exhortations, and has since become a cliché.
[2] Although militarily insignificant (the *Scheer* sunk only one ship and managed to shell Dikson Island), it was bad for Soviet morale as it showed how powerless the Russians were to defend their own Arctic seas.

'It's all in there,' he muttered, pointing to his head. 'I don't need to take notes.'

I wasn't sure that I believed him, so I persisted. From time to time I had noticed that he leaned over and altered the compass setting in front of the pilot. Had we been flying in a random pattern or did he know where he wanted to go?

'It certainly wasn't random,' he said with what might have been irritation. 'We were flying in a very precise pattern and I knew exactly where we would be going.'

It was time to broaden the subject to the whole field of ice navigation. Was it an art or a science? Did some people have a talent for it? Valerii Mikhailovich thought for a long time.

'My first reaction was to tell you that it is a science,' he said. 'But I am beginning to doubt if this is the case. In fact the older I get the more I believe that it is an art. But,' and he paused, 'there's an awful lot of science in it too. For example, you've got to know about meteorology and navigation as well as seamanship.'

I remembered a conversation I'd had a few months earlier in Washington. I had gone to visit the United States Coastguard, who are in charge of the American icebreaker fleet, because I wanted to know what they thought of their Russian counterparts. As it turned out, the American Coastguard were as ignorant as they were prejudiced about Russian icebreakers. They began by warning me of the dangers of radiation on *Arktika*.

'I hope you've finished raising a family,' said one man with lots of scrambled egg on his peaked cap. 'Because if you haven't I suggest you take along some lead BVDs.' His colleagues guffawed.

One of the things I wanted to know was whether the Russian ships had any medical staff aboard. The answer in Washington was clear enough.

'Nope.'

'So what'll happen to me if I get ill?'

'Don't.'

At least we ended on a more upbeat note. Having sneered at the Russians' primitive conditions and unsophisticated technology, the head of the Ice Section of the United States Coastguard became serious for a moment.

'You gotta admit one thing,' he said, 'those guys know more about sailing ships through the Arctic than anyone else on earth.'

Looking at the hydrologist on *Arktika* I knew he was right.

When Valerii Mikhailovich returned to the ship, did he, I asked, tell the captain where to steer? He laughed.

'Oh, no. Nobody ever tells the captain to do anything. All I can do is to advise him and hope he follows my advice.'

Does he?

'Yes. This particular captain does, but then we've known each other for a long time and we both respect each other.'

Had he ever been in a helicopter crash?

'Oh, yes. Often. It's really quite a dangerous job, I suppose. But fortunately we rarely fly much above fifty metres and you can't do a lot of damage to a helicopter if you fall fifty metres.'

Had he ever been scared?

'No. Never.'

I got up to leave the room, but Valerii Mikhailovich hadn't quite finished.

'It's going to be a long trip,' he said. 'Looking at that ice this afternoon I think it will take us another week to reach Cape Chelyuskin. I hope you are not bored already.'

I thought he was joking. On the map it looked as if Cape

Chelyuskin was a day's sail away. The hydrologist must have read my thoughts. 'The ice conditions are bad and they're going to get worse,' he said. 'And at the moment we are doing no more than six miles every four hours. Work it out for yourself.'

On my way out of the dining room I passed a table where a solitary grey-haired figure was finishing his meal. It was Dimitri Nikitin, my guide round the nuclear reactor. I pulled up a chair and joined him for a glass of tea.

'Why don't you come with me to the control room?' he asked. 'I am just about to go on watch.' It seemed like a good idea, since the only alternative was to torment poor Leonid in the radio room with inane questions about the Inmarsat phone system which never seemed to work.

In the control room Dimitri was greeted by a good-looking young man in a singlet which was obviously designed to show off his exceptional figure. Vadim Rusanov was a body-builder who passed the time in *Arktika*'s gym pumping iron and studying himself in the mirror. There was, admittedly, a lot to study. Dark curly hair sat on top of a square face with regular features. This in turn was supported by a squat, thick neck. Sprouting from his shoulders, and emphasised by his sleeveless singlet, were two enormous arms which bulged in strange directions. The rest of his body consisted of a large chest, a narrow waist and two trunklike legs. A sort of Arctic Ozymandias.

Dimitri exchanged some words with the engineer he was relieving and beckoned me over to a chair in front of a large console showing a schematic diagram of one of the nuclear reactors. Vadim was sitting in the equivalent chair in front of an identical bank of lights and switches monitoring the second nuclear reactor. Two more crewmen were looking at other functions, not directly connected with the reactor, while the fifth man on duty was Leonid

100

Razumovsky,[3] the radiation safety engineer, whose bald head and goatee beard made him look uncannily like the young Lenin.

Everyone in the control room was wearing dosimeters, which looked like aluminium fountain pens, in their breast pockets, except Vadim who had clipped his to the neck of his singlet.

'We wear them all the time,' explained Vadim, 'and every day we take them to a machine which automatically checks how much radiation we have been exposed to. It's a safety device for people who work with the nuclear plant.'

I was about to leave when Dimitri asked me if I would like to see the engine room. Surely, I protested, he wouldn't be able to leave his post – particularly one as important as checking on the reactor?

'Oh, yes,' he replied, 'that will be no problem. One of my colleagues will do my job for me, and then I will do his when I return.'

I followed Dimitri out of the control room and forward towards the middle of the ship before turning into a small passageway and climbing down two steep companionways. He opened a large steel door and led me into a cavern, painted cream and illuminated by neon strips.

The first thing I noticed about *Arktika*'s engine room was how quiet it was compared to conventional ships with their big diesel engines. Here there was no motor, since the nuclear reactors were in a separate compartment altogether. Instead there was a labyrinth of pipes feeding into three large steam turbines which were driving the same number of electrical generators. From these sprouted three long shafts which drove the propellers on the outside of the hull.

[3] A year later he was to marry the ship's secretary, Ludmilla Chernova.

Not a lot of attention had been paid to safety. There were unguarded belts and pulleys which were completely exposed and bits and pieces which stuck out inconveniently – even dangerously – into the walkways. In Britain the Health and Safety Inspectorate would have closed *Arktika* down. But this wasn't Britain and there probably wasn't a Health and Safety Inspectorate.

From the engine room Dimitri took me forward to the galley. At this time in the evening I had expected to find it empty, but a blonde woman was stacking white and rye bread she had just baked into a cupboard, while on the other side of the room a bedraggled man with lank hair and a grubby white overall was cutting up carrots into a vast saucepan of soup.

Since the soup was invariably the best thing about every meal, I found myself behaving a bit like royalty going walkabout.

'I would like to compliment you,' I heard myself saying, 'on the excellence of your soups.'

Dimitri translated this pompous pontification and I waited for the reply.

Silence.

Dimitri repeated the speech again.

Still silence as the man continued cutting carrots and staring into the bowl. Was there something the matter, I asked Dimitri.

'No,' replied Dimitri. 'I do not think he likes foreigners.'

My royal progress moved on to the maintenance workshop which was situated on the lowest deck of the ship. We walked into an ill-lit space to find a man soldering a small piece of electronics, using a magnifying glass to see what he was doing. Dimitri chatted with him while I cased the joint. On the other side of the room on the workbench which ran the length of the bulkhead was a bowl containing two goldfish. It was the first and only time I had seen an aquarium which itself was below sea level. I wondered if the goldfish realised this.

9 The Gulag

The following evening there was a knock on my door. I opened it to find Dimitri and Vadim, both dressed in black leather jackets and blue jeans.

'We hope you are not occupied,' said Dimitri, who was clearly the spokesman for the delegation. I replied that, far from being occupied, I was actually trying to find things to do.

'Good,' replied Dimitri, 'we wished to discuss things with you.' This sounded a bit ominous, so I offered them a coffee and cleared enough of my junk from the sofa so there was a space to sit.

I poured the coffee, asked them if they took sugar or milk powder, and waited for them to tell me what was on their minds. Dimitri and Vadim were sitting side by side like two prim sisters, with their hands folded in front of them, looking at their knees. The silence continued for what seemed like a very long time before I realised that this was simply a social call.

The obvious solution was to ask them about their families. They were, it seemed, both twenty-seven, both married with one child each. Dimitri came from Leningrad, Vadim from Lvov in the Ukraine.

Another silence during which Vadim looked at Dimitri

and Dimitri looked at Vadim. I sat back, equally ill at ease, hoping that they might ask me about my family, or what I thought about the weather. They did not. Shyness had numbed them into immobility. It was up to me to do inside my cabin what *Arktika* was doing so effectively outside – break the ice.

Would they, I wondered, like a glass of whisky?

'Yes, thank you,' said Dimitri. Once again whisky did the trick. Within minutes I was hearing all about their foreign travels on board the training ship they served on when they were at naval college in Leningrad.

'It was a huge schooner,' explained Vadim, 'which used to go on cruises loaded with naval students.' I vaguely remembered seeing a photograph of a Russian schooner taking part in one of the Tall Ships races. Yes, they confirmed, that was the one.

Dimitri liked Greece best, while Vadim preferred Copenhagen. A gentle argument then erupted about whether the Greek climate (which was clearly preferable) outweighed Danish food (which was also superior).

'I'll never forget,' said Vadim, 'when we left Copenhagen and we sailed out past that mermaid sitting on her rock. I felt as sad as I do when I leave home. Really sad.'

'Come off it,' giggled Dimitri. 'It was the girls and not the mermaids that you liked. And the beer, of course.'

Vadim grinned.

The conversation then turned to the only topic which everyone on *Arktika* always wanted to talk about.

'You wait,' said Dimitri, his eyes shining with the fervour of a religious fanatic, 'now that Boris Nikolayevich [Yeltsin] is President, you'll see things move in this country.' He was beginning to sound like an editorial in *Readers Digest*. 'Just wait until we have a real free market

105

and you'll see what Russia can really do. She's been held back for the last seventy years. Just you wait.'

Touched as I was by this enthusiasm for capitalism, I thought I should sound a note of caution. I pointed out that in a free market it would be perfectly possible – indeed likely – that the Murmansk Shipping Company could no longer afford to operate nuclear icebreakers. In fact the whole Northern Sea Route might not even make economic sense.

My two visitors pondered this for a while before Dimitri replied gravely, 'You are right, I suppose, but even so I won't mind because in a way I have nothing to lose. I just know that we shall have to go through a very difficult stage in our country before things get better. But it will be worth it.'

With supporters like this, Yeltsin's worries must be over, I reflected. Quite how representative Vadim and Dimitri were was another matter. Besides, it was relatively easy for them to talk bravely like this when they both had good jobs on a comfy icebreaker.

As they left the cabin they noticed my suitcase sticking out from below the sofa.

'You have broken it,' said Dimitri, looking at the handle which had been ripped off when I caught it on a bulkhead door the day I joined the ship. The lack of handle was going to be a bit of a problem when the time came to leave the *Arktika*, but I assumed I would just have to make do with string.

'May we repair it?' asked Vadim, almost nervously, as if he was asking me a favour. I was happy to agree, and contributed two bars of chocolate to ease my conscience.

Bed came early that night, but sleep didn't. A combination of the sunlight seeping through the gaps in the curtains and the fact that the ship seemed to be bumping

106

around more than before, meant that after a couple of hours I gave up any attempt at sleep and instead went up to the bridge.

If the captain's dress was anything to go by, he had been suffering from the same affliction. He was wearing track-suit bottoms and a very baggy T-shirt. For someone who almost invariably wore his uniform, this was a serious aberration. Always a small man, he suddenly looked vulnerable, like someone caught without their false teeth. I suppose that is why uniforms were invented in the first place.

'The ice is getting worse again,' said the captain. We managed to travel 200 metres before it stopped us completely and we had to back up 150 metres and take another run at the wall, which grew increasingly thick. At that moment we were using the simple straight-ahead battering-ram approach, but there are various other techniques of icebreaking which can be used in different conditions. Instead of simply putting your bow back into the slot it cut the first time, it is sometimes necessary to make three different incisions in the ice, 'a bit like the branches of a tree', explained the captain.

'Oliver,' said Sergei from his position by the port window, 'would you like to drive an icebreaker? It's like a very big combine harvester. A *kulak* like you will have no trouble at all.'

I moved over to where the throttle levers were on the port side of the bridge and, when *Arktika* had once again come to a halt in the ice, waited for Sergei to give me the signal. The routine was normally the same. Hard astern with the right engine, hard astern with the left and leave the centre engine unused. After half an hour I reckoned I'd got the hang of this icebreaker driving.

'You can go to bed,' I told Sergei. 'Now that I've been

trained, I'll do the rest of your watch for you.' And indeed it would have been a good watch to have chosen, since we had just put our clocks one hour forward yet again and this particular watch would last for only three hours. It was bad luck on the people who were off watch and found that they went back to work an hour sooner than they had thought.

'Yes,' said Sergei, 'but they gain on the westbound trip.'

My second attempt at sleep was only marginally more successful than my first. Every few minutes I could feel the ship coming to a gradual stop in the ice and then begin to move slowly backwards. This part was perfectly tolerable. But when we gathered speed again to hurl ourselves at the ice, the whole ship vibrated and some loose bits of tin on the crane outside my porthole made a terrible chattering. Then, when we were doing about six knots, we once again smashed into the ice and came to a shuddering halt some 200 metres nearer to Pevek.

I was, it seemed, very lucky to be able to go to Pevek. In seven years on icebreakers, Sergei had been there twice. Only one or two atomic icebreakers a year are sent to Pevek, the rest work in the western sector of the Northern Sea Route. I had assumed this voyage was a routine milk run for *Arktika*, but it was just the opposite.

The next day conditions had improved slightly so we were managing to travel almost a mile before backing up. When this did happen Maxim continued the training Sergei had started the day before and I worked the telegraph and put the engines hard astern. When I had become proficient at this particular task, I graduated to the next level of responsibility, which consisted of saying '*Zarubko*' to the helmsman. This was the instruction for him to put his bow into the same place it had been before we went astern. Given another decade or two, I would be a fully qualified icebreaker officer.

Every day one of the watch officers would ink in our course on the large map of northern Siberia which had been put up on the after wall of the bridge. And every day we would get nearer to the single most prominent landmark on the whole of the Siberian coast, Cape Chelyuskin. A few days earlier I had asked the captain if I might be allowed to go with the *ptichka* when it flew to Cape Chelyuskin to collect the mail. He was non-committal.

That morning he approached me as if he had an important message to deliver.

'I am sorry,' he said briskly, 'but it will not be possible for you to go ashore.' I obviously looked disappointed. 'I am afraid that we were instructed by the authorities in Murmansk that you should not go ashore at any point on the Northern Sea Route.' The news was getting worse and worse because I had assumed that I would have to spend a few days – and maybe longer – in Pevek while I waited for a ship to take me down to Vladivostock.

Sergei, when he heard this, giggled.

'It's because he's worried you could break your leg ashore,' he said.

To mollify me the captain did at least promise that I would be able to land on some of the Arctic islands which we passed. This cheered me up enormously.

It was a good morning for seals. For some odd reason they appeared out of nowhere and were sitting on the edge of the channel we had cut through the ice. The day before I had seen only a few seals from the helicopter. At first I thought they were simply lying on the ice in the middle of nowhere, but as we approached they slipped through tiny holes back into the water.

The sun was shining brightly and the thermometer registered 1.5 degrees Celsius. Eight kilometres off the starboard bow was a long row of low islands, the tops of which were clear of snow, showing dark brown patches of rock or lichen. We were entering the Matteson Straits; to the south lay Taymyr Island and to the north the Nordenskiöld Peninsula, named after the first man to sail through the North East Passage.

Nils Adolf Erik Nordenskiöld, together with Nansen and Amundsen, was one of the three greatest polar explorers who have ever lived. Born in Finland to Swedish parents in 1832, his first passion was Spitsbergen, which he surveyed, according to a contemporary, 'with an accuracy hitherto unattained in any Arctic land'. After a series of Arctic expeditions, including two attempts on the North Pole and the most northerly latitude ever reached by a ship, he determined to complete the North East Passage. Ever since Sir Hugh Willoughby in 1553 mariners had been trying to find this route through to the east, but for over three hundred years they had all failed.

Backed by two merchants, the Swede Baron Oskar Dikson and the Russian Sibiryakov, Nordenskiöld bought the *Vega*, a strongly-built 300-ton ship, which he filled with enough food to last for two years. Together with three other cargo ships which had been chartered by Sibiryakov to take freight into central Siberia, he set out from Tromsø on 18 July 1878. One month later they had reached Cape Chelyuskin and by 28 August they were at the mouth of the Lena, where the last cargo ship left them. Conditions had been almost perfect, but by early September, after they had passed Cape Shelagski (a few kilometres east of *Arktika's* destination of Pevek), the ice began to close in. On 28 September, only 180 kilometres from the Bering Straits, they could go no further.

It is a mark of how lucky Nordenskiöld had been in the previous year that only on 18 July 1879 did the ice break and allow them to move again. Two days later, on 20 July, they reached the Bering Straits. Nordenskiöld described the scene: 'At eleven o'clock in the forenoon we were right abreast of East Cape,[1] and with colours flying from our masthead we saluted with our little cannon the eastern-most point of Asia. As soon as we came out of the ice south of East Cape, we noticed the heavy swell of the Pacific Ocean. The completion of the North East Passage was celebrated the same day with a grand dinner, when the last of many of our delicacies disappeared.'

One hundred and two years later I was following in Nordenskiöld's footsteps, but that afternoon I was not at sea. I was up with the *ptichka* again. We began by flying our normal zig-zag pattern some 80 kilometres ahead of the ship until Valerii Mikhailovich was satisfied that he had seen all there was to see. At that point the history lesson began.

We climbed to around 500 metres and headed towards the mainland, which was the north-west edge of the Taymyr Peninsula. Just after we crossed over the shoreline, Valerii Mikhailovich tugged my sleeve and pointed to a cluster of dark marks against the snow.

'Gulag,' he shouted against the noise of the engine.

I was looking at the remains of Biruli camp, which nestled in a small ice-filled inlet on this desolate coast. The pilot put the helicopter into a hover and we lost altitude. Gradually I could make out the skeletons of wooden huts, which were roofless and derelict. There seemed to be no pattern or system to their location, unlike the Nazi concentration camps which have been preserved in Poland. There was no visible fence and no watchtowers. It could, I reflected, have been the remains of a lumber camp – except for the fact that we were 800 kilometres

[1] Now called Cape Dezhnev.

from the nearest tree. We were twice that distance from the nearest city.[2]

Seen from the air, these frozen remains of the Gulag seemed antiseptic and impersonal. It was as if I were looking at a diagram on a map, not at a place where human beings had lived, worked, starved and died in conditions which I could not even contemplate. In winter the temperature would have fallen to −40 degrees, and even that day in late June it was still only hovering around the freezing mark.

I began to understand why the *zeks* (prisoners) in the Arctic Gulag referred to the rest of Russia as 'the mainland'. Although it was not an island, it was so far from civilisation, separated first by the tundra and then by the taiga, that it was as isolated as any island could ever be.

After a few minutes we set off towards the north east, disturbing a herd of reindeer which had been grazing in a snow-free valley. Far in the distance I could make out a string of islands, one of which appeared to be inhabited. As we came closer I could see a cluster of wooden huts surrounding what looked like a radio mast. Was this another branch of the Gulag?

We circled the island twice as the pilot looked for a flat landing space and eventually came down with clouds of snow blowing in all directions. When the rotors had stopped turning, Valerii Mikhailovich passed a chart back

[2] On my return to England I was idly looking at the *National Geographic* map of the world when I noticed that among the very few settlements marked on the northern Siberian coast was Biruli. Having so recently seen that it consisted of nothing more than a few wooden skeletons, I wrote to the *National Geographic*, pointing this out. Four months later I received a letter from Washington: 'Upon recite (sic) of your letter, newer map sources have been reviewed and indicate that the town no longer exists. We have, therefore, corrected all of our map plates of the region to no longer include the town of Biruli.'

112

to me and, pointing at a tiny dot among a series of other dots, announced, 'Tirtov Island.'

Valentin, who had been riding shotgun in the rear of the helicopter, offered me a pair of tall leather boots. I refused, safe in the knowledge that my high-tech gore-tex-lined American boots would be lighter and drier than the primitive leather wellingtons. Only then did Valentin, ever polite, put them on his own feet.

The moment we got off the hard shingle beach I saw why Valentin had suggested a change of footwear. The snow, which I had assumed would be ankle deep, came up to my thighs. Struggling to what appeared to be a mossy patch, I found that this was almost as spongy as the snow. By then my feet were both cold and wet, and I had been walking for less than five minutes.

The rest of the party, consisting of Valerii Mikhailovich, the helicopter pilot and Valentin, who had shouldered the rifle and looked like a Siberian fur trapper, had reached the first of the four shacks which lined the beach. Above them on higher ground was a relatively new pale green portakabin which stood next to a trestle tower.

Sodden and very cold, I eventually reached the shacks. They had been solidly constructed in wood, with double-glazed windows and brick chimneys. Yet the Arctic had long since managed to force its way inside, smashing open the doors and lifting the roofs. Snowdrifts had piled up in what used to be the kitchen and strips of flowered wallpaper fluttered in the wind. In one room I found two iron bedsteads with rotting mattresses sagging on rusty springs.

Archaeological skills were not necessary to date the settlement. A calendar on the wall showed August 1977. It was an eerie feeling to look out across the frozen sea and wonder what these rooms must have been like when Tirtov Island was inhabited. What did these men do? How did

113

they spend their time? What did they think about during the winter? Why did they desert the place?

On my way back to the helicopter I noticed something rusting on the shingle. I picked it up. It was an old rowlock. Once upon a time someone must have rowed a boat on this sea. It seemed impossible.

Back in the *ptichka*, instead of returning to *Arktika* as I had expected, we turned towards the shore and headed for a tiny piece of rock which stuck up out of the ice like a rabbit turd in the snow. As we got nearer I saw that on top of the hill were two stone cairns. Once again we circled circumspectly before landing on a fairly level patch of brown earth, which turned out to be a bog. The small lump of rock called Nabludeniy (observation) Island is worth a footnote in the history of Arctic exploration.

In 1900 the Imperial Academy of Sciences in St Petersburg sponsored an expedition led by an aristocratic Baltic geologist called Baron Eduard Toll. An old Siberian hand, Toll had spent a lot of time exploring the Siberian coast. On one of his expeditions he had discovered a complete and perfectly formed mammoth buried in the ice. On another he thought he had caught sight of the mountains of the mysterious and mythical Sannikov Land.[3] His final expedition was an assignment by the Academy to find out if this land really did exist north of the New Siberian Islands. Toll set sail on his ship, the *Zarya*, but heavy ice forced him to winter on Nabludeniy Island, where he marked his camp with the twin cairns we had seen from the helicopter.

The following season Toll succeeded in reaching the

[3] There was a strangely similar myth in the North West Passage. John Ross on his first expedition in 1818 thought he had seen a range of mountains which appeared to be blocking Lancaster Sound. The Croker Mountains, as he named them, were later found to be imaginary and Ross became the laughing stock of the British Navy.

114

New Siberian Islands, and in doing so the *Zarya* became the first Russian ship to sail past Cape Chelyuskin. After wintering off the coast of Kotelny Island, Toll and three companions set off across the frozen Laptev Sea to Bennett Island, from where they planned to meet up again with the *Zarya*. But the ice proved too strong for the ship, and by the time it eventually did arrive at Bennett Island the crew found only a message announcing that Toll's party had started south towards the mainland. They were never seen again.

The four of us wandered silently around the two cairns, thinking our own thoughts. I tried to imagine what it would have been like to spend the winter there ninety years ago, but found that my imagination would not stretch that far.

At the foot of one of the cairns was the remains of a rusty trap.

'Polar fox,' muttered Valentin, and relapsed into silence.

I dug up a clump of moss with my hands and found the earth soft and soggy in the top seven centimetres or so. Below that was the permafrost, a hard layer on which I could make no impression at all. And yet in a sheltered corner behind a rock the first faint signs of green growth were appearing through the soil. In less than a month this whole hillside would be alive with Arctic flowers, and another six weeks later it would all be turning brown once more.

Later that afternoon the captain and the hydrologist clustered round the charts to show me where I had been. They were obviously pleased that I was taking an interest in the exploration of this part of the world. Beneath their tough exteriors, they felt quietly passionate about the Arctic. I liked them the more for it.

I also liked them the more for their ideas and opinions.

A few days later I was receiving a lecture about ice from the hydrologist himself.

'You realise,' he asked me, 'that there are different sorts of ice?' I said that I knew about thick ice and thin ice but I hadn't thought much about any refinements which might be added to this list. The expression on Valerii Mikhailovich's face should have warned me. It was as if I had told a butcher that beef consisted of fillet and rump. Half an hour and two textbooks later, I was beginning to realise that the subtleties of ice were as profound as the subtleties of colour, smell or texture.

'Of course,' said Valerii Mikhailovich, 'all of this was discovered by a Russian.' I knew that Russians had discovered television, penicillin, rockets and – for all I knew – gravity and the wheel too, so I tried to conceal my scepticism. 'The man's name,' continued Valerii Mikhailovich, 'was Kolchak. Admiral Kolchak.'

A tragic, talented and moodily messianic man, Alexander Vasilyvich Kolchak had been Commander of the Black Sea fleet before the revolution. After the Bolshevik triumph and the withdrawal of Russia from the war, Kolchak was so appalled by what he felt was his country's shameful desertion of its allies that he volunteered to join the British army and serve in Mesopotamia. But it never quite worked out. He got as far as Singapore before, at the suggestion of the British, he turned back. From there until he reached Siberia a few months later, the sequence of events became cloudy as various Western powers tried to use Kolchak as a figurehead around whom they hoped the non-communist forces would rally. For a brief moment it even looked as if this might happen when, at the age of forty-five, he organised a *coup d'état* in Omsk which installed him – in name at least – as Supreme Ruler of all the Russias.

In the following months tragedy and farce combined to

116

write a chapter of hopeless history. Kolchak, who had set up an incompetent and corrupt government in Irkutsk, was eventually betrayed by the Czech Legion which had also been fighting Trotsky's Red Army. After torture and interrogation by the Reds, he was executed on 7 February 1920 and his body was thrown into a hole in the ice of the frozen Angara River. A brave man to the last, Kolchak's self-control in his final minutes was described in the official soviet account of the execution as being 'like an Englishman'.

The hydrologist sensed my recognition and it gave him pleasure.

'Kolchak was a very great man,' he continued. 'But not many people know about his naval career as a young man. Did you know, for example, that he had been a hydrologist like me? He was on Toll's expedition. What's more, he left his mark in more ways than one. If you look on the charts you will see that just to the north of us here are two islands, Alexander Island and Sophia Island. He named the first after himself and the other after his wife.

'But that's not why he is a great man,' said Valerii Mikhailovich. 'It was while he was with Toll that he began to study the different sorts of ice. Eventually Kolchak came up with the classification which we still use today.' I was impressed. But not half as impressed as I was by the hydrologist's next and final observation. 'Alexander Kolchak was a Russian patriot.'

I had no doubt that Valerii Mikhailovich Losef had been, and probably still was, a member of the Communist Party. It would have been imperative for him to join to rise as high as he had in the Arctic hierarchy. And yet there he was describing one of the great Antichrists of the revolution as 'a Russian patriot'.

Was the Pope still Catholic?

117

10 Boris's empire

I was beginning to feel more at home on *Arktika*. I knew my way around the ship and thought I had a rough idea of who everybody was. However, one afternoon, on our way back from a sauna, Maxim announced that he was going to the shop. I had no idea that a shop even existed, so I followed him to a dark little hole two decks below the galley and up near the bows.

As if entering a speakeasy, we knocked on a door which was opened by a tall but stooped man with thin, stringy, yellow hair which hung down in front of his right eye. He was wearing a *telnyashka*[1] on which a gold crucifix necklace looked a bit out of place. In the dim light cast by a single small bulb, Boris Kapotov looked older than his thirty-six years. The overall effect was that of a bookie's runner who supplemented his income collecting rent from delinquent tenants. On the crew list Boris was described as the chief cook, but it was obvious that running the shop was a sinecure to which he devoted a lot more time than supervising the galley.

Seeing Maxim, who was evidently an old and valued customer, he beckoned us into the gloom of a small

[1] The trademark of the Russian sailor. A navy blue and white striped jersey which is usually (but not always) worn beneath the shirt.

118

compartment in which there were shelves of biscuits (hard and not very nice), Russian shampoo, Austrian coffee (I had wondered where Alexander's Viennese blend came from), soap from England (made in Oxford), canisters of dried lentils and beans. There were tins of Spam from Holland and fish from Russia, bars of chocolate with sputniks on the wrapper, razor blades and eau de cologne from Moscow. There was absolutely nothing I wanted to buy.

Did Boris have any vodka? A grin and the faintest of nods towards Maxim to check that I was kosher.

'Yes, for dollars.' A long pause. 'And with the permission of the master,' together with another grin. I had the overwhelming suspicion that if I produced the former, the latter would not be a problem.

We went out into the dark passageway and up towards the forecastle. Boris, jangling like St Peter, selected a key from his key ring and unlocked an industrial-sized padlock. Inside was a refrigerated store full of apples. It was clear that, like all Russian fruit, these had been badly bruised long before they ever reached the ship. They were looking very sorry for themselves. So were the limp spring onions and sagging cucumbers. I wondered what vegetables we would be eating in the weeks between there and Pevek.

But there were some things in Boris's treasure house which looked good, particularly the wooden barrel containing green peppers in brine. Others, equally tantalising, were full of pickled cucumbers – a dish which Russians do better than anybody else on earth.

From the vegetable department we moved on to a less attractive location, the meat store. Here, also protected by locks which would have been excessive in a top-security prison, were slabs of beef and next to them, very forlorn, a solitary plucked fowl.

'It's a goose,' announced Boris.

With half a century of agricultural experience behind me, I begged to differ. It was far too small to be a goose. Indeed, it would be lucky to be a chicken.

'No,' insisted Boris. 'It's a goose.'

I didn't argue, but wondered why an icebreaker would need a single goose.

Maxim bought two tins of condensed milk and a salami which Boris had produced from behind a pile of boxes. The payment for these was, as in all the best company stores, knocked off the wages, so no cash ever changed hands.

The existence of the shop explained how the crew members managed to be so rotund yet eat so little in the dining room. They patronised Boris's tuck shop and spent their off-duty hours grazing in their cabins. It also explained where Maxim was able to find all the goodies he had provided for our post-sauna feast.

The tour over, Boris invited us for a coffee in his cabin. Boringly clothed pin-ups and a football poster from Mexico '86 were the main decorations, apart from a black and white photograph of his daughter in Leningrad. On the desk was a large and ancient calculating machine and a typewriter, suggesting that Boris had clerical as well as culinary duties. He explained that ten people worked in the galley with him. Of these two were women.

'They aren't such good cooks as men,' he said, 'but they're a lot better at cleaning. Men are very sloppy.'

Was I satisfied with the food, Boris wondered. I told him it was good, which it certainly was if compared to the norm in the USSR at the time. How did it compare with the food on the Canadian ship I had sailed on the previous year? Extremely well, I said. Which was no exaggeration, although I didn't have the heart to tell him that the Canadian food had been very bad indeed.

Boris had another question. Was vodka cheap in Britain?

This was hard to answer since it all depended on your definition of cheap, but certainly compared to the price of vodka in Russia, it was extremely expensive.

'Gorbachev made a terrible mistake with his anti-alcohol campaign,' said Boris with evident passion. 'He turned the people against him. So now he will be remembered just like Brezhnev.'

I protested. Brezhenev did nothing memorable, but at least Gorbachev, whatever his mistakes, had achieved many very good things.

'I disagree,' he replied. 'I'm not saying they are the same, but I am saying that both will be remembered in the same way.' He paused to savour his political testament before continuing with a bit of rhetoric. 'How do people feel about Brezhnev today? Well, that's also how they'll feel about Gorbachev when he is history. And for me that can't happen soon enough.'

I was about to demur when Boris jumped in again.

'Of course you in the West love him, but then you don't have empty shops like we do. Mikhail Sergeivich Gorbachev has only been good for the West and not for the Russian people.'

It was hard to argue with men whose wives were at that moment standing in food queues back in Murmansk.

We had another cup of Brazilian Nescafé and the conversation drifted round to pay and conditions. By then two of Boris's henchmen had appeared and the population density in his small cabin was beginning to feel like downtown Jakarta. Everyone wanted to know what pay British seamen received. I didn't have a clue and, for once in my life, decided not to make it up.

'I'm really pretty pissed off,' said Boris, who by then was getting into his stride, 'because I work like a bull for very long hours on this ship and I don't get paid any more money for doing so.'

'But neither does anybody,' said Maxim, cutting another slice of salami. 'You know damned well that all the sailors in Morflot [the Soviet Merchant Navy] are paid a salary and not by the hour, so why should you complain?'

Boris looked a bit sheepish and then continued, 'So you may wonder why I work as hard as I do then?' It was another of his rhetorical questions so, as a guest drinking his coffee, I felt I should at least nod vigorously. 'To make sure,' he said triumphantly, 'that *Arktika* stays the best icebreaker in the fleet.'

Strangely enough I believed him. This wasn't hype or bullshit. It was – I am certain – an example of the extraordinary morale on board that I had felt ever since leaving Murmansk.

With some difficulty I managed to steer the talk away from wages and living conditions round to one of my favourite topics, food. Where, I wondered, would Boris like to go if I could take him out to a meal anywhere in the world?

'Paris,' came the reply. And what would he eat when he got to Paris? 'Oh, I don't know, but it would have to be something I'd never tried before and I expect there are lots of things in that category in Paris, aren't there?' At this point Maxim, who had been watching a cartoon on TV about a mole and an elephant, rejoined the conversation.

'It's my dream to go to Paris, too, and what's more, I know just where I would like to go. I'd go to my own personal restaurant which is called, of course, Maxim's. I'm told it is very good and very expensive. With a name like that it would have to be good.'

That evening Sergei was in pensive mood when he came on watch. I told him about my visit to Boris.

'He is a very rich man,' said Sergei.

I repeated the story about vodka being sold 'only for dollars and only with the master's permission'.

'The rouble is nothing in Russia today,' mused Sergei. 'Only food. That's the only thing which matters. Food.' He stared out of the open window of the bridge and shouted to the helmsman to steer to starboard to miss a low range of ice hummocks which were dead ahead.

With 75,000 horsepower behind us, why was it necessary to miss them, I wondered.

'You must remember that a hummock is really a small iceberg,' explained Sergei. 'And like an iceberg, it has a ratio of 1:7. So if that hummock there is one metre above the surface, it has seven metres below the water. And seven metres would stop this icebreaker easily. That's why it is better to steer round them.'

Small pools of water were beginning to be visible on the otherwise unmarked surface of the ice. This was the first sign of melting. In a few weeks this area would be open water; it was unbelievable. From time to time the sun threw a shadow on what seemed like a line through the ice. It looked almost like the sort of lead Valerii Mikhailovich might have spotted from the *ptichka*.

Sergei corrected me.

'It's not a lead in the usual sense. It is the mark left by the *Rossiya* when she returned to Murmansk last November.'

I was amazed that any mark would remain in the ice for seven months, but Sergei once again explained.

'You can find marks in the ice which have remained there for years, but what we're following now is obvious to anyone who knows about these conditions. It's the sort of thing any experienced Arctic navigator should make use of.'

The reason we were following the mark was that the ice in what had been *Rossiya's* wake was fractionally thinner than the surrounding ice, and this saved both energy and time.

The forecast was beginning to look better. The *ptichka* had just landed and Valerii Mikhailovich brought with him the news that there was open water east of Cape Chelyuskin. From then on it was just possible that we would have an ice-free run all the way to Pevek.

I stood silently while the hydrologist sketched an ice map of the conditions he'd been looking at that afternoon. He drew quickly and fluently, filling in the different sorts of ice with coloured pencils. It seemed a terrible waste of talent to have a man like Valerii Mikhailovich Losef spending his time sitting up in a helicopter.

When he had finished the map he noticed me standing behind. He grinned shyly, put down his pencils and rested his chin in his hands as he stared far off to the starboard bow. There was a long silence while I decided whether to ask him the question I'd been thinking about for some days.

Had he, I wondered, ever wanted to be a captain? Another long pause while he thought about it.

'I'm really too old now,' he mused. 'I'm fifty-six and they look for younger captains these days. But it would have been good in some ways.'

I thought he had finished, but after a few seconds he started again.

'A friend of mine who was hydrologist on the *Lenin* has just been appointed captain of the latest nuclear icebreaker, *October Revolution*, which will be completed later this year.'

I could feel Valerii Mikhailovich's sadness, but his face remained as impassive as ever.

124

Late in the evening the captain came on to the bridge clad in his fetching dark blue tracksuit with a turquoise stripe down the arms and leg. I told him he looked like a Soviet athlete at the Olympic Games.

'No, I'm the trainer,' was his reply.

It was after eleven o'clock and tomorrow, I remembered, would be Midsummer Day. Back in England it would be the longest day of the year, but in the Arctic there is no such thing. From the moment the sun ceases to fall below the horizon until the day it starts again, all the days are the same length – twenty-four hours. The one thing which would make tomorrow different was that the sun at midnight would be higher above the horizon than on any other day. But how high? It was the sort of useless information which I craved and on *Arktika*, stuffed with scientific and navigational aids, it should not be hard to find the answer.

I asked Sergei if perhaps he would like to take the measurement at midnight for me. I assumed he had a sextant somewhere on the bridge.

'You don't need a sextant,' he said with more than a touch of irritation in his voice. 'You can do it yourself.'

It was late after a long day of heavy ice and I realised I had become a nuisance. I was gathering up my pencil and the notebook in which I had been copying down positions from the log when Sergei turned towards me again.

'If you want to measure the sun, you only need your *kulak*.'

I had obviously failed to understand the joke, but I smiled back at him and walked towards the door which led out on to the deck.

'No, no,' said Sergei. 'I don't think you understand what *kulak* means.' I told him that I understood perfectly well, but I couldn't see the connection between a prosperous peasant farmer and the sun's position above the horizon.

'I knew you didn't understand,' came the reply. 'In Russian "kulak" means a fist. It was because of this that the rich peasants were called *kulaks*. They were tight-fisted.'

It was an interesting bit of etymology, but it still didn't appear to have any connection with taking the sun's measurements. Sergei could see my bewilderment.

'Your fist is eight degrees,' he said patiently, as if teaching a slightly retarded child. 'If you hold it up and put the bottom of your fist on the horizon, you can get a rough measurement. And what's more, it's surprising how accurate it is. Just to give you an idea, I reckon that at midnight tonight the sun will be one and a half *kulaks* above the horizon.'

This was good stuff, like knowing how to use your watch as a compass or how to stop a charging rhino with your belt buckle.

Maxim arrived on the bridge, as usual, a few minutes before his watch was due to begin. I told him about my new-found knowledge, and also about Sergei's prediction that the sun would be one and a half *kulaks* above the horizon at midnight.

'We can easily check this,' said Maxim, who had obviously never thought about it before. He opened several drawers before finding a wooden box containing the ship's brass sextant. 'I haven't used one of these for ages,' he said. 'In fact I don't think I've actually used one since I was at naval college. Maybe I've forgotten how.'

He had not forgotten, and a few minutes later we had a small ceremony. As the international time signal announced that it was midnight, Maxim squinted through the sextant, adjusted the slide, put it down and read off the degrees from the instrument.

126

'Eleven degrees,' he announced solemnly, 'give or take a bit.'

'See,' said Sergei, as he moved towards the door, his watch over. 'One and a half *kulaks*. If you happen to have a small *kulak*.'

11 A walk on the ice

It was to celebrate the one and a half *kulak* sun that I
decided to take a bath the next morning. Not just an in-
and-out dip but a serious immersion which lasted two
hours and had to be topped up with hot water (no shortage
of that with two nuclear reactors) four times.

I emerged pink, wrinkled but extraordinarily clean to
find that *Arktika* had stopped. Around us the level
ice stretched to the horizon like Saharan sand. The
sky was clear, the sun bright and I was as happy as could
be.

On the bridge I noted our position: 76.27N 97.14E. We
were just opposite Tirtov Island, where I had landed two
days earlier to visit the deserted polar station. Just over a
hundred kilometres away to the north east was Cape
Chelyuskin and the beginning of the Laptev Sea.

The reason for our halt was 'routine engine maintenance', or that's what I had been told by the congenitally
taciturn chief engineer, Sergei Markin. To my suspicious
mind it all sounded a bit like the calm voice from the flight
deck informing passengers that 'we are turning back to
Heathrow as a normal precautionary measure'. *Arktika*
had, after all, just emerged from an annual overhaul in
Murmansk two weeks earlier. Anyway, whatever the

reason, we were due to remain in the ice for the next twelve hours, so I might as well enjoy it.

The gangway had been lowered on to the ice and already two groups of men were starting to play football with orange life rings marking the goal posts. Not wishing to take too strenuous exercise, I declined the offer to play right back for the starboard side. Instead I decided to go for a walk.

'You'd better take this with you,' said Sergei, holding out what looked like a World War II vintage flare pistol.

I refused, saying that I had always been frightened of guns and this one looked particularly fearsome.

'You'll be a lot more scared of a polar bear if you meet one of them, so I suggest you take this in your pocket.'

Sergei's argument was strangely compelling, and I lumbered off down to the gangplank with a pistol and four flares in my parka.

Two cooks from the ship's bakery were standing at the bottom of the steps shaking out old flour sacks. The white dust which was blowing in the strong wind disappeared the moment it touched the ground because it was exactly the same colour as the snow.

My first job was to circumnavigate *Arktika* to get a seal's eye view of the ship. As I walked up towards the bows I noticed how bulbous the hull was compared to those of conventional ships. From close up the bow, which had spent the last week smashing through the Barents and Kara Seas, looked anything but aggressive. I ran my hand over the smooth and sensuous curve of steel as if I were stroking a horse's neck. Only when I looked at where the base of the bow met the ice did I see any sign of *Arktika*'s strength. The snow had parted to reveal the hairline fractures in the ice which had crackled out ahead of the ship and would, when we got under way again, buckle and break.

At the stern the channel which we had cut through the ice was already beginning to freeze again. Floating, as if in a giant gin and tonic, were ice cubes the size of council houses. These conditions did not deter one optimistic sailor who stood for hours on the edge of the ice with his fishing rod. I didn't see him catch anything.

Striking out away from the ship, I headed for what looked like a hummock a kilometre and a half away. It might well have been ten kilometres away because it is almost impossible to judge distances in the Arctic with no reference points from which to get a sense of perspective. The snow, which from the bridge had looked like King Wenceslas's variety, turned out to be deep but neither crisp nor even. Instead it was soft and full of holes into which I sometimes sank up to my knees. Just to make life even more uncomfortable, a wind was also blowing, making the −5 degrees temperature feel far colder than the thermometer said.

In the afternoon I managed to persuade both Sergei and Maxim to come with me on to the ice. Sergei relieved me of the pistol and interrupted the second soccer game by firing red and green flares over the ship. We walked up to the bows and took a series of silly pictures of each other appearing to push *Arktika* backwards out of the ice. Like all jokey photographs, it seemed funnier at the time than when the pictures eventually came back from the chemist.

Back on board, we decided to invade Alexander's cabin in the hope that he was brewing a pot of his Austrian coffee. He was. He was also listening to a country and western tape by Merle Haggard I had lent him the day before. As he sat slumped behind his desk, I told him the story of the one and a half *kulak* sun and he yawned good-naturedly.

'I wouldn't get too excited if I were you,' he said. 'The

130

sun will be higher in two days' time than it was yesterday, but that's simply because we'll be further north then.'

So much for my profoundly significant astronomic event.

A ringed seal enjoyed a far more significant event that day. I was up on the open bridge looking at the world through my binoculars when I picked up the *ptichka* approaching the ship in the distance. As I watched the orange and blue helicopter get closer, I noticed a movement on the ice below her. A few hundred metres to the *ptichka*'s left was a polar bear which was moving in an odd fashion, walking in the same crouched position that a cat uses when it stalks a bird. I followed the direction of the bear and saw that almost directly under the oncoming path of the helicopter was a group of seals sprawled round a hole in the ice like Hollywood producers round a swimming pool. The bear, which had lowered its body so that its stomach almost touched the ground, decided it was time to charge. In great big lolloping strides, it ran towards the recumbent seals at exactly the moment when the helicopter passed directly overhead. The noise of the motor must have frightened the seals and they slid back into the sea. The bear had been foiled by less than ten seconds. Somewhere below the ice of the Kara Sea was a seal who should, if he had any conscience whatsoever, have been offering a silent prayer of thanks to Valerii Mikhailovich Losef and his *ptichka*.

In my cabin Raisa was doing some cleaning. I smiled synthetically at her and received the genuine article in return. She took me by the arm and led me to the chest of drawers in my bedroom which she opened to reveal the laundry she had just returned. Not only had she darned my socks, but she had ironed them too. What a woman. My only problem was that I had still not eaten the *semyachki* she had given me at the beginning of the voyage. The taste and crunchiness were lovely but I hadn't mastered the knack of extracting the kernel of a sunflower seed and spitting out the husk without having to insert fingers into my mouth to fish around for loose detritus.

I confessed my sunflower problem to Sergei, who laughed.

'It makes sense,' he said. 'Raisa is a Ukrainian and *semyachki* are to Ukrainians what chewing gum is to Americans. They're born with sunflowers seeds in their mouths.' He suggested that I ask Raisa for lessons in sunflower-seed spitting.

That afternoon I was making my way down to the helicopter deck in time for Valerii Mikhailovich's usual reconnaissance flight when I saw the captain coming in the opposite direction. He looked as if he was on his way to a meeting at some ministry in Moscow, dressed in full uniform, complete with peaked cap, dark overcoat and carrying a black briefcase. Behind him came Sergei, who was also in uniform.

'Don't let the *ptichka* go without us,' said Sergei breathlessly, 'we'll be back in a moment.'

I was relieved to see that at least Valerii Mikhailovich was dressed in his customary brown sweater and ragged blue parka, and beside him Valentin looked his normal sinister self with dark glasses and a black flying suit.

The engines had been warmed up and the two boys had unhitched the helicopter from the cables which attached it to the deck, but there was still no sign of either the captain or Sergei. I asked Valerii Mikhailovich what was happening, but he just shrugged his shoulders and grinned. Eventually the two officers arrived, clutching at their caps as they ducked under the whirling rotor.

We took off, circled once round the ship and swooped low over the ice, heading due east. The ice was beginning to melt fast and puddles of milky turquoise liquid were forming where before there had been nothing. Occasional huddles of seals slithered back through their little holes when they saw us, but otherwise the world was empty and white.

After half an hour low brown cliffs appeared in the distance. Sergei leaned across and handed me a folded chart.

'Cape Mogilniy,' he shouted above the engine noise, pointing to the map. As we came in over the shoreline the snow seemed to disappear. Only in the narrow gullies between the hills did a few patches remain in the sheltered spots behind rocks. The hill which we were circling looked in colour and consistency like a chocolate sponge cake. On top of the cake there appeared to be two small monuments. Valentin picked a landing area and we came in on our final approach. This time neither snow nor dust blew away as we sank gently on to the ground.

I scrambled out through the rear door and found myself standing in a bog, with water oozing up around my boots. One hundred metres away, silhouetted against the sky, were two crosses, both surrounded by a chain link fence. The bigger of the two, as thick as a telegraph pole and about three metres tall, was a conventional cross. The second, slightly smaller, was a Russian orthodox cross with three cross-pieces, the lowest of which was on the diagonal.

The larger cross marked the grave of Alexei Nikolaievitch Zhokhov, who had died of uraemia, aged thirty, on 28 February 1915. Zhokhov had been a lieutenant on the expedition led by Vilkitsky[1] who, with the icebreakers

[1] A year later I was describing my voyage to an elegant Mayfair antique dealer of Russian extraction. 'My great-uncle,' he announced languidly, 'discovered the North East Passage.' His great-uncle turned out to have been A. I. Vilkitsky, whom he last saw as an old Russian émigré living in Brussels.

Taymyr and *Vaygach*, achieved only the second successful navigation of the North East Passage, and the first from east to west. The Vilkitsky expedition also discovered Severnaya Zemlaya (North Land), a group of islands which must hold the record for having been given the most names in the shortest period. Vilkitsky originally called them Zemlaya Nikolaya II after the Tsar, but within a decade they had been renamed Lenin Land. For some reason this was later changed to the less political Severnaya Zemlaya, and so they remained until 1992 when once again the islands were given their original name of Zemlaya Nikolaya II.

Vilkitsky, who was in command of the *Vaygach*, seems to have disliked Zhokhov, and didn't keep his feelings private. Eventually tensions between the two ran so high that Zhokhov was transferred from the *Vaygach* to the *Taymyr*. The move seems to have affected him profoundly and when the Arctic night started, Zhokhov, who had once been a cheerful member of the crew, went into a depression from which he never recovered. He refused to eat and, according to *Vaygach*'s doctor, 'from the first few days of January, practically speaking, he began fasting. . . . He began to spend the whole time in his cabin and would sleep all day. . . . He would not appear for supper at all.' The doctor from the *Taymyr* was summoned to give a second opinion, but by the time weather conditions allowed him to make the journey across the ice Zhokhov had died.

Dr Starokadomsky, the *Taymyr*'s medical officer, described the funeral ceremony: 'They dug the grave not far from our crates of provisions. Then a driftwood cross was erected over the grave. Zhokhov had desired that the cross erected over his grave should, without fail, be driftwood with a small icon and a board on which he requested that a poem he had written be carved. Two of the officers, "soul-mates" of the dead man, insisted on the exact observance of the last wishes of the deceased. On board they prepared artificial flowers and leaves from a thin sheet of brass, and fastened them together into a wreath with wire. They painted the wreath with oil paint. The funeral took place on March 9th. A large procession headed ashore with the coffin. A brass plate was fixed to the cross, with the poem engraved on it.'

The brass plate was still there when I stood in front of Zhokhov's grave. The poem read:

> Beneath the block of ice
> of the cold Taymyr
> where, with his gloomy baying,
> a frightened arctic fox
> alone speaks
> of the dreary life of the world
> the exhausted swimmer will find peace.
>
> The radiance of
> the morning aurora will not shine gold
> on the delicate lyre of the forgotten swimmer.
> The grave is deep
> like the Tuskaror chasm
> like the loving eyes
> of a dear woman.
>
> Were he able
> to admire them again
> to look at them, albeit it from afar,
> death itself would not be so harsh
> and the grave might not seem so deep.

The other cross marked the grave of Ivan Ladonichev, a stoker on *Vaygach*, who had died that winter of peritonitis.

With the wind howling and the frozen Kara Sea stretching out in front of us, Cape Mogilniy (Cape of the Graves) was like an Arctic Golgotha.

Meanwhile the captain, who had found a dry spot of ground, opened his briefcase and was spreading out a picnic consisting of bread, salami, apples and a half-bottle of vodka. We began by drinking a rather solemn toast to all the brave men who had explored the Arctic. Then, munching our sandwiches, we stared out to sea and thought our thoughts.

Although it was sunny, the wind on that exposed hillside was strong and I was beginning to feel chilly when the hydrologist took the bottle from the captain's briefcase where it had been lying. I picked up my small glass in readiness for the inevitable refill, but Valerii Mikhailovich Losef had other ideas. Walking slowly over to the graves, he stopped in front of Zhokhov's.

'They were brave men,' he said. 'They need a drink more than we do.' And he poured some vodka out of the bottle on to the brown earth.

There was another pause while he paid his silent respects before he walked to Ladonichev's grave and poured the remains of the vodka on to the earth. Valerii Mikhailovich Losef, hydrologist and veteran of the Arctic, was giving the two men a drink to warm them as they slept under the soil in the permanent ice of Siberia. I cried a little.

We ate the salami and I, as usual, declined the apple.

'Why don't you eat apples?' asked Sergei.

'I do, sometimes,' I lied. I hadn't the heart to tell him that I only liked apples if they were in reasonable condition and not bruised and soggy.

Our small party went for a slow walk along the cliffs where Valentin stooped down and beckoned me. There, in the fine, puffy soil, he had found some flowers growing. Blue and purple, about one third the size of a violet, they were managing to bloom very close to the soil, surrounded by brown and red moss and lichen. How anything could grow in those conditions, when the sea was still frozen solid, was a miracle. Yet summer was not far away. A small stream was trickling down the gully into the sea; the snow was beginning to melt on the south-facing slopes. Below us in a valley I noticed some polar bear footprints. I pointed them out to Valerii Mikhailovich, who shrugged like a man for whom polar bear prints were not worth thinking about.

Valentin was beckoning. It was time to go back to the ship. We gathered up the remains of our picnic and scrambled into the helicopter. As we rose slowly from the brown cliff I looked back to the two wooden crosses and wondered how many ships had sailed past them as *Arktika* would do in a few hours.

Later, at dinner, the captain announced that he had a souvenir for me. I went up to his cabin where he presented me with an illustrated book about the Second World War. It had a long inscription in Russian, ending with the English words 'Let there be no more wars'. I thought this a pleasant, if somewhat unoriginal, act until I got back to my cabin and switched on the BBC World Service. Only then did I realise the significance of his gift. That day was the fiftieth anniversary of Hitler's declaration of war on the USSR. Operation Barbarossa started on 22 June 1941. I felt both stupid and ungrateful.

At 17.20 we crossed the 100 degrees east longitude.

Raisa and Tatiana, rouged and perfumed, were out on the helicopter deck that evening. In spite of the cold, they had dressed up like two Italian women walking arm in arm on their evening *struscio* through the piazza. I fell in behind them and circled the deck slowly because their stiletto heels meant that they tottered rather than strode. After several circuits Raisa looked round and noticed me for the first time. She and Tatiana stopped, unlinked their arms and, without a word, swept me off like a hooker between two prop forwards in a rugby scrum. They felt softer than

137

rugby players, and smelt a lot better too. The two women continued their conversation as if I were not there, which meant that they had to lean forward to see each other from time to time.

When eventually the cold became more than they could bear, they detached themselves from me and swung out of orbit. Instead of going inside, Raisa waited for me to come round again. She dug into her pocket and produced three boiled sweets which she gave me with a kiss. I was sad that Tatiana took no part in this manoeuvre, but instead stood against the railing looking cold and impatient.

As I continued my circuits alone I remembered what it was like being at prep school in post-war Britain when the gift of three sweets was an important transaction. Here I was back in a land of shortages where I was never offered a second helping of anything in the dining room and where the highest form of hospitality was to give food.

The sun fell lower, so that after half an hour I could see my shadow on the ice each time I walked forward along the starboard side of the deck. *Arktika* must have been travelling very slowly, since a brisk walker would have overtaken us. I calculated that we were probably doing no more than three miles an hour.

I liked my evening walks when everyone else was inside watching TV. I liked looking at the surging wake with its chunks of ice being thrust up by the propellers and the channel which cut through the ice and stretched astern curving back to the horizon. Even though the temperature had risen as high as six degrees in the early afternoon, it had by then fallen to zero. With a sharp wind blowing in from Siberia it felt chilly indeed.

An hour before midnight, I went up to the bridge for what had become my regular nightly glass of tea with Leonid. The tea was brewed in a tiny teapot with a strainer

138

1 Valerii Mikhailovich drew an ice map after every flight on the *ptichka*.

2 Yuri repairing electrical circuits, watched by Maxim (r) and Sergei (l).

3 Captain Ulitin.

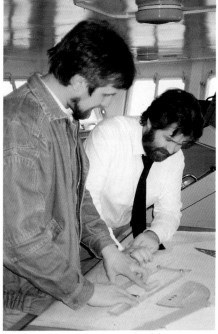

4 Maxim (l) and Alexander (r) at the chart table.

5 The graves of Lieutenant Zhokhov and stoker Ladonichev.

6 A toast to the memory of the early Arctic explorers.
(l to r) Sergei, Captain Ulitin, Valerii Mikhailovich, helicopter pilot Valentin Albansky.

7 Mother and baby walrus.

8 The polar bear did not like being chased by a helicopter.

9 *Arktika* at speed in heavy ice.

10 Captain Ulitin's enthusiasm for music usually overwhelmed his talent.

11 Valerii Mikhailovich at the deserted polar station.

12 The author dwarfed by the bows of *Arktika*.

13 *Igrim*.

14 Larissa Mikhaila, *Igrim's* doctor.

15 Anatoly Shmaglienko, *Igrim's* chief mate, played a mournful guitar.

hanging from the spout, and the resulting strong liquor was diluted with hot water from a nearby samovar.

There was very little radio traffic at that time of night, so Leonid passed the time by watching the evening movie which was piped throughout the ship. It was an American film with Dutch subtitles and a Russian summary in voice-over. This resulted in some oddities, like when the hero said, 'Samantha.' The subtitle faithfully recorded this as 'Samantha' and the Fedor, Ivanovich Chaliapin Russian voice echoed (in basso profundo), 'Samantha.'

I looked around the radio room for alternative amusement and found it in the shape of the Morse key which sat on the table in front of Leonid, where it had almost been hidden by an ashtray full of cigarette ends. Could he, I wondered, give me a demonstration of this machine?

Leonid found this an odd request, like being asked to demonstrate the use of a knife or fork, but he shrugged his shoulders and burst into action. His finger zapped up and down so fast I could hardly see it, and the resulting sound was unstopping and unstoppable. Like a jazz drummer in the middle of a particularly complex solo, Leonid went into a sort of trance. Maybe good radio operators have an inbuilt sense of rhythm which, when they are working, blanks out the rest of the world.

He looked like a man who would happily blank out his own little world. He didn't like icebreaker work, he told me, but there was no alternative if you happened to live in Murmansk. In the old days, when things had been better, he worked on freighters and saw the world.

'I went to South America and West Africa,' he told me gloomily. 'The heat was wonderful.' He took another sip of tea. 'I haven't felt sun on my back for years now. I wonder if I ever shall again.'

12 Cape Chelyuskin

The dove may have brought Noah an olive leaf, but Valerii Mikhailovich in his *ptichka* brought me a medal. He had been up that morning, not looking at a flooded world but making contact with Cape Chelyuskin. According to the dictates of the KGB, I was not allowed to accompany the *ptichka* on the flight lest I contaminate the inhabitants of this, the most northerly point on the Eurasian landmass. So I stayed behind and tried not to sulk in my tent.

I was still trying when the hydrologist knocked on my door and entered. He was even more ill at ease than normal, refused a cup of coffee and a seat, preferring to stand in the doorway. Eventually he produced from his pocket a large bronze-coloured medal which was about seven centimetres across.

'I am sorry you could not come,' he began, 'but I found this for you.' And he handed me the medal. At first I thought it was one of those chocolate coins which come in children's Christmas stockings because it was very shiny and a lot lighter than I had been expecting. I was in the process of stammering out a thank you when he interrupted me.

'It is a little bit special,' he said. 'This medal is only given to men who have spent a winter on Cape Chelyuskin.

Perhaps you can understand that there are not very many of them.'

It was more than adequate compensation for my not having been allowed to land on the cape. I turned to put it safely with the rest of my treasures in the desk drawer. When I looked up Valerii Mikhailovich had disappeared.

Tea was especially good that afternoon, consisting of *vatrushka*, a sort of Russian hybrid which results from crossing a ring doughnut with a bagel. The hole had been blocked up and was used as a container for either jam or, more usually, sour cream. The problem which confronted me was how to spread butter on my *vatrushka*. If you cut it like a bagel the jam leaked out; there had to be a simple Russian technique. To discover this required the most subtle gastronomic espionage. Thus, while pretending to study both the horizon and the bustline of Tatiana, I was actually keeping a close watch on my neighbour, the chief mate, Vladimir Kulikov. The experience was rewarding, since he appeared to break all the Western rules of dough-nut (or bagel) eating. Instead of cutting it crossways as I had anticipated, his solution was to cut slices off around the edge, slathering huge chunks of butter on each as he went, leaving the centre growing ever smaller until, as the final orgasmic act of pure greed, he ate the jammy hole whole.

Maxim was bored. He had played an unsatisfactory game of Grand Prix Racer on the computer and, with Owdoyoudo at the wheel, there was not a lot for him to do on the bridge.

'What is the difference,' he enquired, 'between to offer and to suggest?' When I had explained, he nodded gravely and returned to his work on the navigation chart.

The table on which the chart was spread out looked much like any other chart table on an ocean-going ship.

141

But there was one difference. There was no sign of a pocket calculator. When I mentioned this to Maxim he grinned.

'The best calculators are in here,' and he tapped his forehead.

As he did so I felt *Arktika* roll gently to port. I braced myself against the rail and, a few seconds later, we began to roll back again. This was strange, not to say impossible, since there was little wind and – even more significant – we were in fast ice, so there could not possibly be any waves.

Maxim watched my face register surprise and then, I suspect, a bit of concern.

'What's the matter?' he asked with ill-feigned nonchalance. I told him that I could swear I had felt the ship roll, though it appeared to be impossible.

'You were correct,' said Maxim, like a Professor of Naval Studies. 'We did roll. And we are going to roll again very soon.'

The explanation was that the captain had decided to try to increase our icebreaking efficiency by reducing our width. This could only be achieved by emptying our ballast tanks and thus sitting further out of the water. The rocking motion I had felt was the effect of the ballast tanks being emptied, and we were now two metres higher in the water than when we left Murmansk.

The snag was that while this manoeuvre works well when the ice is fast and smooth, it is actually counterproductive if the ice contains hummocks. If and when we experienced these conditions again, explained Maxim, we would have to reverse the process and sink back down to our normal – and more stable – position in the water.

Crime and Punishment was interrupted that afternoon by Maxim suggesting another sauna. This time I agreed enthusiastically. I had even bought my own pair of flip-

142

flops from Boris in the shop. The only thing I lacked was a felt hat to protect my hair.

Yuri was waiting for me and had brought a thermos of special herbal tea which he said we would drink after the sauna. I made a mental note that about a third of the crew were circumcised, which was a much higher proportion than I would have expected to see on a British ship.

This time the sauna was less traumatic because at least I knew what to expect, which is why I refused Yuri's offer of being hosed down by high-pressure Arctic sea water. But his massage was even more strenuous than the last. After my second session in the sauna, which was a heart-stopping 114 degrees Celsius, he laid me down on a marble slab in the adjoining shower room. Before I could lie on the stone it first had to be cooled because, like everything in the neighbourhood of the sauna room, it was too hot to touch. Eventually, after buckets of cold sea water had been poured over it, the slab was adjudged to be touchable. The fact that an egg would have happily fried on it did not seem to worry either Yuri or the small *kot* of people who had gathered to watch the *kulak* be tortured.

Yuri pulled out of his plastic bag a bar of soap and a pair of gloves which had been made from industrial pan scourers. He then proceeded to treat me like a saucepan covered with cold scrambled egg.

At this point a man dressed in a tracksuit and wearing a large and floppy felt hat entered the room, got undressed in silence and marched into the sauna. Ten minutes later he emerged and sat, slumped on the wooden benches, while we drank Yuri's tea. His black hat gave him a sinister air, as did his resolute silence. Once again he rose to his feet, stretched twice and walked into the furnace of the sauna. This process happened one more time before the silent

143

stranger, after an ice-cold sea-water shower, dressed and disappeared.

I asked Maxim who the mystery man was.

'Oh, him,' came the reply. 'He's the nuclear safety officer.'

Was he always as taciturn as that?

'No. Not at all. He's usually a very sociable chap. But you must understand he's recovering from an awful hangover. I came off watch at four this morning and he was completely plastered then. I'm even surprised he can walk now, and it is sixteen hours later.'

I offered a silent prayer for the safety – and sobriety – of the nuclear safety officer's deputy who was, I assumed, keeping me radiation-free.

Back in the sauna itself, after I had been made to lie down on the top (and hottest) bench, Yuri dipped his leaves in the water, sprinkled the hot rocks to produce steam, and proceeded to hit me with the leaves. It wasn't either stimulating or relaxing. Just the opposite. I felt as if I was being smothered and drowned at the same time. It was also impossible to speak. I did manage to ask what sort of tree I was being beaten with.

'They are maple,' said Yuri. 'You know, like the Toronto Maple Leaves hockey team. Or like the Canadian flag.'

After the sauna, I felt that etiquette demanded that I offer my friends a whisky. This was accepted enthusiastically. Maxim's cabin was agreed as the venue. I arrived with my Cutty Sark to find him cutting up some of Boris's salami. He had also contributed two bottles of beer and some *Narzan* mineral water. Yuri appeared carrying the remains of our last post-sauna party, together with a bottle of kvass which he had made himself. I had never been keen on kvass, a non-alcoholic drink made from bread. It is supposed to be very thirst-quenching, but to me it tastes like slightly sour dishwater. Yuri's did nothing to change my opinion.

At this moment the chief nuclear engineer, Valerii Petrovich Mansvetov, a bald, grizzled man whom I hardly knew, knocked on the door, took one look at what was on offer and went scurrying back to his cabin, to reappear carrying a large decanter of brilliant red liquid which turned out to be his own home-made cranberry wine.

I asked why it was that Russian saunas were so much hotter than their Finnish equivalents. Yuri had an opinion.

'I think it's because we Russians are natural extremists. We like things to be the biggest and the best – and also the hottest. Imagine our having a cooler sauna than the Finns. Impossible.'

We finished the beer and decided to make the whisky last longer by mixing it with the mineral water. By this time Sergei, the moustachioed computer freak, had also joined us, so Maxim's small cabin was becoming very overcrowded. Nature may abhor a vacuum, but Russians abhor a half-empty bottle, and my Cutty Sark was the proof.

It was during this increasingly alcoholic interlude that the following story was told.

Napoleon, with one of his marshals, is on St Helena. The marshal is reading a newspaper in the sunshine. He turns to Napoleon and says, 'If only we'd had this weather we'd never have been defeated at Waterloo.' Napoleon nods. Minutes pass and the marshal says, 'If only we'd had the Red Army on our side we'd never have been defeated at Waterloo.' Napoleon grunts. Minutes pass. The marshal says, 'If only we'd had *Pravda* as our newspaper nobody would ever have *known* we'd been defeated at Waterloo.' Napoleon is asleep.

Valerii Petrovich said that his cranberry wine was not really ready to drink.

'It's still too young,' he announced, swishing it round his mouth like a negociant from Beaune.

I asked him when it would be at its prime.

'Tomorrow.'

At midnight, with the buildings on Cape Chelyuskin clearly in sight, the bridge suddenly came to life. Sergei, who was going off watch, shouted from the starboard side, 'Oliver, come and look.' I walked over and stared at the shore through my binoculars. 'Look,' he said, 'two walrus. One is very old.' Sure enough, where the smooth sea ice met the rough shoreline ice, two animals were lying down. They were certainly bigger than seals. At that point one began to move, and walked on four legs towards the shore. It was a dog.

By now the entire bridge had assembled to witness a sight that even Grigorii Alexeivich Ulitin had never seen before – a dog with a walrus. Perhaps, I suggested, the walrus was ill. Or, volunteered Maxim, there was not enough water for him. But whatever the cause, it was an extraordinary sight to see two such different animals only a few metres apart.

The observation party had by now moved on to the small deck astern of the bridge to get a better view. And as we peered through our binoculars we began to notice that the walrus was disintegrating. Suddenly it transmogrified into two more dogs. The mystery was solved. There had never been a walrus at all; only three dogs lying on the ice in such a way they appeared to be a walrus to the crew of an icebreaker passing three kilometres away.

Cape Chelyuskin should be one of the great names of geography, like the Cape of Good Hope and Cape Horn. It is, after all, the last and most northerly bit of Asia. In

146

practice nobody in the West has ever heard of it, unless they happen to specialise in Siberian geography. The same applies to the most easterly tip of the Soviet Union which sticks out into the Bering Straits and nearly touches Alaska. Who has ever heard of Cape Dezhnev?

As we approached the Vilkitsky Straits which separate the mainland from Severnaya Zemlya, an exceptionally officious radio operator from Cape Chelyuskin kept insisting that *Arktika* identify herself. This irritated Sergei.

'He should open his eyes and look for himself.'

Finally he and Maxim decided that I should reply in English, announcing that this was Her Majesty's Ship *Arktika*, representing the British Merchant Marine. I was all set to do this when Sergei had an attack of nerves and – rightly, I suppose – realised that this joke could backfire badly. The captain might have not seen the funny side to it if his ship had been boarded by Russian soldiers. I therefore kept silent.

We were actually abeam of Cape Chelyuskin at around two o'clock in the morning. Swirling fog made visibility difficult, but through the binoculars I caught occasional glimpses of a cluster of huts, some fuel tanks, radio masts and other assorted buildings. I gathered from Valerii Mikhailovich that the camp was shared between the military, who operate a radar installation, and the scientists, who have a weather station. The latter has the record for the coldest average temperature in Russia throughout the year, amounting to −15 degrees Celsius.[1]

For the first time in the voyage I found myself feeling a real, albeit undeserved, sense of achievement at having

[1] The coldest place in Russia – and indeed the Northern Hemisphere
– is the town of Oymyakon, below the Arctic Circle in eastern
Siberia, where the temperature has been as low as −68 degrees
Celsius. In the summer, however, it can rise to over 30 degrees.

reached this landmark. Most of my predecessors seem to have shared this excitement. The log of Nordenskiöld's *Vega* read, '19th August 1878. Anchored at 6 p.m. off Cape Chelyuskin, latitude 77 degrees 36 minutes 36 seconds north, longitude 103 degrees 25 minutes east, in four fathoms water. Raised flag on mainmast. Fired five shots from cannon. Issued extra rations to crew: two ounces cheese, five ounces sugar per man.'

Nordenskiöld himself was a bit more enthusiastic in his personal diary: 'We have now reached a great goal, sought after in vain for centuries. For the first time a ship lay at anchor off the northernmost cape of the Old World.'

Fifteen years later another Scandinavian, Fridtjof Nansen, sailed past the cape on the *Fram*, on the first stage of his epic drift across the Arctic. He too was moved by the moment and wrote, 'In honour of the occasion all hands were turned out, and punch, fruit and cigars were served in the festally lighted saloon. Something special in the way of a toast was expected on such an occasion. I lifted my glass and made the following speech: "Skol, my lads, and be glad we've passed Chelyuskin."'

After the oration there was an organ recital. Nansen showed his good taste and common sense by leaving the concert and climbing up to the crow's nest to take a last look at the most northerly point of the old world.

The Scandinavians may have treated the event with a combination of reverence and excitement, but the last foreigner to have passed Cape Chelyuskin, some fifty-one years before me, was distinctly underwhelmed by the occasion. Captain Eyssen, the conscientious German sailor in command of the *Komet*, permitted no celebrations.

'It was,' he noted, 'a glorious trip through the Vilkitsky Strait with a blue sky, half moon, midnight sun. Everything was there except there was no ice.'

I would have loved to celebrate our passing of Cape Chelyuskin and entry into the Laptev Sea, but for the crew of *Arktika* it was just another landmark on our journey east, much as Scotch Corner is on the road to Edinburgh.

We hadn't been in the Laptev Sea for more than a few hours when I took off in the *ptichka* for what I thought would be a routine flight in search of new leads. Only when I saw that Alexander, Sergei and the two other helicopter pilots were joining us did I realise that our destination must be somewhere special. Beside me in the rear, a pair of battered blue skis had appeared since the morning's flight.

'In case of a forced landing,' said Valentin, with a stainless steel grin. It was rather reassuring, although I wondered which of us would be given the skis if we needed them.

For the first hour it was a normal reconnaissance flight fifty metres above the rapidly melting ice. Then, as if Valerii Mikhailovich had seen all he needed to see, we turned abruptly towards the shore. Passing the usual tide mark of driftwood, which was surprising since there was not a tree within 800 kilometres, we flew over sandbars, inlets and lagoons.

Eventually we landed on a shingle beach a few metres from the frozen surf. To describe the spot as desolate would be pointless since everywhere in this part of the world was equally so. With the exception of a ship's mast on a nearby promontory, Cape Amundsen had no visible features.

The point was named, of course, after Roald Amundsen, maybe the greatest Arctic and Antarctic explorer of them all. In Britain he is known simply as the man who beat Scott to the South Pole, but he has an incredible list of other achievements to his name, including being the first man to navigate the North West Passage, which had defeated every sailor since Martin Frobisher.

From where the helicopter landed it looked like any other bit of coast on the eastern side of the Taymyr Peninsula. Only when Valerii Mikhailovich led us towards a pile of stones did I begin to see why we had stopped there.

The stones turned out to be a slight depression in the beach, around which lay the rusting detritus of an expedition, including old barrel staves, wooden crates and lengths of wire. I picked up one piece of bleached wood and read 'Case No. 1095. Sprague Warner & Co. USA'. Fifty metres further along the beach was a low hut, perfectly camouflaged since it had been built out of shingle and roofed with wood from the packing cases. A single tiny window looked westwards.

It was here that Roald Amundsen's expedition on the *Maud* had wintered in 1918. His original objective had been to reach the Bering Straits and then put the *Maud* into the ice and drift across the North Pole towards Svalbard. Nansen had started further west in 1893[2] and had managed to get to within 600 kilometres of the North Pole. Amundsen reckoned he stood a good chance of succeeding where the other Norwegian had failed.

He was wrong. The *Maud* expedition was dogged by bad luck. During the first winter Amundsen himself suffered a series of accidents, including breaking a shoulder when he fell off the gangplank, being mauled by a polar bear and then, as if these were not enough, almost suffocating from the carbon dioxide given off by a faulty lamp. The following summer the ice, as it sometimes does in these parts, refused to melt and the expedition found that they were trapped for many months, until eventually on 12 Septem-

[2] Just north of the New Siberian Islands.

150

ber 1919 the ice cracked and they were able to reach open water.

One of the crew, who had been suffering from severe headaches, decided to go home to Norway. He was joined by a colleague who felt it was too dangerous for a single man to walk across Arctic Siberia alone. The two men set out for Dikson, some 800 kilometres to the west, but they never arrived. One of the bodies was later found a few kilometres from Dikson; the other disappeared completely.

Meanwhile Amundsen's bad luck continued. He managed to travel for only eleven days before once again the ice closed in and he was forced to winter on Aijon Island at the mouth of Chaun Bay. The following summer, still suffering from the after-effects of his near-suffocation, Amundsen decided to put into Nome in Alaska before setting off into the ice. No sooner had the *Maud* reached port than another four members of the crew announced that they too wanted to go home. In spite of the fact that this left Amundsen with only four men to crew a relatively large vessel, he insisted on pressing on, but his luck continued to be bad. After damaging a propeller and injuring another crew member, he accepted defeat and, nearly four years after the *Maud* had set out from Tromsø, she limped in to Seattle. The expedition had failed.

Eventually the *Maud* was sold to the Hudson's Bay Company and was renamed the *Baymaud*. For a few years she was used as a supply ship in the Canadian Arctic, but was later moored at Cambridge Bay where she served as a floating warehouse, a machine shop and a wireless station until eventually she sprang a leak and was abandoned.

Twelve months after I left *Arktika* I found myself in Cambridge Bay, where the hulk of the *Maud* is still visible. It was a strange feeling to have seen the mast on one side of the Arctic ocean and the hull on the other.

151

I spent half an hour wandering around the beach, poking through the remains of the stores hoping that I might find something memorable. I didn't. Further along the beach was another heap of stones, half buried by a snowdrift. This had been the kennels for Amundsen's thirty dogs, and the old iron rings to which the animals had been tethered were still attached to the walls. Eventually, with the wind rising and time running out, Valerii Mikhailovich called us back to the helicopter.

Once in the air, I assumed we were on our way back to the ship. But instead of flying out across the ice, we hugged the shore. As the *ptichka* came in to land a cloud of white gulls flew up into the air, like confetti in reverse. They were followed a few seconds later by a squadron of geese who, needing more time to prepare for take-off, waited almost until we had landed before voting with their wings.

From the chart I saw that we had landed at the Unga River, a brittle stream which was tumbling down the rocks from a miniature glacier no more than ten metres high. The earth was soft and spongy but, unlike all the other places at which I had landed, this valley was full of colour. Red and yellow lichens covered the rocks, and behind the bigger boulders, protected from the wind, plants were already blossoming into vivid purple flowers. As I walked towards the glacier at the head of the valley I found myself having to pick my way between birds' nests made from fluffy feathers and containing brown-grey eggs which were bigger than bantams' but smaller than chickens'.

I wondered if this tiny valley had ever seen a human being before. Certainly its freshness and delicacy made it feel as if it hadn't. I sat on a rock and gulped it all in with the heightened sensitivity one has when one knows one will never return. And I remembered Nikel with its dead landscape, its black snow and its stinking streams.

13 A fire on the bridge

Arktika stopped again the following day. It was, I was told, another 'routine maintenance'. This meant that the *ptichka* stayed tied to the deck and I tried to re-establish my less-than-passionate relationship with Dostoyevsky. I was lying on my bunk feeling irritated by Raskolnikov when Alexander appeared.

'Coffee?' he asked.

It seemed like a reasonable proposition. Alexander was the great coffee connoisseur on the ship, which is why I had given him small quantities of the French and Italian coffee I had brought with me from Soho. He had decided that morning to settle his indecision once and for all by having a blind tasting of my two coffees, as well as the Austrian coffee he had bought from Boris's shop.

A kettle of water had been boiled and three jugs were lined up along the shelf which ran the length of his cabin. In front of them three cups, three saucers and three teaspoons were ready and waiting. Like toy racing cars at the start of a race, they were all numbered individually.

We had agreed not to use either sugar or milk powder lest these detracted from the taste. We circled the cups warily, not wanting to pick up the coffee the other might wish to taste first. Eventually I chose cup number two and took a tiny sip. Should I swirl it round my mouth before spitting it out? It was far too hot to do that, so I glugged it back. It was like, well, coffee. A little bitter maybe, but nothing special.

We should, I suppose, have cleansed our palates between cups. But with what? A macaroon, a cream cracker or perhaps just toast and Cooper's Vintage Marmalade.

Cup number one, I was distressed to find, tasted very similar to cup number two. In fact I thought it was the same coffee. I paused to look at Alexander. His eyes were closed and he appeared to be smiling in his private world as he concentrated on activating every last tastebud. Only when they were all in perfect working order did he move on to the next stage. He sucked the coffee down past his larynx and into whatever comes next between tonsils and bladder.

'Mmmm, very good,' he crooned, his eyes still tight shut.

I realised I would have to pull myself together and show a bit more enthusiasm. No, a lot more enthusiasm, if I were to survive at this level of coffee tasting.

I picked up cup number three and tried to look reverential as I swished the stuff round my mouth. I needn't have bothered because, once again, Alexander was oblivious to anything but his tastebuds. His eyes were closed and he had gone into a caffeine-induced trance. More sucking noises and then he emerged back into my world, eyes bright and smile beatific. He could say only one word.

'Wonderful.'

Eventually we decided on the batting order. The Italian coffee was the best, which will be good news for Camisa Bros in Old Compton Street. Alexander liked his Austrian coffee second and the French coffee (also from Soho) last. I agreed with him — for diplomatic and not gastronomic reasons – although in practice I had found it impossible to tell the difference.

By then Alexander was on a high induced by coffee, excitement and novelty. With Willie Nelson twanging away for the third time that morning, we sat down to play *shish besh*, a Russian version of backgammon. It was good practice for my Russian numbers and even though I lost comprehensively, I learned to count up to thirty.

Arktika's oil-change, tappet adjustment or whatever the nuclear equivalent was had been completed by 18.00 hours and once again we were under way. Looking at my map of the USSR, we still seemed an awfully long way from Pevek. The shortest route would take us almost due east from Cape Chelyuskin, north of the New Siberian Islands where Nansen had put the *Fram* into the ice at the start of his three-year polar drift. But the experts seemed to think that this would certainly run us into heavy ice. So it seemed likely that we would continue to hug the coast, just as we had done since leaving Novaya Zemlaya.

Within an hour of starting again, we ran into very thick ice indeed. Once more *Arktika* had to transform herself into a battering ram, backing up by at least one ship's length every time we came to a halt. It did not make for a comfortable night.

The following morning, with the ship still behaving like a slow-motion version of a fairground ride, I ran into Valerii Mikhailovich in a passage. I muttered something about it being rather uncomfortable and he laughed.

'There's only another five kilometres to go and then we are in open water,' he said.

This I had to see. Armed with my binoculars, I ran up to the bridge and stared out across the whiteness. There was no sign of open water and, what was worse, there appeared to be a storm brewing. The sky ahead was dark and threatening.

Were we in for some rough weather, I asked Sergei, pointing at the blackness which contrasted so starkly with the colour of the ice?

'No,' he said, 'it's only the reflection of the water. You shouldn't be worried.'

It was, I later learned, what Arctic sailors call 'a water sky'. The sky is a reflection of the surface below, and when the surface ceases to be ice and becomes sea, the sky above appears a bit darker. When the opposite happens and an area of ice reflects a pale patch in the sky, this is known as a 'snow blink'. In the old days before radar and helicopters, icebreaker captains would scan the horizon looking for a water sky. Once they had found the small dark patch, they would steer towards it.

Half an hour later we reached open water. I found myself anticipating this event with enormous and irrational excitement, so I made sure I was standing at the bows when, for the first time in almost ten days, we found ourselves surrounded by calm ice-free water. Immediately our speed rose to eighteen knots and, instead of needing 90 per cent of the power the reactors could produce, we were back to a modest 40 per cent. Up on the bridge everyone seemed to relax – except for Valerii Mikhailovich, who knew that he and his *ptichka* were redundant.

But not for long. Within twenty-four hours the ice had returned again, although this time we seemed to be able to keep up a much higher speed than we had managed before. Maybe the ice was thinner, or maybe our stops for routine maintenance had discovered some extra horses in the engine room. Either way, the line on the map in my cabin lengthened a lot each evening.

One morning I went up to the bridge to find that we

156

were surrounded by a combination of ice floes, low cloud and a myriad of mobile fog banks, all of which combined to make navigation difficult. Valerii Mikhailovich was by then back on active duty. Even if I hadn't heard him go clattering past my porthole, I would have known from his voice which came over the radio in short bursts.

Sergei, wearing sunglasses and baseball cap against the glare, was standing by the port side windows with his right hand poised over – but not actually touching – the throttle levers. In a loud, clear voice he was giving instructions to the helmsman. In Russian there are no separate words for port and starboard, simply *levo* and *pravo* (left and right). The helmsman would answer by repeating the command in a softer voice.

Valerii Mikhailovich's voice came over the radio again, and Sergei translated for me.

'He says that in fifty kilometres we shall be in the New Siberian polynya, which may possibly last all the way to Pevek.'

This sounded like good news. For the first time since leaving Murmansk, I was beginning to find ice tiresome. The novelty had worn off and I looked foward to a smooth sea and a peaceful bath. I was also looking forward to the next landmark on our course. Called Pestchany Island, Sergei had told me it was 'the walrus capital of the Arctic'.

The walrus, as it happens, plays a small role in Arctic history. Soviet historians, who were keen to show that in the sixteenth century Russians had sailed into the Kara Sea long before the Dutch and English, pointed out that the so-called fish teeth (i.e. walrus tusks) were appearing in the markets of Constantinople during the tenth century. From this they deduced that the Pomors, a seafaring people from around the White Sea, had sold the ivory to the merchants of Novgorod, who in turn took the stuff to Constantinople.

The theory is that walrus ivory was to Arctic exploration what spices were to Western discoveries – the valuable commodity in search of which sailors pushed ever further east. Academics are still arguing about this facet of early Arctic history but, as was often the case in the USSR, chauvinism and politics tended to obscure the original question.

During a stroll round the decks in the cold sunshine, I stopped to watch three seamen cleaning one of *Arktika*'s two spare propellers which were lashed down next to the helicopter hangar. These objects, looking like the Henry Moor sculptures which sit in front of parliament buildings, were kept in case the ship damaged a propeller in the ice. Quite how they could be fitted without the help of a dry dock and lifting equipment remained a mystery.

I opened the door to the bridge to find wisps of black smoke and the unmistakable smell of an electrical fire. My immediate reaction was, naturally, to panic and rush for a lifeboat, but since none of the bridge's occupants looked remotely concerned I tried to appear equally nonchalant and asked Sergei what had happened. It seemed that the electric kettle used to make tea in the *chaikana* had boiled all the water and, as a result, had melted its wiring. As I spoke, Owdoyoudo came in from the deck, carrying the smouldering object from where it had been exiled to cool down.

A few minutes later it was 11.30, time for Sergei's daily report to the crew, which gave our position and any other information which might be interesting. I had already decided that these addresses were not sufficiently inspirational, and so wrote him a speech for that morning which began:

> Peasants and Workers of *Arktika*, I must report to you that
> the bridge is on fire. The cause of this disaster is uncertain

but we cannot rule out sabotage. As Comrades will know, *Arktika* has a viper in its bosom in the shape of a capitalist *kulak* masquerading as a writer. We have him under close surveillance. However, thanks to the leadership of Our Great Helmsman, Comrade Captain Grigorii Alexeivich, the damage has been contained and we are proceeding on our course of 111 degrees towards the Socialist Motherland. . . .

I took this up to the bridge where Maxim translated it for the captain. He listened, slightly puzzled, before breaking into the ghost of a grin.

'I hope you don't publish that,' he said. 'If the international organisation which controls nuclear installations hears about a fire on the bridge they will be extremely upset.'

I promised I would make it clear that a dash of poetic licence had been used to convert a smoking kettle into a fire on the bridge. I could see, nonetheless, that Grigorii Alexeivich remained unconvinced as he went below for lunch.

During the evening watch that day I asked Sergei if the captain had really understood that I was making a joke.

'It is a very serious subject for him,' explained Sergei gravely. 'Besides, I don't think he has much of a sense of humour.' And then he added quickly to atone for any possible disloyalty, 'But he is a very good captain.'

In the radio room Sasha was on watch. He was a chubby and friendly young man whose English was as poor as my Russian. In Murmansk he had sported a bushy red beard. Then, to my confusion, he cut it off, but that morning it appeared to be growing again. I had gone to see if I could do anything to improve the reception of my little Sony radio since for the past forty-eight hours the BBC World Service had become increasingly faint. Sasha gave me a length of wire with which I was able to connect my set to one of the ship's aerials strung between two masts. The result was amazing. Whereas that morning I had been unable to get the BBC at all, I now had perfect reception. The first programme I heard turned out to be a discussion of the works of Pasternak, which somehow seemed to be much more meaningful than if I had heard it back home in England. But then pastis always tastes better in France and even tequila is drinkable in Mexico.

For the first time I was beginning to feel twinges of boredom. Maybe it was the fog, or the fact that the *ptichka* rarely flew, or that the cabin seemed stuffier than usual. Whatever the cause, the days began to drag.

I found myself spending more and more time walking round the helicopter deck, but I had to be very choosy. The cliché of an army marching at the pace of the slowest was excruciatingly true on the helicopter deck. Most of the people who used the circuit did so for social reasons and came out with a friend to saunter round the deck looking at the view and chewing the rag. I, on the other hand, had but one end in mind, to get as much exercise as possible in as short a time as possible. Which explained the great contrast in styles between my shipmates' shambolic stroll and my brisk middle-class Anglo-Saxon gait.

The disparity between us meant that I had either to perform various intricate overtaking manoeuvres, accelerating hard and braking sharply, or else to pretend I was an army and slow down to the speed of the slowest. The solution was to pick my times carefully so that I would be alone and unhindered.

On my second attempt that day to find an empty deck, I succeeded and started to stride round and round in clockwise circles, feeling virtuous and very British. However, after twenty minutes, in spite of my Arctic parka with its

160

wolf-fur hood, the cold, damp wind had penetrated to the sensitive bits. Only then did it become clear why my fellow walkers had stayed inside.

Back in the cabin I couldn't face Dostoyevsky, so I turned on the television. It was a black and white film starring a very young Robert Redford, George Segal and Zero Mostel. I watched for a few minutes and was relieved to learn that the Russian for a 'double Jack Daniels straight up' is a double Jack Daniels straight up. On the other channel there was a saccharine little cartoon about two storks who were bringing up a family and were threatened by an ugly vulture.

My boredom had by then reached a level at which the only solution lay in alcohol. This was no easy realisation as I had made a firm decision at the beginning of the voyage that on no account would I ever be reduced to drinking alone. The resolution had so far survived untested, but now I went to the cupboard and poured myself a moderate Cutty Sark which I diluted 50/50 with water before sitting down at my desk. No sooner had I done so than the telephone rang, before I had even taken a sip. It was Dimitri, who asked if he could come round.

Two minutes later there was a knock on the door and in he came, carrying my suitcase. He had repaired the handle perfectly. How, I wondered, had he managed to make such a superb job?

'I got the ship's turner to make me two new brass screws.'

Struggling to express my gratitude, I realised I had the solution in my right hand.

'Would you like a whisky?'

'Yes, please. I had never before drunk whisky until you gave us some the other day. Vadim and I liked it very much.'

161

We sipped our scotch, talked about the weather and how long it would take to reach Pevek. Eventually Dimitri looked at his wrist, announced that his watch was starting and excused himself. As he turned to leave he said, 'Would you like a party tonight with Vadim and me?'

That would be lovely, I replied.

'I will come for you when my watch is over.'

I felt like Cinderella being escorted to the ball.

Less than a minute had elapsed since Dimitri left when there was another knock at the door. It was Raisa with the laundry. She had, as usual, ironed my socks and had also darned the holes in the elbows of my sweater. Indeed, she had darned them so finely that when she came to show me, she could not even find where the holes had been.

After lots of sign language, in which I tried to mime gratitude, love and pleasure, she sat down on the sofa and motioned for me to do the same. Thus began the serious stuff of family photographs. First came her two very pretty daughters, both of whom showed strong likenesses to their mum. Then her husband, who looked like a slob, and finally her parents, who were younger than I had expected. Either their picture had been taken a decade ago or Raisa was lamb dressed as mutton.

Out of a plastic bag came two small packets of maca-roons and one large packet weighing at least a kilo of what would have been called Rich Tea Biscuits back in England. How could Raisa have known about my craving for these biscuits for the past week? As a totally inadequate substi-tute, I had been reduced to filching rusks from the carboard box in the *chaikana*.

I rather think that she then asked whether she should bring me some butter. At least I caught the word *maslo* and she pointed to the fridge. I shook my head and said I

162

could manage very well without butter, thank you. That was the cue for Raisa's trademark, *semyachki*.

It was the moment I had been waiting for. I put a seed into my mouth, chewed vigorously and then fished around with my fingers before extracting some of the husk. Raisa looked puzzled. She obviously had no idea that I was asking for her help in the art of sunflower-seed eating. I repeated the process and she looked even more puzzled. I offered her a seed, but she shook her head. It was no good; I was going to need an interpreter if I was ever going to get this across to Raisa.

It had been a lovely evening. My suitcase had been repaired, my resolution not to booze alone remained intact. I had a heap of biscuits and sunflower seeds. I'd also been invited to a party.

14 The Laptev Sea

Dimitri's party turned out to be a rather dismal affair. He and Vadim had produced a tin of Spam, a hard boiled egg, a sliced apple and a tomato. The three of us sat under a black and white photograph of Arnold Schwarzenegger and drank from a tiny bottle of industrial spirit while we looked at still more family photographs. Dimitri's wife was an exceedingly pretty woman, with brown eyes, a large mouth and perfect teeth. His four-year-old daughter looked equally cute. Vadim's family was less good looking, which was only fair since he was better looking than his buddy.

They both admitted that life was getting harder, both at home and on board *Arktika*.

'I had to spend half a day looking for food when I was in Murmansk the other week,' said Vadim. And, he continued, the portions served in the dining room on board had also become a lot smaller in the past three months. As a result both he and Dimitri had been forced to spend more money buying extra food from Boris's shop.

We finished the small bottle of alcohol and Dimitri opened the porthole and pulled in a string at the end of which was a plastic bag.

'Our fridge,' he grinned, producing a half bottle of real vodka.

164

How often did they drink vodka?

'Once a month, on average,' replied Dimitri. 'Of course there are people on board who drink it a lot more often, but they are rich. Besides, it's not really good for body-builders.'

The best thing for body-builders was regular sleep, which seemed like a good idea to all of us.

We had left the pack ice far behind and were then in open water with only a few ice floes visible. These were often big, as much as a kilometre across, and on them we would see large colonies of walrus who, unlike the seals, were unafraid of a huge ship with its turbulent wake.

According to Sergei, walrus lived on a diet of what he called 'shells' which, if Lewis Carroll was accurate, probably meant oysters.

One morning he asked, 'Why do you in England have a company called Shell but no company called Walrus?'

I reflected for a moment and came to the conclusion that this was an example of Sergei's humour. I laughed uproariously and he seemed pleased.

The captain, as usual, wished me a good morning and solemnly shook my hand. This time he also gave me his visiting card which had an English version on one side and Russian on the other. I wished him a happy birthday because that day was his fifty-eighth birthday, an event which was taken very seriously on *Arktika*. A party had been being planned for some days by a few of the officers. I knew none of the details except that I had been asked – even ordered – to lead the singing of 'Happy Birthday' in English.

Lunchtime was one of those moments of profound disillusion, like the day you realised Father Christmas did not exist or that your parents had affairs. In this case I was, as usual, wrestling with the salt shaker. Russian table salt consists of large, coarse granules and Russian salt shakers have very small holes. Whether this is a deliberate method of restricting salt intake, or simply one of these coincidences which litter the Soviet Union, I shall never know. What I shall henceforth know, however, is that one of my profoundest beliefs was revealed as fallacious.

In a moment of exasperation with the salt shaker, I turned to Sergei and said,

'Of all the places in the world we shouldn't have any problems getting salt, it's here in Siberia.'

Sergei looked blank – which he quite often did when he didn't understand my English. So I repeated my observation and received a similarly uncomprehending stare. I tried once more, but this time at dictation speed. Sergei was clearly exasperated.

'Yes,' he said, 'I understand what you say, but I do not understand why you say it.'

I explained how for every British child the ultimate deterrent, if they did not eat their greens, pick up their clothes, brush their teeth or polish their shoes, were the salt mines of Siberia.

Another blank stare.

'But there are no salt mines in Siberia,' said Sergei. 'The salt in Russia comes from many places, including the Urals, and a town called Balkash on Lake Balkash in Kazakhstan. But no salt comes from Siberia.'

He might as well have told me that no coffee comes from Brazil or no rice from China. And then I remembered that no coal comes from Newcastle, no cheese from Stilton and no hats from Panama.

The captain's birthday was marked not by the playing of solemn music, the declaration of a holiday for all hands or even a tot of vodka. Instead it took the form of a gastronomic extravaganza which left *Arktika*'s crew gasping.

166

For that day only each table contained a small bowl filled with a pale grey sludge which looked like library paste but tasted unmistakably like mustard. I remembered my birthday party in Murmansk when Vladimir Yevseyev had offered me mustard as if it were myrrh or frankincense. All around me people were not just putting it on their three strips of meat, they were spreading mustard on bread, putting it on mashed potatoes and one of the radio operators was eating it neat off the end of his knife.

It all went to show that food snobs like me pay more attention to rarity and cost than to inherent quality and taste. If one day I woke up to find that truffles were being grown like carrots throughout the fens, I might not be quite so appreciative of their subtleties. It would, I thought, be a long time before I took mustard for granted again.[1]

We received a radio message that afternoon from the icebreaker *Yermak*, which was working near Pevek. Ice conditions, she reported, were very bad indeed.

The name Yermak originally appeared on the Siberian scene in 1584 when the Cossack Yermak Timofeyev conquered the Khanate of Sibir[2] and began the process of eastward colonisation which ended only when the Cossacks reached Kamchatka in 1697.

Two hundred and fifty years later the name Yermak reappeared when it was given to a ship used in Arctic exploration by the Russian P. P. Krusenstern. That particular *Yermak*, like so many of its predecessors, was crushed in the ice and sank. The next *Yermak* appeared in the shape of the world's first purpose-built icebreaker. Commissioned by an enthusiastic but unlucky Russian admiral called Makaroff, it was built in Newcastle-on-Tyne in

---

[1] My good intentions did not last long. I still leave small heaps of mustard behind on my plate.
[2] The area surrounding the modern city of Tobolsk.

1898. Makaroff's unfulfilled ambition was to sail this vessel to the North Pole.[3] With her revolutionary egg-shaped hull, *Yermak* looked unlike any other ship of her time. This design, which was able to withstand enormous ice pressure, became *de rigueur* for all succeeding icebreakers. Anyway, the *Yermak* was a great success and remained in service until 1961.

Admiral Makaroff did not, sadly, enjoy such longevity. He died in 1904, aged fifty-six, during the Russo-Japanese war when his flagship, the *Petropavlovsk*, struck a Russian mine in Port Arthur Bay and sank with all hands. Yet today Makaroff is one of the heroes of the Soviet Arctic. His portrait, showing a be-medalled figure with a large forked beard, hung over Alexander's desk in his cabin.

That afternoon, I was sitting in my cabin in my post-sauna underwear when the phone rang. It was Andrei Cherepukhin, the fourth mate, suggesting in his fractured English that I should come up to the bridge. I clambered with my camera up the two staircases to find the whole ship listing badly as we altered course hard to port.

'Look, look,' cried Andrei.

Out of the port windows was a collection of ice floes, but instead of being white, they were brown. Through my binoculars I could see why. A colony of walrus was lying tightly packed together on the ice. Brown and flabby with huge tusks, they seemed to be watching nothing in particular. *Arktika* continued her sharp turn so that we were only fifteen metres from the animals, and still they did not move. They reminded me of the old saw that you could fit the population of the world on to the Isle of Wight. This must have been the entire walrus population of the Laptev Sea and it was fitting on to a handful of ice floes.

[3] In 1977 a surface ship did eventually manage to penetrate the polar ice and sail to the North Pole. That ship happened to be *Arktika*.

Suddenly there was another shout from Andrei, who had moved to the starboard side of the bridge. There, on a tiny floe, was a female walrus with her baby, which could not have been more than a metre long. She too watched *Arktika* with equanimity before sliding off into the water, followed by the calf. Through the clear green water I watched them swim in circles before they disappeared under a big chunk of ice.

'I have never seen that before,' said Andrei.

Neither had I.

Walrus were not the only excitement that afternoon. Not long after I'd returned to my cabin Maxim appeared, grinning broadly.

'Look,' he said. 'I am Russian millionaire.' He was carrying a folder in one hand and a small bundle of banknotes tied with string in the other. 'This,' he said, waving the package in the air, 'is 5000 roubles. I am rich.'

A slight pause while he wondered whether I might not take him seriously.

'No. I joke, of course. This money is not mine, but I am banker for the ship. It is my job to keep the money.'

I wondered why he needed 5000 roubles in cash when we were at least 1500 kilometres from the nearest shop.

'It is for when we reach Pevek,' he replied. 'The crew will want to spend money, but I don't think that 5000 roubles will be enough. What do you think?'

Not knowing the cost of living anywhere in Russia, least of all in a small town on the Chukchi Peninsula, I kept quiet.

The millionaire left, only to be replaced by a lonely Sergei Tomilin who entered, slumped down on a chair and, after a long silence, came up with an opening gambit which I hadn't come across before.

169

'I thought,' he said gravely, 'that you might like to understand how our nuclear reactors worked.'

Sergei began by explaining that there were two reactors, each of which had four pumps and four steam generators. The latter heated water to 300 degrees Celsius in the so-called first circle. However, the pressure was so high (130 kg/sq cm) that the water could not turn to steam. This heat was then used to heat the second circle of water, which produced steam because, though the temperature was also 300 degrees, the pressure was a mere 30 kg/sq cm.

The steam thus produced drove two turbines, each with a shaft on which a generator was mounted. The electricity produced by these two generators went to drive three electric motors which in turn provided power for the three screws. After driving the turbines, the steam was then condensed and used again in the second circle.

This was all very well, but I wanted to know what happened when the bridge asked the control room for more power, as we had done during the week we were in pack ice at 90 per cent power. Was moving the throttle lever on the bridge forward the same as stepping on an accelerator in a car? The answer was no. Sergei explained that with a nuclear reactor, unlike an internal combustion or steam engine, you didn't increase power output by feeding more fuel into the motor. The output from the reactor was, roughly speaking, constant. The only way to increase the actual horsepower was to pump more water into the second circle, thereby producing more steam, more electricity and more power at the screw.

Sergei himself was one of the small team who went into the reactor room every eight hours to check that everything was functioning properly and to monitor dials. The radiation level in the reactor room itself was higher than in the rest of the ship, but not dangerously so. Indeed, the nuclear

170

safety team claimed that the radiation levels in the living quarters of the ship were lower than those occurring naturally outside. I saw no reason to disbelieve this claim, but I did wonder with which part of the world we were being compared. The natural radiation from some granite rocks in, say, Cornwall, is relatively high compared to other locations on the globe. Perhaps *Arktika* was being compared to Penzance.

The seminar over, I was about to relax when Sergei told me the real reason he had dropped in to see me. He wondered whether I could possibly help one of the crewmen who had a problem.

Hoping the problem didn't involve religion, sex or politics, I nervously agreed to do my best. Sergei disappeared and returned a few minutes later with a large man in a boiler suit wearing a neat goatee beard.

'This,' he said, 'is Oleg Zhelezny. He is a motorman.'

Oleg's father-in-law, it seemed, came from a small village in the Ukraine, near what is now the Polish border. His brother, Stepan Tichonovich, who had been born in 1927, was captured by the Germans in 1944 and spent the rest of the war in a prisoner-of-war camp. Some time after the war, the sensible Tichonovich decided to emigrate to England rather than returning to his native Ukraine. The problem Oleg faced was how could he get in touch with his long-lost father-in-law's brother?

I tried to explain that this wouldn't be an easy task since there were fifty-six million people in the United Kingdom and the only information we knew for certain was this man's name.

'Ah,' said Oleg (who was being translated by Sergei), 'I have a photograph of him if that would help. It was taken fifty years ago.'

Once again I found myself pouring Arctic water on the

poor man's hopes. His appearance, I suggested, might possibly have changed since the photograph had been taken.

Oleg had another idea.

'Stepan wrote to my father-in-law back in 1978, or was it 1979? I don't remember, but somewhere around then.'

Perhaps his father-in-law had kept the letter with an address on it, I ventured?

'No, he didn't,' said Oleg. 'At the time my father-in-law was the chairman of a state farm and he was very nervous about having received a letter from abroad so he tore it up.'

This incident did at least show how much things had changed in the Soviet Union during the past two decades, but it did nothing to help my search for the missing Stepan Tichonovich. I did, however, promise to write to the Ukrainian organisation in London in the faint hope that they would know of the missing man and where he could be found.

This appeared to be more than enough to make Oleg happy. It was even possible that the act of speaking to an Englishman had taken a weight from his mind.

15 Captain Ulitin's birthday

The party to mark Captain Grigorii Alexeivich Ulitin's fifty-eighth birthday was a formal affair. For the first time since coming on board *Arktika*, I wore a tie. The other seventeen guests were dressed in full uniform when we gathered in the boatswain's cabin. After rehearsing 'Happy Birthday' twice, we formed a crocodile led by Alexander carrying a large pink cake which had been baked by Boris that afternoon. On top of the cake was a birthday card with a Russian inscription on one side and, inexplicably, the English words 'Keep Smiling' on the other.

The procession reached the captain's cabin and was ushered in by Raisa in her full ceremonial state uniform of scarlet dress, scarlet shoes, scarlet lipstick and newly permed hair done up in a mound à la Betty Grable. The actual performance of 'Happy Birthday' left a bit to be desired, because some of the choir had stage fright and the remainder seemed to have forgotten the words. Throughout this musical extravaganza the captain smiled coyly.

The gifts were presented with great solemnity. Alexander produced a bunch of maple twigs (although I had yet to see the captain in the sauna); Valerii Mikhailovich gave a book, my contribution was a bar of fabulous pink Camay soap, which I hoped Grigorii Alexeivich would eventually give to Mrs Ulitin. The best present by far came from Sergei Markin, the senior chief engineer. It was a hip flask made of beautifully turned stainless steel which had been machined, he explained, by the nuclear engineers. In a country where quality goods are tatty and everyday things just plain shoddy, it was the best-finished object I had seen, showing what good engineers can achieve if they have the tools, the materials, the time and – most of all – the incentive.

The captain's table wasn't large enough to seat eighteen people, so the party was split into two. On the main table sat the captain in his normal position under Lenin. On his left was Yuri, fresh from a sauna and glowing accordingly. On his right was the ship's doctor, a Georgian called Vladimir Sabashvili who, with his grey lank hair, sunken eyes and an emaciated frame, looked like the 'Before' section of the old Horlicks advertisement which used to begin with the washed out wreck saying to his GP, 'But doctor, I even wake tired.' Next to him was the surgeon, Andrei Lazur, bearded and bald, with gold teeth, tinted glasses and very hairy arms.

On the surgeon's left, and opposite me, was the boat-swain, Stepan Lushney, a short, bald, cheerful man who said nothing but smiled a lot. Then Slava Melikhov, the chief engineer, big, bearded and happy, in contrast to Vladimir Okhlopkov, the chief nuclear safety engineer, looking, as always, sinister with his small goatee beard, short black hair and slightly oriental expression. Sergei Markin, with his droopy moustache and eyelids to match, sat next to Vladimir Korotkov, the chief radio engineer. The table finished with Maxim, myself and a spare place for Sergei when he came off watch.

At the far end of the room, under the Kirov and the adoring Caucasian peasants, Valerii Mikhailovich presided over a little table consisting of Oleg Popolitov, the chief electrical engineer, a rat-faced little man with strands of limp black hair and a stooped appearance, and the three helicopter pilots, Valentin, Oleg and Sergei, none of whom appeared to have any restrictions on their vodka consumption even though one of them would probably be flying within twelve hours.

The evening began inevitably with a series of toasts, including 'to the captain', 'to women', 'to sailors everywhere' and finally 'to wives and girlfriends. May they never meet.' These were drunk from small vodka glasses on which the letter 'L' had been engraved. The captain explained that they had been a gift from an old friend of his who had once been captain of the icebreaker *Lenin*.

It was a mark of how much I had been accepted by the crew that we did not have to undergo the usual Soviet toasts to Peace and Friendship, Britain and the USSR and all the other clichés which were invariably proposed when foreigners were present. Eventually the serious business of eating and drinking got under way. Beer, mineral water and vodka were on the table, but they were often hard to distinguish since they were all in the same shaped bottles and if, as often happened, the label had been washed off there was no way to distinguish water from vodka without tasting it.

Raisa, preceded by a shock wave of 'Moscow Nights' perfume, bustled round serving a series of *zakuski*, among which were mackerel, salami, pork laced with giant cloves of garlic, cranberries with cabbage and mayonnaise.

I was crunching my way through another garlic clove when I noticed that most of the assembled company were making for the door. There had been no signal and certainly no lifeboat drill had been called, so I assumed the watch was changing and they were all going off to their posts.

Four minutes later they all trooped silently back and sat down to carry on eating where they had left off. Only later did I discover that this had been a smoking break which took place in the passageway outside the captain's cabin. Throughout the evening these interludes became a regular feature, but I was unable to detect who had decided it was time for a fag, and what the secret signal was to announce this fact.

After these intervals the seating arrangements changed at random. At one point I found myself sitting next to Valentin, who took a gulp of mineral water and leaned over close to my ear.

'I have three dreams,' he whispered, 'and I hope you will not laugh.'

I assured him that I took dreams very seriously; indeed the voyage on *Arktika* had been a dream of mine.

'First I would like to play the forte piano. Second I would like to fly an American F4 Phantom fighter, and third I would like to speak good English.' He raised his vodka glass and we drank to his dreams. Valentin was a superb helicopter pilot and a lovely man.

Exactly two hours and approximately two dozen toasts later, I could eat no more. This, however, was the signal for half a roast chicken and french fries to be brought on. My neighbours tucked into the lukewarm bird like hungry polar bears. Hiding food on a plate is a technique I had perfected since my days in the nursery. The last time I had needed the skill was a few years earlier when I was being entertained to a civic lunch by the mayor of a village high in the mountains of central Crete. A plate of heaped spaghetti and rabbit was placed in front of me and, as a special treat, I had been given the animal's head, complete with ears and eyes. I loathe rabbit at the best of times, and the sight of the head made me feel sick. The solution was to appear to enjoy the food while concealing the little beast beneath a tumulus of spaghetti.

My fellow guests were far too busy eating to notice what I was doing with my plate. I had just completed an artful composition of chicken carcass when I looked up to see Raisa in the doorway with a platter containing yet another bird. She put it down in the middle of the table, beamed and retreated. I remembered the plucked fowl Boris had shown me in the cold store a few days earlier and had insisted was a goose. I owed Boris an apology. It was a goose. And what was more, it had been roasted and garnished with apples and tomatoes.

The appearance of the goose had a profound effect on the previously silent boatswain, Stepan Lushney. He jumped up and grabbed a large carving knife with which he split the bird down the middle to reveal cranberry and apple stuffing. There was a groan from the over-fed audience.

Vladimir Korotkov looked at the fowl on the plate and announced, 'A goose is a stupid bird. It's too big for one person and too small for two.' This observation triggered off a whole series of goose stories, which culminated in the chief mate recounting that on one icebreaker he had served on, a goose had flown in the porthole of a cabin and had promptly been plucked and then eaten by the crew. The captain, not to be outdone, insisted that the previous year on the icebreaker *Kiev* a goose had laid her eggs on the stern while the vessel was still in Leningrad harbour. When the ship eventually sailed the crew transferred the nest to a cabin and left the window open but the goose, who had apparently gone shopping, was unable to find the nest. The ship's doctor rigged up a form of incubator but, unfortunately, didn't realise that 50 degrees was far too hot to hatch goose eggs and only managed to cook them.

At midnight the party broke up and I went to bed.

It was, not surprisingly, an awful night. I had drunk too much, the cabin temperature oscillated between Arctic and tropical and – as if that were not enough – we hit our first two-year-old Canadian pack ice. And nobody packs ice like the Canadians.

The next morning I looked out over an icescape of indescribable filth. I could have been in a sewage disposal works somewhere in the West Midlands. Instead of level white nothingness, there was a grey mishmash of sludge. The ice itself was dark and honeycombed, and on the surface lay puddles of black water. Really black. It was as if I had been transported back to Nikel and was watching the ice melt after the winter.

Sergei explained that the ice in the Arctic rotated very slowly round the North Pole, and that this ice had come from Canada, where it had been formed two years earlier. During this time the salt had been leached out and the ice had become a great deal harder, which explained why we had managed only 25 miles during the previous watch. I asked him why the ice was so filthy and he did not appear to know.

'Maybe it is the mud from the Canadian rivers,' he suggested.

At midday we had been at sea for exactly two weeks, had travelled 2773 nautical miles and were further east than Sydney. We had passed through three different seas, the Barents, Kara and Laptev, and were then in the fourth, that most remote patch of water, the East Siberian Sea.

The main topic of conversation on the bridge that morning was what to do with me when we reached Pevek the following evening. My visa did not include Pevek among the towns I could visit and the captain was therefore unable to let me go ashore. After a lot of pressure from me, he at last agreed to radio the Pevek office of the Murmansk

178

Shipping Company and ask them to approach the KGB on my behalf. I wasn't optimistic.

It was beginning to look as if I would have to wait until a ship sailed from Pevek for Magadan or Vladivostock and then change vessels at sea. I remembered as a boy looking at terrifying wartime photographs of ship-to-ship transfers by boatswain's chair, and wondered if the same fate awaited me.

Throughout the voyage I had been keeping a diary in my laptop computer. Compared to the galumphing old personal computer on which Maxim played strip poker, mine was the latest word in technology, small, light and totally portable. Computer-literate members of the crew used to make pilgrimages to my cabin just to see it in action, and I took great delight in running programmes like Flight Simulator to keep them amused.

That morning, while I was up on the bridge copying the ship's positions over the past twenty-four hours into the computer, I had a flash of inspiration. Compaq, the manufacturer of my laptop, would undoubtedly pay serious money for a photograph of one of their happy customers sitting all alone on an ice floe in the East Siberian Sea using their computer. I could see it clearly. A half-page photograph of me would appear in every computer magazine in the Western world, together with an enthusiastic endorsement about 'how it had worked perfectly in the most difficult conditions'. Nobody need ever know that conditions on a nuclear icebreaker were no more arduous than conditions in an office block overlooking High Holborn.

The snag was that to achieve this objective I would need a partner, or specifically, a photographer. I put the idea to Maxim who, incipient capitalist that he was, became very excited indeed.

'How much money will they pay you?' he wondered. While I was pondering this legitimate question he continued babbling. 'A million pounds? No, probably less. Half a million pounds?' A pause. 'And if they do, how much will you pay me? It should be a lot of money since you will be very rich because of me, won't you?'

Without waiting for any financial commitment from me, Maxim galloped off across the bridge and had a brief but intense conference with Alexander. Whatever he said must have been pretty forceful because that afternoon *Arktika* came to a complete halt in the ice, which by then had reverted to the white and level variety.

I began to understand how egg-shaped and bulbous *Arktika*'s hull was when I climbed down a rope ladder on to the ice. Instead of descending a vertical wall as I had expected, I found that the nearer I got to the ice the more overhung the hull became, and the more difficult it was to cling to the ladder. Eventually I reached the ice and waited for Maxim to throw down the props we required. These consisted of a folding seat and an orange life ring with the words ARKTIKA MURMANSK written in English. We had decided that this would be necessary to prove to the rest of the world that I had been in the Siberian Arctic and not on a frozen lake in Minnesota.

I sat down, composed my features and tried to look both busy and professional, tapping away at the keyboard while Maxim danced around me like a polar dervish snapping with the camera. After twenty minutes of intense creativity, I climbed back up the ladder, hoisted the props on board and the icebreaker set off again towards Pevek. Had I been a Madison Avenue advertising agency it would have cost me a million dollars to do what I had just done for free.

In the meanwhile I had a new project to occupy me, the procurement of a *telnyashka*, the horizontally striped jersey which Russian sailors wear under their jackets. I had tried to find a navy surplus store in Murmansk but they did not seem to exist, so the only possible way to get hold of one was to buy it from a crew member. As I had just realised about my laptop, the solution lay in advertising. My campaign began that afternoon with a brief notice on the ship's bulletin board announcing that the *kulak* was willing to pay five dollars for a large-sized *telnyashka* in mint condition.

I was waiting for a response when there was a knock at my door and Maxim came in. I assumed he was bringing the first of a flood of *telnyashkas*, but he wasn't.

'I have a small present,' he said. 'It is now near the end of the trip and we felt it would be nice for you to have these.' He held out two small bundles which, when unfolded, were revealed as signal flags. One was red and yellow and the other red, white and blue. 'They represent Whisky and Oscar,' Maxim explained. 'You may remember that we hoisted them when we said goodbye to the *Captain Sorokin* and *Captain Danilkin*. When you hoist these flags in the right order, WO, they mean "Icebreaker support completed. Proceed to your destination."'

I felt like crying, but managed to stammer a 'thank you very much indeed'. There was only one snag. If I were not allowed to land in Pevek, my voyage on *Arktika* could well last a lot longer than Maxim had assumed.

That evening I did my thirty minutes walk on the helicopter deck as usual. As I walked round and round I noticed that the ice had again become very dirty and pock-marked. It looked like aerial photographs of carpet bombing from the Vietnam War.

The next morning there was bad news on the bridge. The captain and I shook hands as usual.

'I have been in touch with Pevek,' he said, 'and there are

no ships due to leave for the east, so you will have to stay with us.' I digested this information while he continued with his news bulletin. 'We have been ordered to proceed to Pevek where we shall drop off two of our helicopter pilots. We shall then continue eastwards and will meet a convoy in the area of Wrangel Island. We shall escort these ships back to Pevek and await further orders.'

In a strange way I was relieved not to be leaving *Arktika*. I had grown very fond of the ship and its crew. But I didn't relish the idea of messing about in the Chukchi Sea for an indefinite period until some hapless cargo ship could be prevailed upon to take me to Vladivostock. So I smiled, wished Grigorii Alexeivich the top of the morning and went in search of Valentin to ask if he could post my letters in Pevek.

I was sitting at my desk adding a hurried PS to my last letter when a knock at the door announced Maxim's presence. He looked a bit embarrassed and wondered if he could ask me a delicate question. I thought he was going to tell me he had VD, or enquire if I had any spare condoms, but instead he said, 'I wonder if it would be possible for you to sell me some dollars. I wish to buy a present for my wife.' He wanted $25 but I rather suspected he didn't want to pay the current tourist rate of twenty-seven roubles.[1] After some restrained haggling, I agreed on an exchange rate of twenty roubles to the dollar. No wonder he looked happy when he left the cabin.

I was eating my rissole and mashed potatoes at lunch that day when I thought I must be dreaming. It sounded as if someone was speaking English, but this was clearly improbable. The words themselves were indistinct but the intonation was definitely American. The noise seemed to

[1] By November 1993, with Russia on the brink of hyperinflation, the rate had risen to over 1000 roubles per dollar.

182

be coming from a loudspeaker in the dining room ceiling. I moved around the room until I located the source and, standing underneath, found that I was listening to the weather forecast from a radio station in Kotzebue, Alaska.

'Well,' said the cutesy, folksy voice so beloved of radio announcers, 'that just about wraps up the weather scene in our nation's greatest state. Next stay tuned for Country and Western Hour brought to you by Vanbergs, for all your household needs.'

Vanbergs might have been surprised to learn that 157 Russians in the East Siberian Sea were listening to their special offer on lavatory cleanser. Back in my cabin I looked at the map and saw that although the projection made Kotzebue appear to be a long way away, we were in fact less than 800 kilometres distant.

16 Hangover

I went to pour myself a cup of tea and found Owdoyoudo
sitting on a low stool in the semi-darkness of the *chaikana*.
On a primitive loom, he was weaving yet another one of
his doormats out of old string. Blinking as I emerged into
the daylight, I saw out of the sloping windows of the bridge
that we had stopped once again, this time in the middle of
a desert of dirty, black ice whose outcrops and hummocks
spewed untidily across the horizon.

Sergei approached, looking worried.

'That ice on the starboard side is grounded.'

I didn't understand what he meant.

'Grounded,' he repeated. 'It is touching the ground and
we cannot break it.'

This seemed impossible, so I asked him to explain.

'The captain has just told me,' he said wearily. 'The sea
is fifteen metres deep here and the ice you see on your
right is also fifteen metres deep. That is why we cannot
move it and that is why we are going astern because we
must go round that ice and not through it.' And sure
enough, with all three engines at hard astern, we started to
move backwards. Only this time, instead of ramming the
offending hunk of ice, we steered hard to port and found
ourselves back in a narrow channel of black, slimy water.

Fifteen metres meant that there were only four metres of water under our keel. It was no coincidence that the captain was in command on the bridge at that moment. Sooner him than me. It seemed a very small margin of safety beneath a nuclear icebreaker.

The *telnyashkas* arrived that morning in the shape of two rather shy seamen who turned up outside my cabin carrying neatly folded – and apparently unused – sweaters. Neither was big enough to fit me, but both would look good on the women in my life. *Telnyashkas*, Maxim told me later, were meant to be pretty tight, a bit like a body stocking. This might make good sense at sea, but I happened to prefer loose-fitting clothes. Anyway, the two sailors went away with five-dollar bills.

The flight on *ptichka* that afternoon was uneventful until the last five minutes. We had flown south for almost an hour until we were in sight of the coast before turning back to the ship. We were flying much higher than usual and from an altitude of 1000 metres the dirty Canadian pack ice looked like a mosaic of discordant fragments – the way a Pompeii pavement might appear from fifteen centimetres away. Blotches of old brown ice were interspersed with clean white ice, thin strips of deep open water and huge puddles no more than five centimetres deep. The East Siberian Sea looked a mess.

After an hour the helicopter cabin was very stuffy. Both Valerii Mikhailovich and the pilot took off their parkas and I was becoming drowsy, so I spread out some cushions on the floor and, in spite of the noise from the rotor and the fact that I was wearing earphones, managed to sleep for a bit. I woke with a start when we began to lose altitude.

We had circled *Arktika* twice and it seemed that we were about to land when the pilot veered off to starboard and touched down on a solitary ice floe. Valerii Mikhailov-

185

ich grinned and motioned me to get out. As I did so, the door slammed shut and the helicopter took off again. I was alone on a small piece of ice no more than a cricket pitch long and probably twice as wide.

It was utterly improbable and almost impossible. There I was standing all alone on an ice floe in the middle of the East Siberian Sea with a bright sun above, black sea and whitish ice in every direction and the cold wind blowing cleaner than clean. Between me and *Arktika* pressure ridges stood like grotesque tombstones sticking up out of the ice at crazy angles. It was like a graveyard after an earthquake. Off in the distance, orange and black in the afternoon sunshine, came *Arktika*. Seeing me, she blew her whistle twice as she steamed past much faster than I had expected. Each time she hit an ice floe puffs of ice spurted up from her bows. And then there was total silence.

It was one of those moments that you realise at the time will stay as a memory for the rest of your life. I stood there with my nerve endings quivering, trying to fix the sight, smell and sound into my memory so that I could summon it up at any time in the future.

This almost trance-like state was interrupted by the return of the Valerii Mikhailovich *ex machina*. With a roar, the *ptichka* descended on to my little island, blowing loose snow everywhere and making me hang on to my woolly hat. I scrambled in, keeping my head down as one always does anywhere near a helicopter rotor. Valerii Mikhailovich turned round in his seat and shouted, 'Was it good?'

How could I possibly answer? It had been better than good. Far, far better.

Back on board, I went straight to the bridge to thank Alexander, who was on watch. At that moment Maxim appeared.

186

'Have you any idea how lucky you've been on this voyage?' he asked. 'I've never heard of anyone else being allowed to do the things you've done. Take those photographs you've just made of *Arktika* from the ice floe. I don't suppose there's a single person aboard who's been able to do that, and I know we'd all love to have a picture of *Arktika* which we'd taken from the ice.'

I agreed, and felt humble and grateful.

Alexander brushed off my thanks as if this sort of thing happened every day.

'You can tell me all about it over coffee this afternoon,' he suggested. At 16.30, therefore, I pushed back the curtain which covered his doorway to find him playing *shish besh* with Sergei while Maxim poured the coffee. I had just sat down on the sofa when the curtain parted again and in came a woman whose face was familiar. We had, I remembered, occasionally passed on the helicopter deck, she wrapped up against the cold and wearing a fur cap while I had my head down against the wind.

Ludmilla Chernova appeared on the crew list as the captain's secretary. Short and not quite plump, she had flashing brown eyes, a wide smiling mouth framed by well-applied lipstick and illuminated by a single gold tooth amongst all the other very white ones. Born in the Altai Mountains near the Mongolian border, Ludmilla had trained as a theatrical producer. Being a typist on an icebreaker seemed a rather drastic change of career.

She grinned a gentle grin.

'The problem,' she explained, 'was that there simply weren't any vacancies in the Murmansk Theatre and I had to do something.'

While the officers played *shish besh*, I continued my interrogation of Ludmilla. Were there, I wondered, any problems about being a single woman among nearly 140 men. It was a stupid question which deserved the answer it received.

'Yes,' came the reply. 'So many problems I won't even bore you with them.' Ludmilla paused, stroked the soft hairs on her forearm and looked out of the porthole. 'But none of the problems are insurmountable.'

She was some tough lady.

After Ludmilla had drunk her coffee, she made her excuses and departed. Not surprisingly, the subject of women came up.

'You might be surprised to know,' said Alexander, 'that every woman on this ship is tested once every three months for various gynaecological problems. And those who work in the kitchen or the dining rooms are tested every six months for AIDS, syphilis and other venereal diseases.'

This sounded like sex discrimination to me, until Alexander confirmed the same tests also applied to the men who work in the kitchens.

Over our second cup of coffee and a Spam sandwich, the talk turned from sex to economics. It seemed to me that the Northern Sea Route in general, and the atomic icebreaker fleet in particular, couldn't be justified when a market economy came to pass in what was still the Soviet Union.

A few weeks after I had left Murmansk, the newest nuclear icebreaker, *Sovietsky Soyuz*, which had been sitting in dry dock when I joined *Arktika*, headed north into the Barents Sea. Its mission was not to escort a freighter to Dudinka, but instead to carry ninety-six tourists to the North Pole before depositing them at Providenyia on the Bering Straits where the icebreaker would pick up another load and bring them back to Murmansk. It was, however, going to be no ordinary outing. The travel agent's blurb

188

promised 'three European chefs and a European catering manager ... and to soothe the body while you let the ship do the work of smashing through the ice, there are two saunas'. The cost of my cabin for one of these trips was £42,000 for two people.

One of the passengers, a rich scientist called David Fisher who paid £15,000 for his ticket, wrote an account of the trip called *Across the Top of the World*. The passengers aboard the *Sovietsky Soyuz*, it seemed, were faced by a series of decisions. They had to decide such difficult questions as whether to eat Beef Wellington or grilled sole and whether to drink a white Burgundy or a *petit château* claret. Thank goodness the resident barman knew how to make a really dry martini.

Eventually, like Marie Antoinette playing in the Trianon, they thought it would be picturesque to order the sort of grub that the natives ate each day. Not surprisingly, the dining room staff suspected that the passengers were joking, and only after much persuasion did they agree to put on a Russian meal. Fisher's description would have made *Arktika's* crew blink with disbelief.

'It's fantastic,' he wrote. 'The waiters and waitresses are dressed in peasant clothing, which is a bit touristy, but the first things they bring out to the tables are pitchers full of vodka.'

If the Murmansk Shipping Company could spare one of its four big nuclear icebreakers for most of the navigation season to ferry rich Americans round the Arctic, then surely it meant that there were too many nuclear icebreakers. The crunch question was simple: were Alexander and Sergei's jobs really necessary?

After a long discussion amongst themselves, Alexander was appointed spokesman. He agreed that there was certainly over-capacity in the nuclear icebreaker fleet, and accepted that this would become even worse when the newest icebreaker, *October Revolution*, joined the fleet that autumn.

'But,' he said with some vehemence, 'there is no question that our jobs are necessary, even if we admit that we don't need such expensive ships – or so many of them.'

I wondered what would happen to towns like Dudinka if they no longer had year-round navigation and instead reverted to the old days when they could be reached by sea only between August and October. The officers seemed to agree that this would not necessarily be a national disaster.

We quickly tired of serious economic argument and instead reverted to what the Americans call locker-room talk. How did they manage the problems of being hetero-sexual sailors at sea for three months at a time?

'It's easy for Sergei,' said Maxim. 'When he gets home again he becomes a sex terrorist.'

This was a new category for me. Did Maxim mean a sex maniac?

'Oh no. Not at all. They're very different. In the Soviet Union a sex maniac is a sick man, whereas a sex terrorist is just a man doing what he was designed to do.'

I was glad my wife couldn't hear this conversation. Was it, I asked, possible for a woman to be a sex terrorist?

'*Terroristka*,' corrected Sergei. But his answer was an unambiguous *nyet*.

Maxim had disappeared, but he soon returned and had a hurried conversation with Alexander in the bedroom.

'Shut your eyes,' he said to me.

I did so.

'Now open them.'

I did so.

There in front of me was Alexander with three gifts, all of which had been made on *Arktika*.

190

The first was the Union Jack.

'Turn it over,' said Sergei. On the other side was the scarlet flag of the USSR with a yellow hammer and sickle.

'You came on board *Arktika* like this,' said Alexander, showing the Union Jack, 'and you will leave like this,' showing the hammer and sickle.

The next present was a thick white doormat. I recognised it immediately. It was the one I had been watching Owdoyoudo weave in the *chaikana* ever since we left Murmansk.

The third gift was a duffle bag. Bright orange with green plastic corners and the word *ARKTIKA* in Cyrillic, it had, Alexander assured me, been made out of canvas by one of the sailmakers on board. Quite why a nuclear icebreaker needed a sailmaker remained unclear, but it was a lovely present.

Yet again I found myself close to tears. Yet again, all I could say was thank you.

My walk on the helicopter deck that afternoon lasted three quarters of an hour, and was brisker than normal. I began just as Valerii Mikhailovich was taking off for his second flight of the day and finished as the ground crew were clearing the deck for his landing.

The sun was trying to set (it wouldn't actually succeed in that location for nearly three more months) and glistened off the patches of open water between the ice floes. The wind, though strong, was warmer than of late, which meant that it was refreshing rather than chilling. Every so often the stern would heave and then shudder as the bow rode up over a particularly hard piece of ice. It would hang for a moment before falling again under my feet, and then would stay level for a few minutes. At other times we would scrape the side of the hull on a submerged wall of ice and *Arktika* would shake violently as if she had hit a rock. All of these movements, and the noises which went

191

with them, were now familiar to me. For some reason far out on the stern all motions were amplified, so the effects on my walk were more dramatic than if I had stayed in the cabin, the bridge or the dining room.

I was alone on the East Siberian Sea in a landscape I had hitherto only dreamed about. I was also acutely aware that my days on *Arktika* were coming to a close. Once again all my senses were heightened by the knowledge that I would never return.

Ahead of us, just off the port bow, towering out of a fog bank, I could see the peak of Cape Chelagsky, rising 470 metres straight out of the sea. This mountain, which is one of the highest points along the North East Passage, marked the entrance to Chaun Bay and the great natural harbour of Pevek.

We eventually dropped anchor at 22.02, sheltering in the lee of Cape Chelagsky with the town of Pevek some fifteen kilometres to our south. I could just make out the buildings, their windows reflecting the low sun. We had travelled 3107 miles from Murmansk and it had taken us fifteen and a half days.

The countryside round Pevek looked like County Mayo on the west coast of Ireland. We might have been anchored off Achill Island. The hills were low, smooth and green. Green. It was a colour I hadn't seen since I left the customs post at Boris Gleb. Nikel was black, Murmansk grey and the North East Passage had varied from white to brown and back to white. Now I could see green again. Come to think of it, I could even smell green when I shut my eyes and took a deep breath. There may not have been any trees, but there was certainly grass. Real grass and not just soggy green moss. It seemed to grow best in the smooth, rounded valleys. Only in a few north-facing hollows was there any snow left.

The light also was similar to that in the west of Ireland, a strange combination of soft and bright, accentuated by the low rays of the sun which cut through swirling clouds of mist to make occasional rainbows. On the tops of the hills small clouds sat like steam from volcanoes.

The anchor chain rattled and the noise vibrated my bedroom's porthole. After a few minutes of silence the second anchor went down and *Arktika* was secure. It was time for a lovely, relaxing, pointless evening bath. But first I had an appointment with Leonid in the radio room. He had insisted that I came while he was on watch that evening.

Leonid also had a present for me. It turned out to be another *telnyashka*, faded and smelling of sweat.

'It is not new,' said Leonid solemnly, as if I could possibly think otherwise, 'but it comes from my heart.' I wondered where he had heard that idiom. Though corny, it expressed what he felt – and what I felt too. I managed to put it on in spite of the fact that Leonid's chest must have been half my size. It was, as a result, a trifle revealing.

Wearing this striped leotard, I pirouetted through to the bridge where Sergei became hysterical.

'I've never seen a *kulak* in a *telnyashka* before. Don't move,' and he rushed off, only to return a minute later with a naval cap (far too small for my big head) which he gave me. 'It is a Russian navigator's cap. Now it is yours.'

It was bedtime when Valentin asked me if I would like to have a vodka with his friends.

'I am going back to Murmansk this evening,' he said. 'The helicopter is taking me to Pevek in an hour.' It seemed churlish to refuse. Besides, I had grown to like Valentin, and to admire his skills in the left seat of the *ptichka*.

The farewell party was being given by Vladimir Korotkov, the chief radio officer. I had only been to his cabin once before where I had been impressed by the mammoth's vertebra which sat on his desk. When I arrived the party was already in full swing. Around a table full of the inevitable *brusnika*, mackerel and meat, were Vladimir, the owner of the cabin; Sergei Markin, the senior chief engineer; his deputy, the bearded Slava Melikhov; and Sergei Ivanov, the youngest helicopter pilot, who was wearing his full dress Aeroflot uniform, complete with gold braided cap. The tipple of the evening was cranberry vodka, which was smoother than the conventional stuff and extremely good. Each glass was followed by the traditional spoonful of the berries themselves.

The party continued for an hour, during which I became instantly popular by producing some Waylon Jennings country and western tapes. Eventually – and after two for the road – we moved up to the helicopter deck to wave the pilots off. There were lots of hugs, quite a few kisses and occasional tears before the blue and orange chopper took off into the low sun.

I had just come to the conclusion that the party was over when Ludmilla put her arm around me and suggested we return to Vladimir's cabin. It seemed like a better than reasonable idea and I followed the crowd back to where we had started. By then the party had reached critical mass so I sat back and watched one of the best sights in the world: Russians enjoying themselves. Ludmilla's role was a delicate one. At first it appeared that she was very definitely the property of the cabin's owner, but as the evening wore on I became less sure. Throughout it all she did a magnificent job of remaining friendly and cheerful and harmlessly flirtatious without encouraging her many suitors. From the safety of the sofa I admired her tact, sensitivity and sexiness.

I watched as Ludmilla tried to dance with two men at the same time. She very nearly succeeded. Eventually

Vladimir admitted defeat and sat down beside me. There was a long silence during which he poured himself a vodka, threw it back and ate a spoonful of berries.

'Do you like *Arktika*?' he asked.

I nodded happily, still preferring to watch the dance floor. Vladimir was persistent.

'You know this ship was not always called *Arktika*.' I nodded again. 'In fact when I first joined her she was called the *Leonid Brezhnev*. The name had been changed the year before.' I clucked sympathetically. 'We never liked the name, but we couldn't do anything about it.' A pause. 'And then one day we decided to go on strike.'

I sat up on the sofa. Vladimir might have been slightly the worse for vodka, but not enough for him to start hallucinating.

'No, really. We went on strike. And eventually we won our name back and the ship has been called *Arktika* ever since.'

It was a good story, but I found it hard to believe. Vladimir had, after all, been talking about a period when strikes were not exactly encouraged in the USSR.

A few days later I was told the background to the so-called strike. It seemed that the crew of the *Leonid Brezhnev* had hit on the idea of a communications strike. They refused to reply to any radio messages unless their ship was referred to as *Arktika*. Within a week the name was changed back to *Arktika*.

Vladimir's nostalgia subsided into silence and together we sat slumped on the sofa. The cranberry vodka had long since run out and had been replaced by a jar of what I assumed was cleaning fluid.

'It's called Chilo,' explained Valentin, who had just joined us. 'It's a slang word for the metal spike we use to make holes in paper.'

The taste, smell and appearance were just like vodka but, as I was to discover, Chilo is to vodka what vodka is to Malvern water. It must be the only drink in the world whose strength varies depending on its geographical location. Chilo starts life as pure industrial alcohol. But when in the Russian Arctic it is used as booze, albeit watered down. The tradition is for it to be diluted to the same percentage as the latitude. Sitting as we were at 70 degrees north, I was happily slugging back liquor which was 70 per cent alcohol, almost twice as potent as normal vodka.

Oleg, the helicopter pilot who had ferried his colleagues to Pevek, returned to find that any drinking restrictions there might have been had long since been lifted. He brought with him from the mainland a bunch of daisies (though where he found daisies in Pevek at nine o'clock at night remained a mystery) which he presented to Ludmilla on bended knee. It appeared that this was a belated birthday present since he had given her nothing a few days earlier when the official celebrations had taken place.

Goaded by this display of chivalry, and desperately trying to keep my place in the queue for Ludmilla's affections, I staggered off to my cabin and returned with two pairs of tights and a bar of Lux soap. The gift achieved the desired reaction. I was kissed on both cheeks and on the mouth and returned once again to the sofa in a state of benign stupefaction.

Sometime towards midnight, for no visible reason, Slava, Ludmilla and I moved down one deck to his cabin, where we continued to drink Chilo. I was vaguely aware of being left alone for ten minutes (it could easily have been an hour as my internal clock had long since ceased to function), which struck me as a bit strange. By then I was past caring, and certainly past being able to show I cared.

196

Eventually our little party broke up at 3.30 a.m. and I wandered off to bed feeling extremely proud that I could both find my way home, and even more difficult, climb the stairs.

17 The Kolyma

Consciousness returned like a tide coming in over an estuary. At five past one in the afternoon I became aware that someone had come into my cabin and pulled the blind down. I staggered out of bed, remembered who and where I was, made a cup of coffee and looked out of the porthole. The weather was a reflection of how I felt. It was grey with gusting sleet and we were surrounded by loose ice, all of which must have blown in on the strong north-east wind. Off in the distance I thought I could make out the shape of another icebreaker moored in the lee of the shore.

As I got dressed it began to be clear that I was suffering from the sort of hangover I had forgotten about since my undergraduate days. Maxim welcomed me on to the bridge.

'I've heard so much about your party. How are you?' I assured him, unconvinced and unconvincingly, that I was well. 'The captain was so worried when you didn't come to lunch that he sent Sergei to see if you were all right. Even Raisa was worried. She wanted to clean your cabin but said that you were still sleeping. I told her,' said Maxim conspiratorially, 'that you were very tired.'

It must have been Raisa who had lowered my blind.

We had, it seemed, raised anchor at just before six o'clock and while I slept *Arktika* had moved to the edge of the

198

pack ice some sixty kilometres west of Pevek. Our orders were to wait there and meet a convoy which we would escort to the mouth of the Kolyma river. The icebreaker I had seen in the distance was the *Captain Khlebnikov*,[1] a sister ship to my old friend the *Captain Sorokin*.

I was not the only one to have felt the after-effects of the party. Slava, it seemed, had been due to go on watch at four in the morning but Maxim told me that he had only just appeared. Someone else must have stood in for him. I wondered how Ludmilla had managed to survive, and whether she had turned up with her steno pad in the office at nine o'clock.

After an hour on the bridge I was beginning to feel queasy. A walk on deck seemed to be the best remedy. Wandering aimlessly back and forth under the orange lifeboats, I was approached by a sailor I had never met before.

'Oliver,' he said in heavily accented English. 'I have a present.' So saying, he removed his belt and gave it to me. It was black leather with a brass buckle embossed with an anchor, the symbol of the Russian Merchant Marine. Nobody had ever taken off their own belt for me before. I had a dim idea of how Queen Elizabeth must have felt when Sir Walter Raleigh took off his cape and laid it in the puddle. All I had in my pockets was a cheap French gas cigarette lighter which I gave him as an inadequate exchange. As usual, I felt utterly helpless at expressing my thanks.

This present-giving was beginning to get out of hand. A

[1] This ship has since been converted into a passenger-carrying icebreaker to take tourists through the Arctic. I met her the following summer when, on board the Canadian Coastguard icebreaker *Henry Larsen*, we passed the *Captain Khlebnikov* sailing eastward through the North West Passage with a load of Champagne Charlies who were paying megabucks for the experience.

few minutes later Alexander came into my cabin with a rubber stamp he had carved himself. On it was embossed:

OLIVER WALSTON
I'M THE FIRST!
'ARKTIKA'
SU91

I searched around the cabin for something to give Alexander before realising that I had the one thing which Russians valued above pearls. A few weeks earlier in New York I had bought myself a pair of Levi's. I had worn them once but discovered that a combination of pessimism and *Arktika*'s low calorie diet meant that they were far too big for me. They would, however, be perfect for Alexander.

For once it was the Russian who was speechless and I felt that honour had almost been satisfied. Later that evening I asked Alexander why he wasn't wearing his new trousers. He was, he admitted, saving them for a special occasion.

I didn't eat dinner that night, preferring to lie in my darkened cabin and wallow in self-inflicted misery. These wallowings were interrupted yet again by a knock on the door. I opened it to find Slava, one of my co-conspirators of the night before. He had obviously survived the ordeal better than I, and was standing with a paper bag in his hand.

'Here,' he said. 'It is for you.'

I opened the bag to find myself looking at a replica of the stainless steel hip flask which he had given to the captain on his birthday and which I had so admired.

'It holds exactly one litre,' said Slava, which seemed fitting since it must have been about the quantity I had consumed the night before.

200

The flask was beautiful and I thanked him massively. The only problem was that I would need hips like a horse if the flask were really to live in my hip pocket.

'No, no,' explained Slava, 'it isn't meant to be carried in your pocket. It is for travelling in your suitcase. It is steel and so cannot be broken and it is curved not to fit your pocket but because it is stronger that way.'

It all made good sense. The snag was that the way I felt I never wanted to touch booze, let alone carry it, ever again.

Raisa stopped me in the corridor and scurried to the cupboard where she kept the vacuum cleaner. With an enormous grin she thrust a small package into my hands, kissed me on the cheek and disappeared. When I got back to the cabin I found that she had given me six walnuts and yet another heap of *semyachki*. Like a squirrel, she must have been saving these throughout the voyage.

It had been a foul day. Not just because of my hangover – which would have made any day awful – but because outside it was grey, cold and trying to snow. Off in the distance the *Captain Khlebnikov* was occasionally hidden by snow flurries. She was apparently one of the icebreakers based in Vladivostock rather than Murmansk. The thought occurred to me that maybe she might be going back home sometime soon and I could hitch a lift with her. In the meanwhile there was more news from the bridge. The office had reported that there were still no ships in Pevek harbour outbound for Vladivostock, and the rumour was that no ship would even arrive from the east for at least a week. There was, however, the faintest possibility that a vessel was discharging somewhere on the Kolyma and might then be heading east.

I missed supper that day, and so celebrated twenty-four food-free hours.

The weather was no better the following day, but at least

there was some activity to look at. Off to our starboard an old freighter, the *Maxim Ammosov*, was inching its way slowly into the notch on the stern of the *Captain Khlebnikov*. It took an entire morning for this manoeuvre to be complete, but eventually the two ships were lashed together and *Arktika* set off to lead this tiny convoy through the ice which had been blown down on to the coast by a north-east wind.

I remembered my recent conversation with Alexander, Sergei and Maxim about the economics of the Northern Sea Route. There was *Arktika* together with a second, smaller icebreaker escorting a single ship the 150 kilometres or so along the coast to the mouth of the Kolyma. All that expensive hardware and all those expensive men were not being used to ferry computer parts, medicines, food or fuel to the settlements of inner Siberia. Certainly not. The *Maxim Ammosov* was carrying timber.

On the bridge the captain met me for the first time in twenty-four hours, grinned and said 'How are you?' I made a bicep-flexing gesture which was meant to convey rude good health, but I doubt if I fooled him much. A man like Grigorii Alexeivich Ulitin could recognise a hangover from one hundred metres in thick fog.

Owdoyoudo, who was starting his watch, managed to convey that the temperature was −1 degree which, with light snow out of a dark grey sky, was a depressing way to end June.

A day later the weather improved a bit. At least it had stopped snowing. Astern of us the *Captain Khlebnikov* was still towing the *Maxim Ammosov*, yet it was clear that ice conditions were worsening. We seemed to be spending as much time going backwards as we did going forwards. Up on the bridge the captain was in command, with his hands on the throttles, giving instructions to the helmsman. Yuri was also up there, staring at the ice and talking to Sergei. Cape Baranov was visible off to the port side, which meant that we were half way between Pevek and the Kolyma River. It was a slow business.

By mid afternoon we had reached the spot at the mouth of the Kolyma where the sea suddenly became a lot shallower so we were forced to stop and turn round. The *Captain Khlebnikov*, being a smaller ship, continued to tow the *Maxim Ammosov* westwards. Our mission over, we set about looking for some ice in which we would bury ourselves. This was a safety measure since it is dangerous to anchor in an area containing drifting ice. Far better simply to wedge ourselves in a large chunk of ice and drift with it.

Facing eastwards again, I could see the mouth of the Kolyma, that most sombre of rivers, off to starboard. Just as in the West Auschwitz has come to symbolise the Holocaust, so also in the Soviet Union has the name Kolyma come to mean the Gulag. Solzhenitsyn called the region 'the pole of cold and cruelty'.

Set up in the early 1930s with the dual objective of mining the local gold and providing a receptacle for Stalin's first great purge, the camps of the Kolyma soon degenerated into primitive killing machines for the endless stream of prisoners who were brought by ship from Vladivostock. Robert Conquest has estimated that the camps of the Kolyma alone killed at least three million people.

The sea was a muddy brown, just as it had been at the mouths of the Ob, Lena and Yenisei. The low hills along the shore were largely hidden by clouds, and some snow still stood in the north-facing gullies. It was a bleak picture. For the first time I felt a bit homesick.

We eventually found a cosy nesting place in the ice and stopped, surrounded by white snow and green puddles of meltwater. Sergei Tomilin, his moustache even droopier than usual, came into my cabin while I was watching the gulls eat the biscuit I had thrown to them.

'Well,' he said lugubriously, 'what did you think of our work just now?'

I didn't understand what he meant.

'Ninety-five thousand horsepower. Ninety-five thousand horsepower.'

I still did not understand.

'Think about,' he said, 'we needed both *Arktika* and *Captain Khlebnikov* to break the ice for that tiny little load of timber. Do you really think that made sense?'

I agreed that it had already occurred to me that it was a mite extravagant using two icebreakers for one little coaster.

'But that's our system in the Soviet Union,' he said, putting his index finger to his temple and twisting it. 'Crazy. Unbelievable.'

'It may have seemed silly to you,' said the captain when I taxed him, 'but you were probably asleep last night when even we found that we couldn't get through a hummock which was at least five metres deep. It was a very difficult situation. Now of course *Captain Khlebnikov* could have managed by herself, but it would have taken a very long time and have been very expensive.'

I remained unconvinced.

Some bad news emerged later that afternoon while we were sitting around between saunas. Alexander revealed that the ship we are waiting for from the Kolyma wouldn't be ready for another four days, so *Arktika* would either spend the time sitting in the ice, or we would be given another job by the office in Pevek. Either way it was turning into a long wait.

In Maxim's cabin with Yuri and Alexander, I turned

down some vicious distillation which Yuri offered from an old Martell cognac bottle. After forty-eight hours the idea of alcohol still made me feel sick.

Over tea I asked Valerii Mikhailovich about the Gulag Archipelago. He wasn't keen to talk about it, protesting that he had never seen it for himself, but eventually he did tell me a bit about the Kolyma. There weren't, it seemed, any camps in our immediate area along the coast.

'The nearest one was Pevek itself,' he explained. 'The town was built as the regional headquarters of Dalstroy[2] and also as a transit camp where some of the prisoners were landed when they had arrived from Vladivostock. The rest were taken along the coast to Ambarchik at the mouth of the Kolyma.'

I wondered if any of the old camp buildings still remained in Pevek.

'Not many, but there are two hospitals for the native Chukchi people which were once part of the camp. Almost everything else has either fallen down or been destroyed. Don't forget,' he continued, 'the Gulag stopped a few years after Stalin's death in 1953, and there've been almost forty years since then.'

The air that day was almost warm, the sun bright and the sea level and white. It could have illustrated a tourist poster. A month later when I had returned home, I looked up 'Kolyma' in *The Gulag Archipelago*.

'I almost left Kolyma out of the book,' wrote Solzhenitsyn. 'Kolyma was a whole separate continent of the Archipelago and it deserves its own separate histories.' He went on to reprint the following eye-witness account of a Kolyma camp.

[2] The Far Eastern Construction Trust, an arm of the NKVD, was based in Magadan and operated all the prison camps in a territory four times bigger than France.

For many months there day and night, at the morning and the evening checks, innumerable execution orders were read out. In a temperature of fifty below zero the musicians from among the non-political offenders played a flourish before and after each order was read. The smoking gasoline torches ripped apart the darkness. . . . The thin sheet on which the order was written was covered with hoarfrost, and some chief or other who was reading the order would brush the snowflakes from it with his sleeve so as to decipher and shout out the name of the next man on the list to be shot.

Loitering around the bridge, waiting for a cable from Pevek about my transport arrangements, I was asked a question by Sergei.

'Would you like to photograph one of these charts with the orange corners?'

Since my camera was with me, I said, 'Yes please.'

This was not the reply he had been expecting.

'No,' he giggled, 'I was only joking. They're classified and you mustn't.'

Would he, I wondered, be sent to the Gulag if I published a photograph of him with a classified chart?

'No, not the Gulag any more, but I'd certainly have problems even though things have changed a lot these days.'

Was there a KGB man on board *Arktika*?

'I simply don't know,' replied Sergei. 'It's always a possibility. When I was working in the Baltic on the icebreaker *Dikson* I knew of two KGB men on board. One was the third mate.'

I assumed that even then the KGB was still not absolutely dormant and that there must have been a representative on *Arktika*. I wondered who it might be. If the KGB had any sense at all they would have hired Maxim, simply

206

because he was the most gregarious, the most louche and the least probable.

We moved our parking place in the ice that morning and pushed another seven miles out from the coast. We had drifted into shallower water, which is dangerous for ships at the best of times, but for hulls containing nuclear reactors, it is strongly discouraged. The ice was beginning to melt so fast it wasn't even safe for me to go for a walk. Every time I looked out of my porthole the puddles of milky turquoise water had grown bigger.

Grigorii Alexeivich Ulitin was grinning. It seemed that the poor old *Captain Khlebnikov* had got stuck in ice at the mouth of the Kolyma and was drifting helplessly with the *Maxim Ammosov*. We could do nothing about it since our draft was too deep for the river estuary. The whole episode showed how tough the conditions were. It was the first day of July and a 22,000 horsepower icebreaker was unable to clear a passage for a small freighter. I remembered the old rhyme which the Gulag prisoners used to sing.

> Kolyma, Kolyma
> Wonderful planet:
> Twelve months winter,
> The rest summer.

A message was waiting for me in my cabin. Could I bring my passport up to the captain? This was a strange request, but I complied immediately and knocked on his door. He was sitting behind his tidy desk. If it hadn't been for his uniform and the gold stripes on his shoulders, I would have guessed he was deputy secretary at the Ministry of Overseas Trade somewhere in a Moscow tower block.

He smiled as I entered, and held out his hand for my passport. I gave it to him and he flicked through until he

207

found the visa, which he studied carefully. Eventually, after much thought, he said 'Good' and handed the passport back. 'Please wait, I must now radio Pevek,' he said gravely as he left the room and climbed the stairs to the bridge.

Something was happening. I resisted the temptation to follow him and instead retired to my bunk to wrestle with Dostoyevsky. The result was, as usual, inconclusive.

Eventually I could stand it no longer and went up to the bridge. The captain was deep in conversation with Alexander. Clutching a sheaf of what looked like telegrams, he noticed me and broke off.

'Ah, *kulak*, I have news for you. It seems as if there are two tankers which will be leaving Pevek in the next forty-eight hours. Are you prepared to travel on one of them?'

For an instant I felt like saying that tankers were not the class of ship I was used to, and I would wait until a cruise liner or a nuclear icebreaker could accommodate me. In fact I agreed enthusiastically and made a brief speech about how grateful I was for all the work he had done on my behalf. The captain waved me away, as if to say that he had better things to do than listen to my ramblings.

Then he changed his mind and said, 'Good. I am happy for you. And now it is nearly goodbye.'

It was another of those moments when, just as at the beginning of the voyage, I had become a great deal more sensitive to all the sounds, sights and smells on board. I knew that within a day or two I would leave the ship and never return. I had to make the most of my last few hours.

That evening I went for an unusually long walk round the helicopter deck. It was cold but dry, with a low sun making the open patches of water shine golden. Some of the crew were even fishing over the rail. Down on the stern deck below me two men were burning garbage in the incinerator. Seeing me above them, one of them looked up and, pointing to the primitive tin box in which the rubbish was blazing, shouted, 'Very good. Not nuclear.'

I was beginning to wonder if I should go indoors for a bit of warmth when Ludmilla appeared, looking elegant in a short overcoat and a fur hat. She walked alongside, put her arm in mine and without saying a word kept up the same brisk pace. Like some form of stylised Highland dancing, our progress round and round appeared to attract other members of the crew. First came Volodya Okhlopkov, who, contrary to his sinister appearance, turned out to be both friendly and talkative. His main interest was in finding out what sort of car I drove in England.

After exhausting the subject of cars and ignoring the presence of Ludmilla, who was still on my arm, he asked me what English women were like. I felt like misquoting Noël Coward and saying that they were upright, straight-forward and downright, but something told me that this form of humour was not what was needed, so instead I became boring and worthy, talking about English roses and other rubbish.

There was a break in the conversation and I remembered that somewhere a policeman was being born, before Volodya started again.

'Here,' he said, unhitching the aluminium dosimeter he wore in his breast pocket. 'Take this, please. I don't think you'll ever need it, but at least it will remind you of your days on *Arktika*.'

It was getting very cold and Ludmilla was turning a pale shade of blue.

'Do you want some tea?' she asked.

I wanted tea very much indeed.

18 Leaving *Arktika*

The tea was administered by Galina Smirnova, the ship's nurse who, with her strong jaw and gold teeth, could have been matron in a Gulag psychiatric ward. Ludmilla, who already had a date for tea with Galina, took me along as her chaperone. The presence of a foreigner in the nurse's tiny cabin across the corridor from the dispensary was a cause for celebration. This took the form of two hard-boiled eggs, mayonnaise, boiled potatoes, bread, butter and a smear of jam.

After the meal Ludmilla led me to her office, a small windowless hole lit by two neon tubes. On a battered wooden desk was an ancient typewriter which sat in the shade of an aspidistra. A bottle of Tippex, two blunt pencils and a faded colour photograph of Ludmilla's nieces were the only bits of clutter in an otherwise empty space. Through a heavy door with a large lock were the archives, a five metre long space lined with filing folders. Not a hint of a word processor anywhere. It looked like Hoylake Urban District Council Planning Department in 1955.

On my way back upstairs I passed Sergei coming down.
'Any news from Pevek about your ship?' he asked.
'No.'

210

'I'm not surprised,' he said, 'they're all asleep in Pevek. Siberia is like Mexico. They sleep all day.'

To get to my cabin I had to pass Alexander's and noticed that the door was open. As I walked by there was a roar.

'Oliver. Come.'

Alexander was alone in his cabin, wearing his new jeans – which fitted perfectly.

'Thank you very much,' he said in his seismically fractured English. 'You have given me such expensive an present and I have nothing to give you.'

I waved him aside with a patronising gesture to suggest that I continuously travelled the world dispensing Levi's jeans as he might sunflower seeds.

'Please,' continued Alexander, 'take my talisman,' and he handed me a tiny model of a fat, bearded figure in a sailor's cap which looked uncannily like himself.

I could not possibly accept this symbol which he obviously treasured.

'Do you want to go home?' he enquired.

By now feeling decidedly homesick, I tried to play it cool.

'Well, yes, in a way. Do you?'

Alexander let out a bear-like growl, threw his arms wide open and said, 'Yes. So much. So much.'

Eventually, after all the diversions, I managed to return to my cabin. The door was ajar and on the table in front of the sofa was a crumpled newspaper in which was sitting what looked like a heap of earth. I picked it up and saw that it was a plant with small, dark red leaves which felt soft like those of a succulent. At the base was a long tap root still covered with damp soil.

There was only one person on the ship who could possibly have had access to plants and soil. I knew that Valerii Mikhailovich had been flying that day, but I

211

assumed it was simply over to the airport at Pevek to collect mail and do some business in town.

I met him on the bridge later that evening and he confirmed that he was the anonymous donor.

'It's called Golden Root,' he explained, 'but the proper name is *Radiola Rozovaya* (Pink Radiola).' The plant apparently grew on the banks of Kolyma River and was used by the local Chukchi people as a medicine.

'If you want to be a real man,' grinned Valerii Mikhailovich, 'you take the root, cut it into four strips and leave them to dry out completely. Then you take the strips and put them into a half-litre bottle of vodka. You must leave them soaking for a few months before it is ready. But remember, you should only take a drop or two at a time. It is very strong.'

I must have looked disbelieving, because Valerii Mikhailovich felt that a testimony was required.

'My father is eighty years old and he's very fit. I'm certain it's because he drinks a bit of this every day.'

The Golden Root was not the only treasure Valerii Mikhailovich had brought back from his foraging expedition that evening. As we were all gathered around the chart table he produced another bundle of newspaper which contained five streamlined, silver, herring-sized fish.

'I saw some Chukchi fishermen on the shore,' he explained, 'so we landed and I managed to buy these.'

Immediately an argument broke out between Maxim and Sergei about what sort of fish they were.

'They're omul,'[1] said Maxim. 'Absolutely unmistakable.'

Sergei, who was more experienced in this part of the world, disagreed.

'Don't be ridiculous. They couldn't possibly be omul.

[1] The most famous fish of Siberia. Omul come from Lake Baikal and are distantly related to salmon.

212

They're the wrong shape, the wrong colour and I don't think you find omul this far east anyway.' Having demolished the opposition with this speech, Sergei proceeded to give his verdict. 'I think they are ryapushka.'

Valerii Mikhailovich, who had been absent during the argument, returned at this point.

'You're right. They are ryapushka.'

It was 10.30 p.m. by the time I was summoned to the *chaikana* by Maxim. There, amid the hardware of the Cold War, were two fishes. They had been salted, just like Dutch matjes herrings, and so only needed skinning and slicing across the backbone. Together with fresh bread, lots of butter and a huge cup of tea, we had ourselves a real Siberian feast.

Those poor rich tourists on their £20,000 outing on board the *Sovietsky Soyuz* would have hated the idea of raw fish on black bread. For me it was the best meal of the voyage. The enjoyment of food is one part taste, one part texture and one part ambience. And the greatest of these is the last. Which is why the ryapushka that night tasted as good as any fish I have ever eaten anywhere.

At around midnight the captain came up on to the bridge. He was dressed in his traditional tracksuit slumberwear, but he obviously wasn't feeling sleepy.

'Good night, *kulak*,' he said.

I rather think he meant good evening, because he went on to enquire whether I would be interested to hear a recording of various Arctic explorers which he had in his collection.

I wasn't remotely sleepy either, so the two of us padded downstairs to his cabin and I sat beneath Kirov while Grigorii Alexeivich set up his old gramophone. Eventually he located the record he was looking for, put it on the turntable and sat down opposite me with a luminous smile on his small face. For the next twenty minutes I sat and listened to a series of voices, mostly speaking Russian. From time to time the captain would interject their names.

'Otto Schmidt,' he would say in a hushed whisper, or 'Amundsen.'

By the time the record came to an end Grigorii Alexeivich was in garrulous form.

'Did I ever tell you about the time we spent the winter here back in 1983?' he asked.

He hadn't, so he did.

'It was October, probably the coldest October there has been for the last century or so. Anyway, I was second master on *Arktika*, which was called the *Leonid Brezhnev* in those days, and we were working a long way west of here around Tixi. Then all of a sudden one day we got a radio message. We should sail at full speed to Pevek. It seemed that fifty-three freighters on their way back east to Vladivostock had got trapped in the ice near Wrangel Island. When we got here a week later we found conditions were incredible. A north wind had been blowing for the past month and the ice, which was five metres thick in places, had been pushed up into huge pressure ridges. What made things worse was that on the way we smashed a propeller and had to put into Pevek to get it repaired. As you saw, there isn't a dry dock in Pevek, so it had to be changed by divers under water. The temperature was 20 degrees below zero, which didn't make things any easier either.

'Eventually we met up with the *Lenin*, *Sibir* and a few other diesel icebreakers, but it wasn't a straightforward job. Just the opposite, in fact. It took us a month of non-stop work and we were fit to drop, but in the end we managed to free the entire fleet. Well, the whole fleet with the exception of a single ship, the *Nina Sagaidak*. She was

214

nipped by the ice and sank. In fact if you go up to the bridge and look on the charts you'll see exactly where she sank because I marked the spot with a red cross. I know it's still there because I saw it this morning.'

So ended Grigorii Alexeivich Ulitin's account of one of the great moments of the Northern Sea Route. It was also my cue to go to bed.

The next day I looked at the map to see where Vladivostock was in relation to Pevek. I was surprised to find it was far to the west of where we were. Pevek, it seemed, was roughly 170 degrees east whereas Vladivostock was a mere 132 degrees. The reason was that Siberia sticks out a long way east of Vladivostock up towards the Bering Straits. Vladivostock is, in other words, west of Tokyo, while Pevek is on the same longitude as New Zealand.[1]

My geographical musings were interrupted by yet another presentation ceremony. Maxim and Sergei Tomilin entered the cabin in line astern and, trying to look solemn and ceremonial, placed a rolled-up piece of paper on my desk. It turned out to be an elaborate certificate, written in both Russian and English, signed by the master and senior officers. The English version read as follows:

---

[1] The remoteness of this part of Siberia is more than just a piece of cartographic trivia. A year later I was in Magadan, a city on the shores of the sea of Okhotsk which had been built by Stalin to administer the Gulag. One of the municipal officials was reciting an endless list of economic statistics when he suddenly stopped. 'Do you realise,' he announced, 'that we are nearer San Francisco than Moscow?' I was digesting this information when he continued, 'We sometimes feel we're nothing more than a colony. Moscow takes all our gold, our diamonds, our tin and our timber, and what do we get in return? Taxes. Look at our roads and our hospitals and you can see how much we need. But Moscow doesn't care.' I could have been talking to a participant in the Boston Tea Party.

USSR
Murmansk Shipping Company
i/b ARKTIKA

CERTIFICATE No. 1

This is to certify that
Name: **OLIVER WALSTON**
Occupation: Kulak

received a full Russian training course of the life saving on board the atomic icebreaker ARKTIKA during the voyage from MURMANSK to PEVEK between 13.06.91 and 02.07.91.

The special syllabus contains as follows
- *high spirit keeping despite the cold Arctic winds and ice in summer time;*
- *training to understand Russian English;*
- *skill to smile during the flights on 'ptichka' (Russian helicopter) in Arctic conditions;*
- *tests with*
    - *hot steam in Russian sauna ('Banya') a lot of times*
    - *a hard seaman's jokes;*
    - *an Arctic special vodka;*
    - *Yuri's massage;*

The ship's decision is to admit
OLIVER WALSTON
as a well-tried and brave man who is the first foreigner to transit the
NORTHERN SEA ROUTE

Latitude 69 degr. 57 min. N
Longitude 163 degr. 58 min. E
East Siberian Sea
1st July 1991. 10.00 GMT

Signed by Master. **G. Ulitin**

Signatures of Course Instructors

Second Master	*A. Barinov*
Chief Mate	*S. Sidorenko*
Second Mate	*M. Shumilov*
Senior Ch. Engineer	*S. Markin*
Chief Engineer	*V. Melekhov*
Ch. Eng. Nuclear Plant	*V. Mansvetov*
Engine operator	*S. Tomilin*
Chief of control systems	*Y. Sevostyanov*
Hydrologist	*V. Losev*

I was about to take the document down to my cabin when I heard some strange noises coming from the chart room. It turned out to be one of the nuclear engineers playing a game called F-19 Stealth Fighter on the computer. The man clearly knew what he was doing and could play the game extremely skilfully.

His mission was to take off from the NATO base at Lakselv in northern Norway and bomb Murmansk. There he was, flying over the same landscape I had been through less than a month before. Names like Nikel and Polyarni flashed up on the screen and gave me a strange feeling. For me they were real towns with real people. I suddenly lost my enthusiasm for war games on computers.

What was still more eerie was the fact that five metres from where he sat staring into a colour computer screen, the real thing was sitting in a darkened room. The actual radar screen, complete with pedals, dials and knobs, for controlling a missile was next door in the *chaikana* where I had eaten fish the previous evening. The engineer could have stopped playing on the computer, walked ten paces and started shooting at real American fighters – always supposing that *Arktika's* armaments had been fitted.

Later that day we raised anchor and set off slowly towards Pevek and the tanker which would take me to Vladivostock. As we approached Chaunskaya Gub, or what some Western atlases call Chaun Bay, the sun disappeared behind a fog bank and it immediately became impossible to see the bows. The bridge was then a very silent place. The only noise was the loud whirring of the gyroscopes. Everybody was either peering through the fog or looking into the radar screens which, with their rubber eyepieces, were like the X-ray machines which used to be in the shoe shops of my childhood, enabling me to see my toes wiggling inside my new shoes.

217

Raisa came in with my laundry – and also brought me some iron rations in the shape of a tin of condensed milk and a jar of cranberries. She was all done up in her finery, a multi-coloured miniskirt and fishnet stockings, smelling (no, reeking) of strong Soviet perfume. I pitied the man who was about to share her evening. It would take him weeks to get rid of the smell. In return for the food Raisa accepted, reluctantly, two pairs of tights. Our relationship ended as it began – but this time I received two kisses and not one.

We entered Chaun Bay and the fog disappeared. The sun came out, albeit weakly, the temperature rose to five degrees, the wind dropped and – most exciting of all – I could once again smell the land. It was the smell of peat and moss and bog and earth, which you don't normally notice unless you've been at sea for a long time. At five minutes before midnight the anchor chain went out like thunder and a sailor hoisted the black cone on our bow which signified that we were at anchor.

Most cities look beautiful from the distance. Pevek, however, was an exception. The town consisted of a cluster of barracks-like apartment buildings painted white, yellow and pale green. There were also prefabricated bungalows of assorted sizes. Along the waterfront a line of derricks hung limply downwards, and at either end of the town two factories produced smudges of smoke which showed black against the very blue sky.

Behind the town a green hill rose steeply with a radar station on its summit, and off to its left was what appeared to be a series of terraces, as if some giant had cut steps into the hillside. Far in the distance when I looked through the binoculars I could see tiny dust clouds showing where lorries and cars were moving along a dirt road.

The surroundings were as beautiful as Pevek was tawdry.

218

White puffy clouds floated above green hills going down to the sea like the Mountains of Mourne. The valleys between were draped with a thin blanket of mist which followed every fold and even tumbled over the edge into the sea. The wind had risen just enough to make Chaun Bay sparkle.

As I looked through my binoculars at the hills far to the east, something caught my eye: a vertical slab of rock which must have been at least six metres high. At first I thought it was part of a ruined building, but then I noticed more and more of the same shapes, grey against the sky. The more I looked the more I saw, scattered over the hillsides, some in the valleys and some on the crests. There seemed to be no pattern to them, so although they reminded me of the statues on Easter Island, I had to assume they were natural outcrops of rock.

It was, as usual, Valerii Mikhailovich who came up with the explanation. These rocks, he told me, were the most characteristic features of the north-eastern Siberian coast. Stretching from Pevek in the west to Cape Schmidt in the east, they varied between five and fifteen metres tall. Called *kigilyakh* by the local Chukchi people or *tchuk* in Russian, the words meant 'persons'. It wasn't hard to see why.

The *kigilyakh* did not appear to interest Dimitri and his buddy Vadim, who were going for a walk round the deck clad in identical leather jackets with dark glasses, both to protect them against the bright sun and to make them look tougher.

Down in her office Ludmilla took my letters, stuck down the flap on one envelope because the lick had not worked and promised that she would pay for the stamps out of ship's funds.

Maxim had summoned me to his cabin.

219

'Sit down,' he said like a headmaster saying farewell to a prefect who was about to leave. 'I think I should tell you that you will be going to a very dangerous place. Vladivostock,' he continued gravely, 'was for many years a closed city. Now it is open it is attracting criminal elements from all over Russia. So please let me give you a piece of advice, Oliver. Don't do anything which calls attention to yourself.'

I was still pondering this valediction when Valerii Mikhailovich came into my cabin, bringing a handful of yet more souvenirs. The first was a Chukchi doll which he wanted me to give to my daughter. The second was a book about Magadan, with photographs showing the labour camps being built, and the third, most touching of all, was a tiny ivory polar bear.

'It is made from the tusk of a mammoth,' he explained. 'You know that there are still a lot of mammoths preserved in the ice in this region. This one has been carved by a Chukchi man and I would like you to keep it.'

By now I was so overwhelmed with the generosity of everyone on board – and particularly Valerii Mikhailovich – that I was unable to say anything at all.

I took off my fancy Casio watch, which contained a barometer as well as all the other normal goodies, and handed it to the hydrologist. He refused. I insisted. He refused and I insisted once again. Only when he had given me his own watch did he agree to take mine.

It was time for a final sauna. Yuri did not arrive until I had left, so Alexander played the role of torturer. It was a sad occasion and instead of emerging relaxed I found myself feeling morbid and morose.

Just after midnight the bridge came to life. My tanker was due to put to sea and we were going with her. It was one of those Arctic summer nights in which the sun, still well above the horizon, had turned the sea to gold. I could feel the summer coming in to Chaun Bay by the hour. Some of the ice floes were so low in the water that they looked like hippos in a river, while others, in the final stage of decomposition, existed only below the surface as ghostly patches of palest white. These looked like enormous jellyfish as they glided past the ship.

Over Pevek the smoke from the power station hung heavy and motionless. Through my binoculars I could see the tanker at her berth. Called *Igrim*, she had a white superstructure and a white funnel with the traditional red band containing the hammer and sickle. She looked awfully small compared to *Arktika*.

The captain noticed me writing in my notebook.

'Last words, eh?'

'No', I replied, 'I'm writing my will. Would you like to be included?' The joke fell flat because I first had to explain to what a will was.

The captain outlined his plan of action.

'We'll have to find some ice first, and that may not be so easy in these conditions.'

Why, I wondered, was ice necessary?

'It is unsafe to come alongside a ship in open water, but in ice it is perfectly safe because we don't move.'

The idea of being transferred from ship to ship in the ice excited my schoolboy sense of adventure.

The two ships were not strangers. During the great freeze of October 1983 which the captain had told me about the previous night, *Igrim* had been the last one to be freed. The icebreaker which came to her rescue was the *Leonid Brezhnev*.

At 01.00 we raised our anchor and moved away from our berth in the roads outside Pevek. The sun was still shining and the sea was as calm as it could possibly be. It was a perfect night on which to depart.

The next morning the sun was even brighter, but there was no sign of ice. The previous night I had asked the captain what happened on an icebreaker if there wasn't any ice. He thought for a moment and replied, 'Well, we'd have lifeboat drill every day for a start. And if that doesn't make the crew find ice pretty soon, nothing will.'

Sergei was in a good mood.

'Things are looking bad for you,' he said cheerfully. 'There doesn't seem as if there'll be any ice for a long time yet. You might as well go back to sleep.' I told him that any icebreaker officer who couldn't find ice on 4 July in the East Siberian Sea couldn't organise a party in a vodka distillery.

This opinion was dutifully transmitted to the captain and hydrologist, who were studying the latest satellite ice charts which had just been faxed to the radio room. It seemed that south of Wrangel Island there would be 30-50 per cent ice cover, but that was a day's sail from where we were. My time on *Arktika* was not over yet.

Looking at the classified chart that morning, I saw that the *kigilyakh* were dotted all along the coastline. By then I couldn't actually see any of them because of thick fog, which also obscured my view of *Igrim*, even though she was only a kilometre astern of us.

The exciting event I had to look forward to that morning was our crossing of the 180th meridian, meaning that we were half way round the world from Greenwich and were about to enter the Western hemisphere. This I felt was enormously significant, like crossing the Equator or the Arctic Circle, and I was all prepared to record the moment for posterity until another thought occurred to me.

I live just south of Cambridge, about eight kilometres from the Greenwich meridian itself. Every time I go to

222

Royston I cross from the Eastern into the Western hemisphere and I don't even think about it. Neither, come to think of it, do I distinguish between, say, Cambridge which is an Eastern hemisphere city and Oxford, which is a Western one. Or Burgundy which is an Eastern wine and claret which is a Western one. So why, I wondered, was I getting so excited about crossing the 180th parallel?

Over lunch Maxim told me that the previous night on his watch the officers from *Igrim* had radioed to enquire about me. How much Russian did I speak? Was I easy to get on with and such like. They were, he said, rather nervous about having a foreigner in their midst. I didn't tell him that I was nervous too.

Sergei appeared, carrying two books about the ancient Russian prison, Pavelin, and also a jar of *kompot* which he said came from his wife and should be considered as her present. I must eat it, he was adamant, with a spoon while drinking tea. Up on the bridge the present-production industry was working flat out. Valerii Mikhailovich, who was somewhat underemployed that day because the fog and absence of ice prevented him flying, decided to draw me an ice map of the entire voyage. He was hard at work with his crayons, colouring in the fast ice, the 90-100 per cent ice and the open water. It occurred to me that I really should present it to the Scott Polar Research Institute at Cambridge for their library, as it would probably be the only example of a Soviet ice map for the Northern Sea Route they had ever seen.

The captain's contribution to the Walston Welfare Fund also appeared in the shape of two bottles of Siberian vodka. 'These are for you,' he stressed, 'and not for the crew of the tanker. You should take them back to England with you so you can remember us when you are at home.' After my experience a few days earlier I was not sure I could ever manage any more vodka, but I accepted the bottles with enthusiasm.

By early afternoon the fog had lifted a bit. Behind us *Igrim* emerged into the sunlight. I could see that she had the words NO SMOKING across her superstructure. She seemed very high out of the water, which wasn't surprising since she was returning empty, having taken a load of fuel to Pevek.

It was decreed by the captain that the changeover point would be at 21.00 that evening. I had five more hours on board *Arktika* and was wandering round feeling unhappy and disoriented. It was becoming all too clear how much I would miss everyone, and how dependent I had become on the routines of the ship, with the regular mealtimes, the walks round the helicopter deck, the sauna and the occasional party. I remembered my last day at school when all the boring things I had taken for granted in the previous five years suddenly became special and memorable. It was happening again.

Just as Valerii Mikhailovich had predicted, the ice began to get more frequent. Once again I heard the old juddering noise of floes hitting the bows which sent a shiver down the entire ship. One was so violent it slammed my cabin door shut, and a few minutes later I noticed that we were going astern. We had, it appeared, just hit heavy ice and we had radioed back to *Igrim* that she should stop while we broke our way through that particular hummock. I wondered what I would feel like in a few hours' time when I was in the following ship and, for the first time, watching *Arktika* ahead smashing its way through the ice.

Alexander came by to tell me that the captain was inviting me for what he called a 'Last Supper' at 19.00. I was happy about this as I had come to like the old boy with his nervous drumming fingers, his glasses often pushed up

224

on to his forehead, his twinkling eyes and his sense of humour. I would miss most of all our solemn handshake on the bridge every morning when he said 'Good morning' to me and I replied with a *'Dobry Ootrah'*. I would also miss watching him and Valerii Mikhailovich hunched over an ice map talking intently. I realised I had been looking at a total of nearly eighty years of Arctic experience, and nearly sixty years of nuclear icebreaking.

The sun burnt through the fog and shone weakly from a pale blue sky with a few clouds. The ice floes grew thicker and more frequent with each mile, so that it began to look as if the captain's original schedule of a transfer at around 21.00 would be pretty accurate. By then we would be somewhere south of Wrangel Island.

Dinner in the captain's cabin was a lovely but sad affair. We talked about poetry and Grigorii Alexeivich quoted both Burns and Byron, which he still remembered after thirty years. Accompanied by Alexander, Valerii Mikhailovich and Sergei, we first sat in his office before moving to the living room, where the table had been set. I wondered how much longer Lenin in his button-down shirt and blue tie would hang on the wall, and what would fill the huge space which would be left when Kirov, his horse and the adoring peasants were eventually taken down.[2]

The meal started with the usual *zakuski*, but instead of the traditional mackerel there were slices of the ryapushka which Valerii Mikhailovich had brought back with him the day before. This was the cause of a long and tedious speech by me on the relative merits of different sorts of fish, and how I preferred fish to meat.

[2] Two years later I returned to *Arktika* and found that both Lenin and Kirov had indeed disappeared. The former had been replaced by Alexander's portrait of Admiral Makaroff and at the far end of the captain's day room was a large blank space.

225

The captain agreed.

'I didn't eat fish until I was thirty-five,' he admitted, 'but since then give me a good omul over beef any day.'

We talked about ryapushka and omul, where they came from and how they were caught. We talked about the Chukchi people and their table manners.

'They use knives,' explained the hydrologist, 'like this.' And he put one end of a chunk of imaginary meat between his teeth before taking an equally imaginary knife and cutting it off.

I was very touched when Valerii Mikhailovich, who had taken a good two weeks to decide that I was not necessarily unmitigated bad news, admitted that he had been wrong.

'I know a captain,' he told me, 'who has a notice on his cabin wall. It says "If you ever see a writer, shoot him." I think in your case this is not the correct approach.'

Maybe it was wishful thinking on my part, but everyone seemed sad to see me go. I proposed a toast to the whole crew, which was answered by the captain. Learning from my previous debauch, I drank only half a glass of vodka at every toast. Sergei, who was about to go on watch, drank nothing at all, and Alexander never did.

And then it was time to go. As I was completing my packing there was a knock on the cabin door. It was Valerii Mikhailovich with a long, thin package under his arm.

'Here,' he said. 'Take this. It is ryapushka and omul.'

He grinned shyly and disappeared.

Helped by Alexander, who carried most of the luggage, I staggered out on to the stern below the helicopter deck. A kilometre away *Igrim* gleamed in the evening sun. Both ships stopped and we began to move slowly astern, guided by Sergei, who had left the bridge and gone to the aft control position below the helicopter deck.

A large party began to assemble. There were crew members who came to watch the fun and special friends of mine who had come to say goodbye. Among these were Yuri and Ludmilla, who embraced me with the sort of passion that only Russians can quite manage.

Maxim was in a brown sheepskin coat, looking like a prosperous bookmaker. I had asked him to be the official photographer so he had my camera round his neck. Sergei Tomilin emerged from the control room, blinking in the sunshine. He handed me a piece of paper.

'It is a poem,' he said gravely. 'I wrote it yesterday and it is for you.'

Our position was 69.36 North, 178.45 East. We had covered 3670 nautical miles since leaving Murmansk and my time on *Arktika* had come to an end.

There was no wind, and a low sun was shining on the very hummocky ice. When the two ships eventually touched, I said yet another round of goodbyes before clambering up a small ladder that a seaman had placed against the tanker's bows, which were about three metres higher than *Arktika's* lower deck.

As I hauled myself up on to the bows, a figure in a fur hat and blue denim jacket appeared from behind the gunwhale and, in good English, said, 'Welcome to our ship. I am Anatoly, the chief mate.'

19 Life on *Igrim*

I turned around to look backwards. The ladder up which I had climbed had already been taken away. Maxim and Ludmilla were still waving, but the rest of the farewell party was drifting back indoors. Below the helicopter deck Sergei was talking into a microphone, communicating with the bridge. Beneath me the sea had started to churn as *Arktika*'s three screws crunched through the ice.

The man who had greeted me, Anatoly Shmaglienko, was good looking in a dissolute way, with high cheekbones and sunken cheeks, dark eyes and lank grey hair which came down below his fur hat. We gathered up my luggage and started to move along the long central walkway from the bows aft to the living quarters. As we did so another figure emerged silently from behind a vent. He appeared to be filming us with a video camera. Weighed down by the luggage I had accumulated in the past month, I concentrated on following Anatoly towards the stern.

The moment I opened the heavy sea door and stepped over the bulkhead I knew I was in a very different ship to *Arktika*. The passageway was brightly decorated and well lit. My cabin, which had traditionally been occupied by the fourth mate, could have come from a North Sea ferry. L-shaped, with a small, windowless sleeping alcove separated from the main room by a curtain, it had two portholes which looked out on to an orange lifeboat, a desk with a broken chair, a wardrobe which also contained a safe, and a sofa upholstered in black-and-white check. The whole effect was Scandinavian formica and stainless steel. The bathroom consisted of a small basin, a lavatory which emptied itself by means of a ferocious vacuum implosion and a shower small enough to discourage anything but the most perfunctory ablutions. There would be no more of the two-hour contemplative baths I had enjoyed on *Arktika*. On the plus side, however, the cabin was light, airy and air-conditioned, so the wild climatic changes of my previous bedroom would not be a problem.

I was still arranging my luggage when the cabin door opened without even a perfunctory knock. A short, sandy-haired man with a moustache to match, a freckled face and a yellow T-shirt entered. He reminded me of Captain Mainwaring in *Dad's Army*.

'Hello,' he said, 'My name is Anatoly Achkasov, I am the captain. I am happy to have you on board my ship.' I was about to tell him that I was equally happy when he continued, 'Would you like to have a cup of coffee with me in my cabin?'

We climbed up two staircases to the deck below the bridge where captains invariably have their living quarters, and entered a cabin which was less than half the size of Captain Ulitin's. The room was dominated not by the desk at one end or the porthole at the other, but by a large refrigerator which had been built into the wall. In between was a coffee table, a sofa and a Japanese colour television set complete with video recorder.

'Cigarette?' asked Anatoly, lighting his with a disposable gas lighter. I could see why the words NO SMOKING were painted in large red letters below the bridge, and was glad that we weren't carrying a full load of petroleum.

After a few minutes of stilted conversation about the ice conditions and the weather forecast for the next day, I began to explain who I was. Anatoly's face lit up.

'A *kulak*? Really? You mean you are a farmer?'

I confirmed it once more.

'Incredible,' said Anatoly. 'I never thought I'd ever meet a real *kulak* because there aren't any left in our country any more.'

I assumed that this was a conversational aside, because Anatoly had paused to light a cigarette from the smouldering butt of the first.

'My grandfather was a *kulak*, too. He came from the Ukraine and he refused to join the collective farm back in the 1930s. I suppose that he was lucky to survive, but he was exiled to the Far East by Stalin and my family have been there ever since.'

Anatoly had never met his grandfather.

'He died before I was born. I don't really have any connection with farming at all. My father worked on the railway all his life and, as you can see, I went to sea.' He paused to pour himself another coffee. 'But I do still have a bit of soil I cultivate.' He got up and walked towards the porthole, under which was something that looked like a cat tray in a city apartment. 'It is my window box,' he announced. 'I planted some seeds here two weeks ago, but they haven't come up. Maybe it's been too cold, or maybe I'm not a good farmer.'

I suspected the latter.

'Would you like to see the bridge?'

We went up the last flight of stairs and found ourselves on a bridge which was also less than half the size of *Arktika's*. The position was radically different, too. Instead

230

of looking directly out over the bows we were almost at the stern with one hundred and fifty metres of tanker stretching in front of us. Beyond the bows, far ahead in the swirling mist, was a very familiar shape.

Poacher – Gamekeeper, Hunter – Hunted, Icebreaker – Tanker. Life was going to be very different indeed on *Igrim*.[1] Instead of always looking astern to the following convoy, I was now looking ahead to the leading icebreaker. We were following the channel which *Arktika* had cut. Watching the *Captain Sorokin* and the other ships which had followed us, it had never occurred to me there was any skill involved in steering a ship behind an icebreaker. Only when I saw the first mate giving instructions to the helmsman did I understand how much concentration was needed. Instead of leaving a straight channel, *Arktika* had been twisting and turning to avoid hummocks, *Igrim* had to follow this track precisely. Any mistake and we ourselves would run into the ice wall and have to go astern and start again.

The ice was massively hummocked, higher than it had been since we first entered the ice two days out from Murmansk. The captain came out on to the deck to the starboard side of the bridge. Pointing at the horizon he said, 'It is like the Sahara. But no sand. Only ice.'

Ahead of us the *ptichka*, tiny against the horizon, was taking off into the low sun. With all that ice, I could see why the hydrologist was airborne.

On my way back to my cabin I was intercepted by the sailor with the video camera.

'Maybe,' he suggested in bad but understandable English, 'you would like to look at my equipment?'

I could think of few things I less wanted to inspect, but

[1] *Igrim* was named after an oil-producing town just east of the Urals situated on a tributary of the Ob called the Sosva.

he was obviously proud of the gadget, so I tried to look enthusiastic. Only then did it become clear that he was actually offering to show me the film he had taken. This was marginally more interesting than looking at his hardware, and I followed him to the crew's dining room where he plugged his machine into the TV set. The resulting movie of *Arktika* and the Englishman coming aboard was surprisingly good. It was certainly better than the normal home video, but maybe I found the subject matter particularly compelling. . . .

Sleep is often difficult the first night on a new ship, but that night was worse than most. I had made my bunk with the single small sheet and thin blanket which had been provided, but an hour later I was still wide awake and very cold. I searched the cabin but there appeared to be no spare blanket, so I spread my parka and small bath towel over the foot of the bed in an attempt to provide a bit of extra insulation. Another hour later I realised I had failed. There was only one solution. I got up, rummaged through my suitcase and found the pair of long underpants I had brought for the Arctic weather I had foolishly expected.

Through the porthole I saw that *Igrim* was enveloped in fog. The heavy ice of the previous night had been replaced by no more than 20 per cent cover of thin ice floes.

I eventually got to sleep at almost exactly the moment we crossed the 180 degree meridian, but at the time I couldn't have cared less. Three hours later, at 7.30, the phone rang. It was the captain politely informing me that breakfast was being served.

Staggering out of bed, I looked for my coffee-maker before I remembered. On *Igrim* all cooking equipment, including electric kettles, was forbidden in crew cabins because of the fire risk. The only solution was to find the kitchen and ask for boiling water. With mug and coffee

232

filter I went downstairs, following the smell of rancid fat. In front of me was a cul-de-sac at the end of which were two doors.

In spite of the fact *Igrim* had a complement of only thirty-five, there were two dining rooms on board. The officers were located on the port side and the rest of the crew on the starboard. At the far end of a long table the captain sat all by himself. He motioned for me to join him. On a greasy plate were three half hard-boiled eggs covered with salad cream. Beside them were some stale white bread, a small container full of hot pepper paste from Georgia and a bottle of Vietnamese soy sauce ('Tiptop quality guaranteed for export').

By then we were in the Chukchi Sea, the fifth and last of Russia's Arctic seas. Over the horizon to port was Wrangel Island, one of the more romantic places in the Arctic. Geographers know all about it because it is one of the very few islands in the world which straddles the 180 degree meridian. Naturalists are even more interested because Wrangel Island contains the highest density of denning polar bears in the world.

A polar bear den is the hole which the female digs in a snow bank in late autumn where, a month or so later, she normally gives birth to two tiny cubs which are no bigger than rats. The difference in size between mother and baby is greater than in any other placental mammal in the world.[2] Throughout the winter the mother remains awake, nursing her young on milk which has the consistency of thick cream and a fat content higher than any other animal with the exception of a seal. Eventually, in the early spring, when they are about the size of a Jack Russell terrier, the cubs venture out of the den. The mother, meanwhile,

[2] An equivalent variation in humans would result in a new-born baby being five centimetres long.

keeps an eye open for wandering male polar bears who seem to enjoy eating their – or anybody else's – children.

Wrangel Island interested me not just because of the polar bears but also because it was a wonderful example of what happens when explorers and politicians collide. The island was named after the man who first imagined it, Ferdinand Petrovich Wrangel, a friend and contemporary of Pushkin who later rose to become the first Governor of Russian America, as Alaska was then called. Wrangel must be one of the few explorers who never actually saw, let alone set foot on, the spot which now bears his name. In 1824, while he was surveying the shoreline of the Chukchi Peninsula, he noticed that flocks of birds often flew out to sea in a northerly direction. From this he deduced that somewhere out in the Chukchi Sea must be a decent-sized piece of land. Confirmation of Wrangel's theory came in 1849 when Captain Kellett on board *HMS Herald* actually sighted the island. Eighteen years later an American expedition under Thomas Long sighted it for a second time and very politely named it after the Russian. Only in 1881 did anyone actually land on Wrangel Island, when an American whaler called G.L. Hooper struggled ashore and did what any red-blooded explorer would do – claimed it for the United States.

There was then an interlude of thirty years before the first Russians set foot on Wrangel Island. The crews of the icebreakers *Taymyr* and *Vaygach* didn't just claim the island for Russia, they actually built a beacon to show that they had been there. This game of musical chairs continued in 1913, when a Canadian hunting expedition led by Vihjalmur Stefansson found that they had been separated from their ship and pitched camp on Wrangel Island for six months until they were eventually rescued. This experience led to Stefansson trying to enlist the support of the

234

Canadian government to claim Wrangel Island on the slightly shaky grounds that they had actually occupied the island for the first time.

Eventually the ownership of Wrangel Island was settled by force, albeit the most exquisitely polite force. On 19 August 1924 the Russian icebreaker *Nadezhny*, which had been renamed *Red October* and reclassified as a gunboat, arrived at Wrangel Island to find the straggling remnants of some Canadian Inuit who had been settled there by Stefansson with the tacit support of the Canadian government, and a solitary American. They were all arrested and taken back to Vladivostock. The Inuit were eventually repatriated by the Red Cross and the American died of pneumonia. Since then nobody has bothered to argue about who owns Wrangel Island.

Arktika had long since disappeared into the fog and from *Igrim*'s bridge it was almost impossible to see the channel itself. Suddenly I heard a familiar voice. It was Sergei on the radio telling our first mate, Anatoly, that the ice would continue for the rest of the day and, as a result, *Igrim* should keep as close as possible behind *Arktika*.

Anatoly must have read my thoughts.

'We are following *Arktika* by radar only. It's just like flying a plane,' he explained. It sounded simple enough, but I could not make the connection between a pale green dot on the radar screen and an icebreaker somewhere out in the fog.

I went back to the cabin and tried to catch up on the rest I had missed the night before. But sleep was difficult. As I lay on my bunk I realised how much I missed *Arktika*. I knew precisely what was happening on the icebreaker. Sergei had been on watch for an hour by then. Maxim was asleep and the captain was in his usual spot on the port side of the bridge, drumming his fingers on the rail.

Meanwhile Valerii Mikhailovich would be standing at his chart table, colouring in the latest ice map. Leonid would be smoking in the radio room and Owdoyoudo would be at the wheel. One deck below Raisa was mopping the passageway outside the captain's cabin. And so on. There they were, somewhere ahead of us in the fog — less than a kilometre away. We might as well have been on different continents.

I was just drifting off to sleep when the phone rang. I knew instinctively who it was.

'I have just made a cup of coffee and wonder if you'd like to join us,' said the captain. It was unclear whether Soviet tanker captains always used the royal we or whether there was a party taking place.

Larissa might have passed for Gina Lollobrigida in the dusk with the light behind her. With her bedroom eyes and red toenails, she was sporadically attractive, but she lacked a certain subtlety. She had tightly curled brown hair, a tight rosebud mouth, tight blue jeans and a tight yellow shirt tied tightly round the waist to reveal a loose midriff. She was sitting on the sofa nibbling a biscuit and smiling at the captain. I got the feeling she had been doing the opposite until I walked in.

'Larissa is our doctor,' explained Captain Anatoly. 'I have known her since she was a little girl.' This qualification was, I assumed, to deflect any impure thoughts I might have had. It did not succeed.

Born in Donetsk, Larissa Mikhaila had trained as a dentist, which made it all the odder that she was *Igrim*'s doctor.

'She is married,' said Anatoly, as if talking about a tailor's dummy. 'Her husband is an engineer on another ship out of Vladivostock, and this is the first voyage she has had on *Igrim*.'

236

Married or not, dentist or doctor, Larissa was clearly the hostess. She poured me a cup of coffee and I noticed her long, varnished fingernails.

'I drink as many cups as Balzac did,' the captain remarked, 'which means at least ten a day.' With his coffee and his continuous cigarettes, he was evidently a prime heart-attack candidate. His faintly florid complexion did nothing to diminish these suspicions. He also looked like a man with a terrible temper.

Far off to starboard a low grey smudge against the sky marked Cape Schmidt. Until 1936 it had appeared on all maps as Cape North, but was renamed after Stalin's favourite Arctic explorer, Otto Julievich Schmidt, who managed to survive the purges which swept through Russia, including the Arctic, like the Black Death.

In *The Gulag Archipelago* Solzhenitsyn tells the story of a three-man Arctic station on Domashni Island, part of Severnaya Zemlya. The chief of the station, an old and respected Arctic explorer called Babich, who was not a party man, was denounced by the only communist, a labourer called Yeryomin. A telegram was sent to Moscow detailing Babich's idealogical misdeeds and, as a result, the icebreaker *Sadko* was dispatched to bring the three men home. Once on board, Babich was immediately arrested on the extraordinary charge that he had been planning to turn the icebreaker over to the Germans.

It was at Cape North in 1778 that Captain Cook, commanding the *Resolution*, had found his way blocked by ice. The presence of a British ship at the eastern extremity of the Russian empire, off the one remaining section of the northern coastline which had not yet been explored, made the chandeliers of St Petersburg rattle. Catherine the Great, terrified lest the English might discover and claim hitherto unexplored land, put together an expedition which would,

237

once and for all, survey the northern shore of the Chukotka Peninsula. Catherine persuaded Cook's assistant astronomer, Joseph Billings, to command the expedition. His first attempt, sailing east from the Kolyma, was blocked by ice, so Billings decided to start instead at the Bering Straits and travel overland. A second party, riding reindeer, succeeded in following the coast all the way from Cape Dezhnev to Chaun Bay, thereby filling in the last gap of unexplored coastline between Murmansk and the Bering Straits.

Cape Schmidt today is the second largest port in the region after Pevek, serving the lead- and tin-mining communities in the hinterland of the Chukchi Peninsula. From out at sea it looked a pretty exposed harbour, with no visible breakwater. I counted five freighters anchored off the town, which was dominated by a red-and-white striped radar installation on a small hill. Behind the hill was a range of treeless snow-capped mountains. I tried to remember when I had last seen a tree. It must have been in one of the grubby urban parks on the edge of Murmansk.

Igrim's second mate, a young man called – inevitably – Sergei, who had a round mongoloid face, came up behind me.

'This is rich country,' he said, 'but the people are not.'

Later that evening Sergei Vladimirovich Kyryshuk, the fourth mate whom I had apparently evicted from his cabin, managed to overcome his shyness.

'Are you all right?' he whispered so softly that I had to ask him to repeat the question.

I said that I was perfectly all right. Indeed I was very well.

'I am so glad,' came the reply, a little louder and more confident than before. And then a long pause. 'I hope my English is good enough for you. I learned it at the Vladivostock Marine College.'

238

I congratulated him and found out that he was aged twenty and on his second Arctic voyage.

At supper that evening the bald, nervous man who was sitting diagonally opposite me announced, 'You are sitting in what was the place of the ideological officer, but he has gone now. Thanks to perestroika he does not exist any more.'

I asked if this was a good thing and Sergei, the second mate, who was sitting opposte me said, 'Of course, it is very good. The first mate did no watch duty. He only watched all of us. He also arranged all our cultural affairs, which meant that his biggest and most important job was selecting the movies and videos.'

The bald man rubbed his eyes and announced in a soft, small voice which seemed far away, 'I was the ideological officer on this ship for three years.' There was a pause before he continued. 'But now I am third mate.'

I hadn't realised that I had been speaking to Valerii Nikolaivich Uvarov, the last tenant of my place at table. Instead of appearing downcast by his demotion, he gave every impression – outwardly at least – of being extremely happy.

Igrim's political commissar might have gone, but his memory lingered on in the shape of some splendidly Stalinist relics which were spattered throughout the ship. The crew's dining room contained the best examples, scarlet banners and slogans exhorting the maritime proletariat to fulfil, and if possible exceed, their targets. I remembered an old schoolmaster of mine who pointed out that to exceed a target is to miss a target.

It wasn't just inspiration that was on offer. Information in the shape of bar charts showing how many litres of fuel *Igrim* had carried that year was also pinned on the ship's noticeboard. But the best display of all was the series of

239

glossy black and white photographs in a glass case outside the officers' dining room. Below each picture was a caption, conveniently written in both Russian and English. The images ranged from standard ones of the Great Patriotic War showing heroic soldiers at Stalingrad, to lyrical scenes from rural life. Amongst the latter my favourites included one showing two groups of peasant girls in native costume lined up on either side of a furrow. A tractor pulling a huge plough was receding into the distance, while in the foreground two men in business suits were shaking hands. The caption read, 'There is unshakeable friendship between the farmers of Moldavia and the Ukraine.' The other depicted an ancient couple, he with a long beard and dressed like Tolstoy in a white smock; she with a Slavic headscarf. They stood in their thatched hovel staring up at the electric light bulb hanging from the ceiling. The caption read, 'Soviet power brings electricity to the village for the first time (1927).' It was Ilyich's bulb.

All these outward and visible signs of political fervour were in strange contrast to the captain's agnosticism. That afternoon he had admitted to me, 'We have no history in this country. It has been hidden from us first by Stalin and then by the other communists. Mind you, I am a communist too. It would be have been impossible for me to be a captain if I had not been a party member.'

20 Our doctor

It was a summer afternoon in Warwickshire. I could hear cattle mooing and a tractor was somewhere in the distance. I shut my eyes and could picture the scene precisely. I had been to the Royal Show at Stoneleigh every year for the past two decades. This time, thanks to the BBC World Service, I was back on the Dowdeswell plough stand, hearing all about the latest model with adjustable furrow widths and trashboards in place of skimmers.

I opened my eyes and saw the grey face of Anatoly Shmaglienko only a few centimetres from mine. He stepped back, embarrassed to be so close.

'I have brought food,' he said by way of explanation. I blinked and got to my feet.

It seemed that, like Raisa, Anatoly was convinced that I was suffering from malnutrition. He put down on the table two tins of condensed milk, several bottles of mineral water and a tin of instant coffee. I happily accepted everything except the coffee, since I still had some of the beans I had brought from London. The trouble was, I told Anatoly, that because I wasn't allowed to have a kettle in my room, I could no longer make my coffee. This fact was beginning to blight my entire existence aboard *Igrim*.

'Oh, don't worry about that,' he replied, 'my cabin is just

241

down the passage and the first mate is allowed an electric kettle. Feel free to use mine.' It was the best news I'd had since leaving *Arktika*.

The rest of the evening was passed with Anatoly drinking glasses of a Latvian herbal tea called *Arbata*. It tasted foul, but no worse than the captain's coffee and much better than the Chilo on *Arktika*.

Anatoly was forty-two, and had been a chief mate for the past ten years. Why wasn't he a captain?

'I don't want the job. In fact, what I really want these days is a shore job, either in the office or on a ship around the port of Nakhodka. I hate all this travelling. It's an awful lot of work and I'd like to see my wife and kids more than I do right now.'

It hadn't always been like that. Anatoly had been born and raised in a small town in the centre of Kazakhstan, near the space centre of Balkonur, where his father had been a lorry driver. For some strange reason he could not explain, the boy who lived three thousand kilometres from the sea had always wanted to be a sailor. He did well at school and was accepted by the Maritime College in Odessa.

How had he ended up in Vladivostock, I wondered.

Anatoly ran his fingers through his hair and looked even more wistful than usual.

'Oh, I don't know. You just go where you are sent, I suppose. Anyway, that was a long time ago and my memory's no good these days.'

He clearly didn't want to talk about that part of his life.

It was late in the evening and already the sun was lower than I had seen it since arriving in Tromsø. It was only barely above the horizon, so it looked just like an English sun an hour before sunset. At this rate we would experience a sunset the following night, after which there would be an hour or so of dusk. I had never thought I would be nostalgic about twilight.

Off to our starboard was another icebreaker, the *Murmansk*, which appeared to be anchored. It occurred to me that when *Arktika* stopped escorting us – which would surely be soon, since we were by now in open water – there would be no fewer than two unemployed icebreakers hanging about in the Chukchi Sea waiting for a convoy – or even a single ship – to appear over the southern horizon.

At 22.40 the moment finally arrived. We were about 110 kilometres north of the Arctic Circle, and about 150 north of Cape Dezhnev, when Maxim came on the radio to say that *Arktika* was about to stop escorting us. She would, he announced, then turn 180 degrees to pass us starboard to starboard.

Feeling deeply depressed, I went out on to the small deck beside the bridge to watch as *Arktika* made a slow circle a kilometre or so in front of us. She seemed to pause for a moment, as if hesitating, before a small wave frothed up beneath her bow. The low red sun made her superstructure even more orange than usual as the gap between us narrowed. When she was only 100 metres away, the sound of her whistle came booming across the sea. Three long blasts. It seemed as if the entire bridge crew had come out on to the deck area aft of the bridge in front of the radio room where Leonid would be rolling one of his impossibly narrow cigarettes. I was so busy looking at the faces through my binoculars that I almost failed to notice the two flags which were fluttering from the halyard. The top one, red white and blue, flew above a red and yellow diagonal. It was, of course, Whisky Oscar. I was very unhappy.

Returning to the *Igrim*'s bridge, I found the captain stalking up and down impatiently.

243

'Come to my cabin, please,' he said in a tone which was nearer to an order than a request. 'We shall have a drink. The day after tomorrow is a holiday[1] and then the crew will drink.' He paused, contemplating his awful fate. 'It is forbidden for the captain to drink that day, so I must drink today instead.' From his breath and his manner it seemed that he had already had a libation or two. 'Come,' he said, 'our doctor will be there.'

I was sitting on the captain's sofa, looking at the panoply of fish and other *zakuski* which had been spread out on the low table, when Larissa walked in. She was wearing the smallest possible denim miniskirt and a T-shirt. There must be a Russian equivalent of 'If you've got it, flaunt it'.

'Here is our doctor,' beamed the captain, introducing her as if we had never met. 'She lives in my neighbourhood of Nakhodka. She is like a niece to me. Or maybe I am like an uncle.'

I produced my last bottle of Black and White whisky and was in turn given a glass of pale brown Petrovskaya vodka. Larissa, to my surprise, did not drink spirits. While the captain drank and puffed on his cardboard tube cigarettes, our doctor sat watching a video of some swivel-hipped pop-singer. I ignored both and instead stuffed my face with three sorts of fish, garbushka, nierka and ryapushka, mushrooms, tomatoes and the Bulgarian tomato ketchup which my host treated as if it were liquid caviar.

Eventually the video came to an end and Larissa turned towards me. I could see that a question was on its way.

'Do you like Benny Hill?' she asked.

It somehow set the level for that evening's conversation, which fortunately was interrupted by a series of toasts. An hour later I felt I had served my purpose and, pleading

[1] 7 July was National Merchant Marine Day in the USSR.

tiredness, I retired, leaving doctor and captain to Benny Hill and whatever.

I was asleep at 4 a.m. when we passed another of the more famous spots on the Northern Sea Route. It was at 68.16 north and 175.51 west, on 13 February 1934 that the Soviet freighter *Chelyuskin* sank, crushed by the ice pack. But this was no ordinary tramp steamer. Under the command of the inevitable Otto Schmidt, the *Chelyuskin* was attempting to repeat the previous year's successful navigation of the North East Passage by the *Sibiryakov*. Everything had gone smoothly until they met heavy ice at the mouth of the Kolyuchin Gulf, the same spot where the *Sibiryakov* had wintered a year earlier. At first it seemed as if all would be well because the ice pack, with the *Chelyuskin* trapped in it, drifted south towards the Bering Straits. By 5 November they had reached the Diomede Islands and were in sight of the Pacific Ocean when Sod's Law appeared in the form of a southerly wind. The ice pack came to a halt and then went into reverse, drifting north again.

The change of direction was bad enough, but infinitely worse was the increasing pressure of the ice on the ship's hull. Within a few days it became clear that the *Chelyuskin* was so badly crushed that it would inevitably sink. The crew of 104, including two children, disembarked on to the ice and, having rescued most of the stores, set up camp on an ice floe. The events of the next two months, which were transmitted by the radio operator, Ernest Krenkel, captured the attention of the world. Eventually, after several failures, a series of aircraft managed to land on the ice and rescued the crew of the *Chelyuskin*. They arrived back in Moscow to be welcomed by Stalin as the personification of all that was best in his brave new world.

The *Chelyuskin* was not the only Soviet ship to be

245

caught in the Arctic ice that year. Only 300 kilometres away from where Schmidt and his crew waited on the ice floe, another vessel was also in trouble. The *Dzhurma* was en route from Magadan to Ambarchik when she too found that she was held fast by the pack ice. But her flight never reached the pages of *Pravda*, let alone the *New York Times*. The reason was that the *Dzhurma* was carrying a very different cargo. Instead of one hundred scientists under the command of Otto Schmidt, the *Dzhurma* contained 12,000 human beings destined for the labour camps at the mouth of the Kolyma River. When the ship eventually arrived at Ambarchik almost a year later than scheduled, not a single prisoner had survived. It may not be entirely coincidental that, knowing how close the two ships were, Stalin refused all American offers of aircraft to rescue the *Chelyuskin*.

A few months later, a journalist from *The Times*, H.P. Smolka, was invited to meet Otto Schmidt at a party given by the Soviet Embassy in London. Smolka, who had obviously been identified as a sympathetic chap, was invited to visit Siberia and travel from Khatanga westward along the coast to Murmansk. The book which resulted, *Forty Thousand against the Arctic*, was one of the supreme examples of naive fellow-travelling nonsense ever written. At one point Smolka was even taken to a labour camp near Dudinka and described how happy and well-fed all the prisoners were. Some, he reported, did no work at all, but the camp guards were sympathetic. They would eventually work, he was told, when they realised the truth of communism and the error of their ways. In fact, as Solzhenitsyn and others have since shown, the camps which built Dudinka and the other Arctic mining cities were every bit as savage as Auschwitz.

246

When I woke the next morning I padded down the passageway to Anatoly's cabin to boil some water for my coffee. He had just come off watch after a calm night during which he had seen two schools of whales. It irritated me that I was woken every morning for breakfast which I did not eat, but that nobody thought to wake me for whales.

On the flat deck above the cargo area two sailors were rubbing down the surface with a compressed air grinder. I hoped they were aware of the dangers of sparks down there, because the entire ship must have been a floating container of petrol vapour waiting to explode. After cleaning the surface, they painted the deck with orange smears so that the view from the bridge made *Igrim* look like an abstract expressionist canvas by Sam Francis.

The temperature was a balmy 20 degrees when we reached the easternmost tip of Asia. The point which sticks out into the Bering Straits had been discovered in 1648 when a Cossack called Semyon Dezhnev had sailed with a group of six tiny *kochi* (shallow-draft sailing ships) under the leadership of a man called Mikhail Stadukhin from the mouth of the Kolyma eastwards along the coast. Without compass or chart they passed the cape which now bears Dezhnev's name and, sighting the two Diomede Islands, where they reported that the natives had big teeth,[2] they were completely unaware that the American continent was a mere 90 kilometres away. Eventually, after the other five boats had all been sunk in the stormy Sea of Okhotsk, Dezhnev and his crew were themselves shipwrecked on the coast. They wandered barefoot and half-starved in a region so barren that not even the native Chukchi were able to live there. After three months, the group came

[2] They actually wore bone labrets in their lips.

247

across the Anadyr River, the valley of which offered some shelter. By then they must have recovered somewhat, because they managed to build a fort and last out the winter, which would have been quite an achievement under normal conditions. Eventually Dezhnev's report of the voyage was sent back to his commander in Yakutsk, where it remained undiscovered until a German historian called Muller found it in the archives some seventy-five years later.

The most extraordinary thing about Dezhnev's achievement was that his voyage in his flimsy *koch* was not actually repeated by a Russian until the steel-hulled steam-powered ships of the late nineteenth century managed to penetrate the ice in the Chukchi Sea.

Cape Dezhnev, with its mountain rising to 742 metres straight out of the sea, was bigger than I had expected. On the shore were three white huts, and behind them on a small mound made from shingle was a little obelisk. This was the village of Uelen, which claims to be the eastern-most settlement in the word, the place where the sun rises first.

On the port side Great Diomede Island showed up as a large lump of brown rock some 25 kilometres away. A few patches of snow remained on the peaks of the hills, but there were no signs of habitation. Behind Great Diomede, completely hidden from view, was the American island of Little Diomede. The 169 degree longitude, which is the border between Russia and USA as well as the International Date Line, runs very conveniently between them.

I had been so busy identifying the landmarks that I had forgotten the significance of the moment. This was it. This was my objective. Six thousand five hundred and sixty-six kilometres after leaving Murmansk, I had completed the

North East Passage and had become the first Englishman to do so.

Adolf Erik Nordenskiöld, the first man ever to sail the North East Passage, had a rather better reason to feel excited. As his ship, the *Vega*, came abreast of Cape Dezhnev at 3.30 in the afternoon of 20 July 1879, flags were hoisted and the crew, in an un-Scandinavian burst of excess, gave four cheers. Nordenskiöld wrote: 'Thus at last the goal was reached that so many nations had struggled for, ever since Sir Hugh Willoughby. . . . Now for the first time, after 336 years had gone by, and when most experienced seamen had declared that this was an impossible undertaking, the North East Passage was at last achieved.'

I knew exactly how Nordenskiöld felt; which is more than I could say about the last foreigner to sail through the North East Passage before me, Captain Eyssen of the *Komet*, who clearly had not enjoyed himself.

'I passed the Bering Straits between 0200 and 0230 this morning,' he wrote. 'This trip has been enough for me; I would not do it voluntarily a second time.'

After a moment of quintessential happiness and excitement, my spirits fell suddenly. The reason was the presence on the bridge of the captain. I knew what he was going to say and had prepared my refusal.

'Come to my cabin and have coffee.'

I declined with as much grace as I could muster.

'If not coffee, have a whisky instead.'

I declined again.

'Please.'

I relented in the face of this rather sad figure for whom I now began to feel some sympathy. Besides, a small drink to celebrate my completion of the North East Passage would be rather fitting.

While I was dozing that afternoon we changed course

and headed south west in order to miss St Lawrence Island, an American chunk of rock which straddles the Bering Straits. Out of the window I saw what looked like smudges on the grey sea. For a moment they made no sense until I gradually realised I was watching a pod of whales blowing water into the air. I knew nothing about whales, but it seemed that they all had Moby Dick-type tails which hung above the surface when they dived. Their bodies were dark brown and glistened in the sunlight.

Soon afterwards we entered the fog, which was destined to last for most of the following week. On the bridge the second mate, Sergei Aprelkov, was blowing the foghorn every two minutes. He pointed into the murk and explained that somewhere out there was the small port of Lavrentia. I wondered if it had been named after Stalin's NKVD chief, Lavrenti Beria, or if there was any connection with St Lawrence Island.[3] Sergei didn't know, but told me that the village was famous throughout Russia for its troupe of Chukchi dancers and musicians.

There was, I learned that day, an old tradition on *Igrim*. Every Saturday evening the galley staff took the evening off and the crew sat down around the tables in the dining room to make a Siberian ravioli called *pelmeny*. I found myself flattening strips of pastry with an industrial-sized rolling pin while around me sailors were cutting up and mincing meat to be used as the filling. In the background yet another tape of *The Benny Hill Show* was on the television.

[3] There was not. St Lawrence Island had been named in 1728 by Vitus Bering in honour of his patron saint. And yet there was a strange and irrelevant connection between Lavrenti Beria and the Bering Straits. After Beria's execution in December 1953, the order went out that all mention of the man should henceforth be expunged. In the fifth edition of the *Great Soviet Encyclopaedia* Beria's photograph and biography were replaced by an article and photograph of the Bering Straits.

My neighbour, one of the engine-room staff, asked me about English beer. Was it true that we drank it warm? I had just finished trying to explain the return of Real Ale when he became very animated indeed.

'If you really like good beer you should swim ashore right now. It's the best beer in Russia.'

We were, it seemed, abeam of Providenya where the water was purer than anywhere else in Siberia, and the beer was correspondingly wonderful.

'They say,' he bubbled, 'that some Americans are think- ing of building a new brewery there, to export our beer all over the world.'

I promised I would keep an eye open at my off-licence for Providenya *pivo*.

The *pelmeny* were delicious. Some people had them swimming in the water in which they were boiled, while others (including me) ate them like orthodox ravioli. I spiced mine up with the dark red Georgian pepper paste which made them splendidly hot.

The captain ate nothing that evening. He had told me that he was trying to lose weight, but my dark suspicious mind made a link between yesterday's alcohol and today's diet. I remembered with nauseating clarity that I had not eaten for almost two days after my party with Ludmilla.

The galley staff on *Igrim* was small, at least compared to *Arktika*. The cook was a shy young man called Oleg whose first voyage, and indeed first job, this was. He had gradu- ated from technical school where, to judge by his skill at carving meat, he probably studied agricultural engineering. His cooking skills were equally basic, but at least he was cheerful and flexible. After my second day on board we had become friends, and he allowed me to fry my own eggs for breakfast. The system worked well until one day I came into the galley feeling less than ravenous and found myself

251

staring at the thawing entrails of some decomposing mammal. From then on I kept out of the galley and confined myself to smiling appreciatively at Oleg when I saw him in the evenings watching Benny Hill.

The two waitresses, Natasha and Marina, alternated in the officers' and crew's dining rooms. Neither spoke English, so we conversed in sign language. Natasha was older and plainer, but was endowed with a smile that more than made up for her lack of charms in other departments. Marina was a brunette with pink cheeks and eyes as big as portholes. How she managed to fend off the attentions of the male heterosexual members of the crew never ceased to astonish me. Maybe she didn't. But whatever her technique she was always happy, friendly, willing and sexy – a memorable combination.

Larissa came down to dinner wearing a denim dress with the top three buttons left open so that Sergei Aprelkov, who was sitting opposite, spent the entire meal ogling and grinning obscenely. I too was beginning to find Larissa's dress sense a little extreme for a scruffy tanker in the Bering Sea. I was ashamed to admit that she gave me some secret pleasure. Maybe it wasn't quite as secret as I had assumed.

The fog, which by then had become permanent, was unlike anything I had seen before. Sometimes it appeared as white as smoke from burning leaves, and other times the darkest grey. Sometimes it made extraordinary patterns over the level sea. Sometimes it was low and flat, just above the water. Sometimes it clung to mountains and made it impossible to see where the fog ended and the land began. In those cases the fog swirling around the peaks where it met the clear sky made an entire mountain range look as if it was moving.

That night I went out on deck, accompanied by a

252

Walkman full of baroque trumpet music. There was no wind, no stars, no view. Only the white foam churned up by our bow. Somewhere off to starboard in the blackness were the volcanoes of Kamchatka. Somewhere off to port the ocean dropped away to a depth of over 7500 metres. It was a strange part of the world.

We were getting close to the point where once again I would see a sight I used to take for granted: sunset. The next evening, armed with binoculars and camera, I went out on deck, where it was getting very chilly. At precisely 20.00 the sun dipped behind the mountains, leaving a big orange stain in the sky and on the sea. As I looked at the horizon something caught my eye between the ship and the sunset. It was the spray blown by a whale. I looked again and saw that three whales were playing around no more than a kilometre from the ship. Their tails were like the one I had seen earlier, T-shaped against the sky. It was another reason to remember that particular sunset.

An hour later the phone in my cabin rang. I knew what it would be, and I was right.

The captain's voice asked, 'Oliver, are you asleep?' When I had satisfied him that I was not, he continued, 'Please come to my cabin for a drink.'

I went up to find him sitting at his desk looking a great deal less than energetic.

'I know what you think,' he said as I entered, reading my thoughts with total accuracy. 'You think the captain of *Igrim* is an alcohol addict. You are wrong.'

I heard the echo of Mandy Rice-Davies. He would, wouldn't he?

'But there are some captains,' he contined after lighting a cardboard tube, 'who are alcohol addicts. Not me.' And as if to stress the point, he got up, went to the fridge and brought out my bottle of White Horse which, I noticed, was just over half full. I reckoned he must have drunk a quarter of a bottle since we had our nip that morning. He also brought out the remains of yesterday's fish which, even though they had dried out a bit, still tasted good with the whisky.

We talked about his family, his life and how hard it was being a sailor. We talked about other members of the crew, and he told me that Anatoly Shmaglienko had also once been an ideological officer in his day.

'I have two friends who were ideological officers before Gorbachev's revolution in January,' he said gloomily. 'But the best mate on *Igrim* is the second mate. He is a very clever man. I like him very much.'

Like so many people whose command of a language is poor, Anatoly sometimes had difficulty in understanding relatively simple sentences. When this happened he would use a phrase which I first found amusing before it eventually drove me mad. Instead of saying 'I don't know' or even 'I don't understand', he would invariably come up with 'Sometimes yes, sometimes no, sometimes rain, sometimes snow'. He would then beam hugely as if to emphasise his profoundly idiomatic command of the English language.

It was during one of these sessions that I gave him one of the two roots of Pink Radiola which Valerii Mikhailovich had found on the banks of the Kolyma. The smaller of the two plants had no real root ball and was in danger of drying out. The captain took it gratefully, planted it in his window box and grinned.

'Now we are both *kulaks*,' he said.

21 The Sea of Okhotsk

It was one of the rare moments when we were not surrounded by fog. Far off to starboard I could see the faintest
silhouette of the volcanoes on the Kamchatka Peninsula.
Anatoly, the first mate, who was never talkative, was
particularly thoughtful that afternoon. Suddenly he turned
to me and said, 'They don't exist any more.'

I'd been staring at the volcanoes and assumed I must
have missed the first half of his sentence. What don't? I
asked.

'The whales.'

By then I was certain that I had missed an entire part of
this conversation. Before I had time to ask another question, Anatoly continued, 'When I first started sailing these
waters – it couldn't have been more than twenty-five years
ago – there were lots of whales round here. Nowadays you
hardly see any. In fact on our trip up to the Arctic last
week we didn't see a single whale.'

What sort of whales?

'Oh, I don't know. I'm a sailor, not a whale expert. But
there were various different sorts. Some of them were very
big indeed and others not much bigger than dolphins. And
another thing,' he said as he unearthed a fresh memory,
'you used to see them in the Sea of Okhotsk and Sea of

Japan, even in the waters round Vladivostock. I won't say they were common, but you saw them sometimes.'

Whales were not the only things which were now absent from these waters. The Sea of Okhotsk had once been the Via Dolorosa of the Gulag Archipelago. Ships like the *Dzhurma, Dalstroy* and *Nikolai Yezhov* (later renamed *Felix Dzerzhinsky*), each carrying up to 12,000 prisoners, would shuttle from Vladivostock to Magadan or the mouth of the Kolyma during the long summer months. Conditions on board were indescribable. Robert Conquest's book *Kolyma, The Arctic Death Camps* quotes the following eye-witness account dating from 1949:

> When we reached the women's hold, the entrance was barred by two armed soldiers, but on seeing our red cross armbands, they let us pass. We climbed down a very steep, slippery wooden stairway with great difficulty and finally reached the bottom. It took some time to accustom our eyes to the dim light of the dingy lower deck.
>
> As I began to see where we were, my eyes beheld a scene which neither Goya nor Gustave Doré could ever have imagined. In that immense, cavernous murky hold were crammed more than 2000 women. From the floor to the ceiling, as in a gigantic poultry farm, they were cooped up in open cages, five of them in each nine foot square space. The floor was covered with more women. Because of the heat and humidity, most of them were only scantily dressed; some had even stripped down to nothing. The lack of washing facilities and the relentless heat had covered their bodies with ugly red spots, boils and blisters. The majority were suffering from some form of skin disease or other, apart from stomach ailments and dysentery.
>
> At the bottom of the stairway we had just climbed down stood a giant cask, on the edges of which in full view of the soldiers standing on guard above, women were perched like birds, and in the most incredible positions. There was no shame, no prudery, as they crouched there to urinate or to empty their bowels. One had the impression that they were some half-human, half-bird creatures which belonged to a

256

different world and a different age. Yet seeing a man coming down the stairs, although a mere prisoner like themselves, many of them began to smile, and some even tried to comb their hair.

'The fog will last until we reach the southern end of Kamchatka,' said Anatoly gloomily. 'It always does. You can count on it. In fact,' he continued, 'it's possible for this fog to stay with us all the way to Vladivostock. It's the right time of year.'

He became silent again and I reverted to my study of ghostly volcanoes through my binoculars. I sensed that someone else had just come on to the bridge. It was Sergei, the second mate. He said something to Anatoly in Russian, who replied with a laugh. What were they talking about, I asked.

'Sergei just asked me if the captain has been up here today,' said Anatoly. Had he? More laughter, of an obviously bitter kind.

'No, of course not. And he only came up once yesterday too.'

Anatoly continued, 'We never know where the captain is or what he does.'

The conversation seemed to be sufficiently indiscreet for me to pursue another line of investigation. What, I asked, did Larissa do during the day?

'She looks after people when they are sick,' replied Sergei.

But what does she do when nobody is sick?

'Probably reads a book or sleeps,' came the reply. Then a pause and a giggle. 'But she certainly works hard at night, there's no doubt about that.' Another pause. 'For one person anyway.'

'Well,' said Anatoly, 'there are probably two or three nights a month when she doesn't work.' Another smirk.

257

A combination of Anatoly and fog was not good for my morale. I crept down the stairs quietly, hoping that the captain would not notice me pass his door.

He was sitting at his desk lighting one of his yellow cigarettes.

'Hah,' he said as I tried to slip past, 'I was about to telephone you. How about a coffee? Our doctor will be coming when she has finished her work.'

For once I had the courage to refuse his offer, although as things turned out I probably made the wrong decision.

Later that evening Anatoly came into my cabin bringing still more food. Two tins of caviar from a fish called mintaya and another tin of the fish itself.

'There's a good Norwegian movie showing tonight,' said Anatoly. 'Why don't you come?'

It seemed a more attractive invitation than the one I had received from the captain, so I went down to the crew's dining room and joined the crowd who were playing cards, reading ancient newspapers and, of course, watching *The Benny Hill Show*.

Eventually the Norwegian film came on. I managed to survive fifteen minutes when I realised that my bed was a far more attractive proposition. But before I reached my bed I first had to run the gauntlet of the captain's door.

It was shut, so I slept well that night.

The captain graced us with his presence at breakfast the following day. His mood, never at its best in the morning, was not improved by the arrival of two tepid eggs. As in all the best Edwardian dining rooms, there was a concealed bell under the table at the captain's right hand. He pressed it three times, which brought Natasha scurrying. Without a word, he pushed his eggs to the side and scowled. Natasha knew what to do, and a few minutes later two hot eggs were laid in front of him.

258

On a tanker going for a walk was a simple operation. No longer did I have to walk round and round a helicopter deck. *Igrim* was 160 metres long, and most of this was the cargo space which stretched from the living quarters up to the bows. Above the tanks ran a narrow walkway just wide enough for two men to pass. For half an hour I marched up and down until the dampness and the fog began to get under my coat.

Entering the living quarters through one of the sea doors I found myself in a near collision with the captain. He seemed genuinely pleased to see me and said – predictably – 'Come and have a cup of coffee with me.' Ready for this thrust, I parried with the fact that I had already had two cups that morning and could not really face any more.

'I have a headache today,' said the captain, holding his temples. 'I had it all day yesterday too. I think it must be to do with the weather.'

I agreed, and asked if he would like one of my aspirins.

'No,' he said. 'Our doctor has already given me some.'

That afternoon I actually found Larissa working as a dentist. After lunch I had relented and the three of us had been sitting in the captain's cabin when a sailor, wearing a safety pin as an earring, walked in without knocking and said something to Larissa. A few minutes later I was passing the dispensary and saw through the open door that the sailor was on his back while our doctor poked around in his mouth with stainless steel probes and picks.

I stayed to watch, and when Larissa had finished patching up the molar, she gave me a conducted tour of her empire. The hospital consisted of two cabins, one of which was called the Isolator. Both had their own bathrooms, complete with proper baths. The dispensary appeared to be extremely well equipped, with drawers full of exotic drugs. The hypodermic syringes were, I noticed, made in Belgium.

259

I was about to make my excuses and return to my cabin, but Larissa had other ideas.

'Let me look in your mouth please,' she said, guiding me towards the dentist's chair. Short of physically resisting, I didn't feel I had much of an option, so I lay back, opened my mouth and thought of England. She poked around for a few seconds before her eyes lit up. 'Gold,' she said, looking at one of my twenty-nine fillings. 'Very expensive in Russia. You have ceramic, too. That is also very expensive.' And with a final 'good', she snapped my mouth shut and gave me a big smile.

That night I was woken by the sound of breaking glass. The ship was rolling in a heavy swell and, for the first time since leaving Murmansk, I could feel the waves beneath us. The noise had been caused by an empty mineral water bottle falling from the table. I had clearly got into unseamanlike habits.

The next morning I faced a far more serious problem. How to boil and pour coffee in a heavy swell. Clutching my coffee filter, I went along the passage to Anatoly's room and filled his electric kettle. As I did so the ship wallowed into a roll which was deep enough to send all drawers in his desk flying on to the floor. I was forced to do without my morning coffee. Life was looking dismal.

On the bridge Anatoly was flourishing. He was not only smiling, which was rare enough, but he was also moving with a speed and vigour which contrasted with his usual languid manner. The waves, he told me, were three metres high and were forecast to be double that by the end of the day. Outside, the Bering Sea looked like the North Sea with a dark grey swell capped by light grey breakers. The helmsman, a Volga German called Wolf, seemed to be enjoying himself, too. He gave me a thumbs up sign and, grinning hugely, pointed to a shape off to port.

'Komondorsky,' he said in a thick, guttural voice.

I looked at the chart and saw we were abeam of the Komandor group of islands. In the distance was the faint outline of Medny Island, a long thin strip of land which was mostly concealed behind the mountains of the nearby Bering Island.

In 1725, a few months before he died, Peter the Great hired a Danish seaman to lead an expedition which was instructed not only to explore the eastern extremities of the Russian empire, but also to find out whether and how North America was connected to Siberia. After three years of preparation, Bering eventually sailed from Okhotsk and, after rounding the tip of Kamchatka, he headed north east. By mid August he had reached the East Cape (as it was then called) and had sighted and named the two Diomede Islands which I had passed two days earlier. By sheer bad luck a fog bank hid the Alaskan coast, but by then Bering had established beyond doubt that Asia and America were separated by water.

What neither Bering nor anybody else knew at the time was that the straits had actually been discovered seventy-seven years earlier by Dezhnev. This fact only emerged when in 1758 Muller published his book which described Dezhnev's voyage and was based on his account, which had lain undiscovered for seventy years in the archives of the Governor of Yakutsk.

Bering, who seems to have been a somewhat timid soul for an explorer, decided that the local Chukchi peoples were unduly warlike and returned to the safety of Kamchatka that autumn. The news he brought did, admittedly, have a profound effect in St Petersburg. Five years later, as a direct result of Bering's report, Catherine the Great organised her Great Northern Expedition. In 1741, Bering set off again, accompanied by a German-born naturalist called Georg Wilhelm Steller.

This time he was marginally more successful. He not only sighted the Alaskan coastline, but actually sent a landing party ashore. Less than a day later, however, worried about the weather, his crew and the ship itself, a sick and apprehensive Bering set sail back to Kamchatka.

By then winter was closing in and the crew was suffering from scurvy. After a disastrous stop in the Aleutian Islands, Bering pressed on and came ashore on what he had assumed to be the mainland. It turned out to be the island which is today called Bering Island.

Things went from bad to worse. The ship was wrecked, disease was rampant and Bering himself fell ill with scurvy. A few months later he died, leaving Steller in command of the straggling remnants of a once great expedition. The German, however, seemed to flourish and spent the winter tramping round the island identifying many of the animals which made his reputation and today bear his name. The most celebrated of these was Steller's Sea Cow, a vast six-tonne mammal which, once the Siberian hunters had learned of its existence, was wiped out within twenty years.

The sea cows may have been extinct for nearly 250 years, but Steller's Sea Lions still swim in the waters around Bering Island. I hung over the rail in the hope that I might see one. I didn't.

I had originally intended to take the Trans-Siberian Railway back to Moscow, but as Vladivostock approached I found myself less and less enthusiastic. I had been at sea for almost a month and, ignoring my flights on the *ptichka*, I had not touched land. The thought of having to share a sleeping compartment for ten days with a man who prob-

262

ably snored, had dirty socks and spoke no English meant that Aeroflot was looking increasingly attractive.

As the swell grew progressively stronger I began to feel the first distant pangs of nausea. Seasickness, I had always been told, was largely psychological, so I gritted my teeth and pretended that I felt nothing.

I asked Anatoly if he had ever been frightened. He thought for a moment before replying.

'Yes, it was in 1971 and we were sailing from Nakhodka to Japan, a trip which usually takes thirty-six hours. Only this time we found ourselves in the middle of a typhoon with waves which were ten metres high. As if that weren't enough, we were rolling 45 degrees. The voyage took four days, during which we neither ate nor slept because the galley was unusable and we couldn't stay in our bunks. I was frightened then all right.'

The sea eventually calmed and the next two days passed slowly. In the rare moments when the sun melted the fog, I stood up at the bows where I had found a spot which was completely sheltered from the wind. There I watched flights of puffins, with bills as brightly coloured as toucans, skim over the sea. But for most of the time we were enveloped in the damp grey fog and I would sit up on the bridge talking either to Anatoly or to his fellow ex-political commissar, Valerii Nikolaivich Uvarov.

One night I had, as usual, failed to get to sleep and so went out on deck. The moon and stars, like everything else, had been blotted out by fog, and even the navigation lights were blurred. Only the foghorn disturbed the peace as I walked slowly round the stern before climbing the three flights up to where a small deck surrounded the bridge. I stayed there for an hour, looking into the dimly lit bridge where the helmsman was behind the wheel and Anatoly was taking a quick nap on the couch aft of the chart table. I felt like a peeping tom intruding into their privacy.

Eventually the night became too cold and I opened the door into the bridge, which was warm and smelled of instant coffee. Anatoly rubbed his eyes and sat up. He had reverted to type and the energy which seemed to galvanise him during the rough period had long since drained away. He lit a cigarette.

'I don't suppose you'd believe it if I told you that my doctor has ordered me not to smoke or to drink.' He grinned. 'I have heart trouble and it's meant to be bad for you to smoke, isn't it?'

I didn't want to get drawn into a medical conversation, so I just grunted.

'That's why I'd like to get a job ashore,' continued Anatoly. 'At least the hours would be regular and I wouldn't have to keep jumping out of bed every four hours as I have to on this damned ship.'

The helmsman muttered something and Anatoly wandered over to the table, where he looked at the satellite navigation system, made a few calculations and marked our position on the chart.

'We're going to have to change course,' he said. 'We're just coming into a military area and those grey ships with guns don't like to see us here.'

I was just about to go below when the third mate appeared to start his watch. It was, I noticed, 4 a.m. Valerii Nikolaivich Uvarov was feeling talkative and clearly wanted a bit of company, even if our language problems meant that the dialogue was not exactly fluent.

Our conversation began, as it inevitably did with any Russian whom one met for the first time, with the situation back home.

'We have serious problems in my country today,' announced Valerii, by way of introduction.

Give me some examples, I suggested.

'Food, clothes and hooligans,' he muttered.

Hooligans? What did this mean?

'It means that neither my wife nor I can go out on the streets of Vladivostock after ten o'clock at night. That's what it means. And we can't buy good clothes any more either. But perhaps the food problem is the worst of all. There is no food in the shops, and what there is always goes before we get to the front of the queue.'

I had heard the same story from everyone I had spoken to since leaving Murmansk. The difference with Valerii Nikolaivich Uvarov was that he appeared not to have the usual almost religious belief that Yeltsin would put everything right.

The reason, it later emerged, was that Valerii felt that everything had been going downhill since Brezhnev, and that Yeltsin would only accelerate the process. In this, I suppose, his judgement was actually better than that of the others I had talked to. His motives were not hard to find. As a former first mate he had been a beneficiary of the *ancien régime*, but he was trying hard to come to terms with the new realities of life.

Had we heard of perestroika in England? he enquired. I confirmed that we had.

'What do you think of perestroika?'

I pointed out that if it hadn't been for perestroika I would not have been standing on the bridge of a Soviet tanker as it slashed its way through the Sea of Okhotsk on a foggy night. For this reason I personally loved perestroika with a passion.

Valerii grinned.

'It was not always good for me. I think you already know

I was once ideological officer on *Igrim* and now I am third mate.' I was about to commiserate when he cut me short. 'At first I was not happy, and my wife was not happy either. My pay was less and I had to work longer.'

Once again I started to make sympathetic clucking noises.

'But then,' he continued, 'I found that I was happy. I had forgotten how to work. For the six years I was ideological officer I never slept well.'

I assumed this was due to an overwhelming sense of guilt, but the reason was simpler than that.

'In those days,' continued Valerii, 'I did not have a watch, so I was never tired like I am now. So I slept badly.'

Valerii Nikolaivich Uvarov was beginning to sound like a born-again democrat. I could hear what was about to come out. And sure enough it did.

'And now I do my work like everyone else on board. I do my watches, which is why I am here right now. No sleep for me these days.'

This was the cue I had been waiting for. I congratulated him on his new-found happiness, reiterated my love of perestroika in general and Mikhail Sergeivich Gorbachev in particular, and tottered off to bed. As I turned out the light I realised that in only three hours the phone would ring and I would hear the captain's voice summoning me to breakfast.

266

22 'It is impossible'

Breakfast the next morning was the worst yet. In front of me was a plate of what looked like watery pale yellow blancmange. On it, or rather in it, were some dark brown chunks. And the whole was surrounded by a pool of opaque water. I assumed that this, like the *pelmeny* of a few nights earlier, was a Siberian speciality, and asked Natasha what it was called.

'Omelette,' she replied.

A few minutes later the captain appeared, took one look at his plate and pressed his secret button under the table to bring Natasha running. A few words of Russian and the omelette was taken away. Three minutes later Natasha reappeared with two perfectly fried eggs.

I congratulated the captain on his power and influence at the breakfast table, flattered him obscenely and told him how much I admired his professional skills, his physique, his intellect and, above all, his grasp of the English language. By this time even he was beginning to feel that there might be a request in the offing. There was, and I too was given two delicious and very hot fried eggs by the ever-smiling Natasha.

Thus fortified, I went out on deck and walked up to the bows. There was something different about the weather, but it took me some time to figure it out. The wind had a warmth to it. We were moving nearer to the Equator.

On my way back to my cabin I met the radio operator, who told me that the captain had been looking for me. I knocked on his door which was, unusually, shut.

'Ah,' said the captain, 'I have been talking about you on the radio this morning. Everything will be all right. Our Mr Nikitin will buy you a ticket to Moscow. You will have no worries at all.' I was about to thank him when he continued, 'The trouble is that we do not know where we are going. One moment they tell me to head for Vladivostock and then they tell me to go to Nakhodka.' I knew what was coming next. 'Sometimes yes, sometimes no. Sometimes rain, sometimes snow.'

My last two days on *Igrim* seemed to drag on for ever. We passed through the La Perouse Straits which separate Russian Sakhalin from Japanese Hokkaido. Valerii pointed out the rock which stands half way between the two countries.

'It is called *Kamen Opasnosti*, or Rock of Danger,' he explained. I could see why. The straits were a mere 37 kilometres wide and, like the Straits of Dover, were full of shipping. Off to starboard on the southern tip of Sakhalin was another French name, Cape Crillon. Looking at the chart was a bit like skimming through the red Michelin guide to Paris. I remembered the Restaurant Laperouse on the Quai St Augustin which had been so good in the 1960s. The Hotel Crillon had at least managed to maintain its standards. The thought made me feel hungry. Even a *croque monsieur* would have been welcome on *Igrim*.

We were then in the eighth and last sea between Murmansk and Vladivostock, the Sea of Japan. What little of it I could see looked just like the Sea of Okhotsk, limpid, grey and bathed in fog. Somewhere out there, far down on the sea bed, was another historic site containing 269 skeletons. We were only a few kilometres from where on 31 August 1983 the Korean Airlines Boeing 747 had been shot down by a Russian Sukhoi 15 fighter.

The captain paid one of his rare visits to the bridge that afternoon, and was in a mellow mood.

'You know,' he said, 'you're not the first writer we've had on *Igrim*. A few years ago a fellow captain of mine entertained a correspondent from *Izvestia* when the ship was in Nakhodka. They had a few drinks and then decided it was time for a bath, so they went down to the sauna, got undressed and went inside the hot room. The correspondent may have had a bit too much to drink because he sat down naked on the hot stones, which are well over one hundred degrees.' He paused to let the thought sink in. 'He cried a lot. We had to get an ambulance for him.'

The story reminded me that, like all Russian ships, *Igrim* also had a sauna. It seemed like a good time to find out how it compared to *Arktika*'s.

There are, I had learned, three schools of thought in the sauna world. The first is, of course, the Finnish School, which invented the process in the first place. They go in for relatively comfortable saunas, with a maximum temperature of 90 degrees which should be built up to from a cool start. The whole tempo is gentle, relaxed and somehow civilised. Birch branches are used because they are light and flexible. Rolling in snow and jumping into icy pools are relatively rare embellishments on an essentially low church, minimalist approach.

Then there is the Perestroika School, which seems to have broken away from the Finnish mother church because it was too effete. In this school the temperature ranges between 90 and 100 degrees, maple branches are used instead of birch twigs, and the sessions are interspersed

269

with very cold showers. Communicants of this religion regard the Finns as essentially decent but unnecessarily timid.

Finally there are the neo-Stalinists, who feel they are preserving the manhood of Russia by insisting that the temperature never drops below 110 and can sometimes be as high as 120 degrees. At this level, as I had discovered, you need specialised equipment like hats and wooden plates to sit on simply to protect the human body from the heat. No wonder *Arktika*'s doctor put a notice on the ship's noticeboard stating categorically that the sauna was too hot and that the temperature could damage your health. And a fat lot of good it did, too. Everybody ignored his warning.

In the neo-Stalinist persuasion everything is taken to extremes. The maple leaves are almost whips and the cold shower becomes a high-pressure hose of the sort normally used by riot police.

Igrim's sauna, as I should have expected on a Finnish-built ship, was all pale wood and smooth tiles. After only one session it became clear that it was run on loosely perestroika lines. Yuri would have considered it sissy and Alexander would have hated the little shower I stood under while lukewarm water trickled on to my scalp. But at least they would have agreed that it was preferable to a wimpish Finnish sauna.

As usual after a sauna, I emerged feeling extremely hungry. I told this to Anatoly when I met him on the bridge a few minutes later.

'No problem,' he said. 'We'll have a party this evening. I'll bring my guitar.'

Viktor, the chief engineer, joined Anatoly as co-host. I produced a bottle of the Siberian vodka which Captain Ulitin had given me, as well as a bottle cranberries, while they came up with some smoked cod's roe, processed cheese and the ultimate delicacy, a tin of Danish frankfurters.

We sat round the low table while Anatoly, looking like something out of a Boulevard St Michel café, strummed his guitar and sang in a soft baritone. Both men smoked incessantly.

'I gave up once,' said Anatoly, 'but then I found myself sailing through the Ekaterinburg Straits back in 1980. We had hit a very big typhoon when our steering gear broke and for the next forty minutes we were beam on to the storm, rocking forty-five degrees. I don't mind admitting, I was pretty frightened and, without actually realising it, I started smoking again, and I've never stopped since.'

I never got tired of listening to mariners' stories.

At 10.30 I made my excuses and left the party, with the strong suspicion that, true to the Russian tradition, they would ensure that all the bottles were empty before the evening ended.

The next morning, after brushing my teeth and shaving, I went along to Anatoly's cabin to boil some water. To my surprise he was there, slumped in an armchair, looking awful. Why wasn't he on watch?

'I am very sick in the head,' he groaned. 'Normally I drink only little vodka, but last night I drank a lot.'

I tried to make sympathetic noises: after my experience the week before I knew precisely how he felt.

I took my cup of coffee up to the bridge where I noticed that the fourth mate had substituted for Anatoly, who by now had staggered upstairs and was huddled in a chair on the port side, looking grey and terrible.

On my return to the cabin the phone rang. It was the captain, who had just received a telegram from his office telling him about my travel arrangements. My air ticket from Vladivostock to Moscow would cost £328, did he have my permission to go ahead and book a seat? I agreed happily and the captain rang for the radio operator to come and take a telegram.

The captain and the chief radio operator were both long-sighted, but the latter had not brought his glasses with him and so had to share the captain's. Thus when the captain was writing the cable, he used the glasses, and when the radio operator read the cable he was being asked to send, he wore the glasses. This was communism at its best.

Poor Anatoly was still looking terrible at lunchtime. After a visit to Larissa's surgery he emerged, hardly able to walk back to his cabin. I asked him cheerily how he felt.

'Very sick' was the reply.

He told me the story of a man who went into a shop and asked, 'Do you have any fresh vodka?' The shopkeeper replied that he did. 'Good,' said the man, 'I'll buy some. I bought two bottles yesterday from another shop and drank them last night. They couldn't have been fresh, because today I feel terrible.' A pause while Anatoly lit another cigarette. 'I don't think our vodka was fresh last night.'

However miserable the first mate felt, the rest of the crew were happy that afternoon. It had just been announced that *Igrim*'s next trip was to Petropavlovsk.

'Thank goodness it's not to the Arctic like this trip,' said Valerii.

Why he didn't like going to northern latitudes?

'It's so much more work,' he explained. 'When you're in ice it means you can't afford to relax for a second. You've got to keep following the icebreaker precisely or, if you don't have an icebreaker escort, you've got to keep your eyes wide open so you don't hit a large piece of ice. I'm always exhausted when I get back from the Arctic, whereas

272

Petropavlovsk is straightforward. Five days there and five days back, most of it open sea.'

The other piece of information which we received was that our destination had been confirmed as Nakhodka.

'Wonderful,' said the captain. 'That's where I live.'

We were talking about the trip and how smooth it had been.

'You've been very lucky,' he said. 'The Sea of Okhotsk is usually reckoned to be worse than your Bay of Biscay. You see my refrigerator?' pointing to a tall white machine half-hidden by a damaged formica panel. I could sense another sailor's story coming.

'A few years ago we were in the Sea of Okhotsk returning to Nakhodka under ballast when we met a typhoon. We started rolling 50 degrees, and because we were so light we rolled a lot faster than normal. Eventually the whole refrigerator was thrown across the room and did a lot of damage.' I was just trying to imagine what it must have felt like when he continued. 'It was worse for the chief mate, however. He was lying on his sofa when the television set broke loose and dropped on to him. It broke his leg.'

That afternoon the sun came out at last. On the deck the wind appeared to be exactly the same speed as the ship, so it felt as if there was no wind at all. I spent an hour at the bows looking at the sea, which was turning a dark shade of blue. Already I was finding it difficult to remember what the ice-bound Kara Sea had looked like. *Arktika* seemed to have existed in a different age in a different world.

We were running down the coast, only eight kilometres away from the Zapovednye Range, a splendid wrinkle of mountains which swept down to the sea. In some of the valleys where the clouds had broken, patches of sunlight lit up the upland meadows with splashes of green. The same sun also lit up the cliffs in sharp relief, showing them as brown and red. I noticed from the chart that one of the larger hills, which dropped sheer into the sea, was called *Krasnoya Skala*, Red Rock. It was easy to see why.

The sea was oily calm and there was no wind. From time to time small fishing villages came into view with white houses and small blue boats clustered around inlets. It was the first time I had been close to any land for a week. Once again I could smell the earth and the trees on the hillsides. They smelt very good.

Eventually the city of Nakhodka appeared round a bend in an enormous inlet. It was a magnificent natural harbour, containing more ships than I had ever seen in one place before. Murmansk was a provincial anchorage in comparison. Far off to the right was the oil terminal where *Igrim* was heading, under the control of the pilot we had just taken on board. In the centre of the city's waterfront was the ornate crenellated terminal from where the Trans-Siberian Railway began and the ferries to Japan departed.

I should, I suppose, have found the moment moving, or at least significant. I had travelled 6635 miles through eight seas on two ships. The trouble was that I felt overwhelmingly sleepy and so instead of standing on the bridge to watch our arrival, I collapsed on my bunk and remained there until the following morning.

I was woken by a man wearing a homburg hat.

'Excuse me,' he said in excellent English, 'but I am Mr Nikitin from the Primorsk Shipping Company. I hope I have not disturbed you.' The fact that he'd just woken me from a deep sleep did not prevent me from assuring him that he had not.

I remembered my conversation with Vladimir Yevseyev in his office in Murmansk. Where was the KGB representative who was going to process all of my films? Mr Nikitin knew nothing about the KGB. Either the KGB had forgotten about me or – far more likely – they didn't give a damn.

An hour later we were in a black Volga car bumping along the main road connecting Nakhodka to Vladivostock.

'I am afraid,' said Mr Nikitin, 'that since today is Saturday, I was unable to purchase your air ticket through Intourist as I had hoped.' This sounded like very bad news indeed, and I braced myself for the inevitable consequence that I would have to remain in Nakhodka for the weekend. 'I was able to buy you a ticket,' continued Mr Nikitin, 'but it came direct from Aeroflot and was issued in my name.'

It turned out to be one of the great travel bargains of all time. Instead of paying £328 in hard currency, as all foreigners were obliged to do, Mr Nikitin had bought the ticket for himself and paid in roubles.

'I must trouble you for 193 roubles,' he explained. A quick calculation showed that at current exchange rates my ticket for the nine-hour flight to Moscow had cost £4.30. I said a silent prayer of thanks to St Nicholas for ensuring that the Intourist office closed on Saturdays.

The lady behind the check-in desk was most apologetic.

'Your flight was meant to depart at midday, but it has been delayed for eight hours.'

I crumpled like a paper bag.

'But I may be able to help you because there is another flight,' she said.

And when did that other flight leave?

'At midday.'

The Aeroflot flight from Vladivostock to Moscow is the longest overland flight in the world. What is more, explained Captain Vladimir Homyakov, for nearly an hour the aircraft is out of radio touch with the ground. I had gone up to the cockpit to escape the crush of the passenger compartment and was surprised to see five people on the flight deck of the IL-62.

In front sat the captain and co-pilot, behind them in the centre was the flight engineer, on the right-hand-side bulkhead was the navigator (next to whom I had been squeezed), and on the other side, behind the pilot, was the radio operator sitting in front of a wooden desk with a Morse key attached to it. I wondered what Leonid was doing in *Arktika*'s radio room.

'Would you like some tea?' asked Captain Homyakov.

I accepted happily.

'Good,' he replied, 'I'll make some.' Unhitching his safety harness, he got up from his seat and squeezed past us into the rear of the flight deck. A few minutes later he returned, holding a large aluminium kettle and a jar of tea leaves which he poured into my cup. The flight deck began to smell of tea. I was flying the friendly skies of Aeroflot.

Meanwhile the other members of the crew were passing the time as best they could. The co-pilot smoked the same tubular cigarettes to which Anatoly Achkasov was so addicted, the navigator read the Vladivostock newspaper, the radio officer appeared to be asleep and the engineer prepared for the market economy by reading a Russian translation of Dale Carnegie's *How to Win Friends and Influence People*.

In front of me was a face mask connected to an oxygen bottle. I put it on and turned the tap until a hiss told me that it was working. I inhaled deeply. No effect. I inhaled again. Still no effect. It was all very disappointing.

As we prepared to land at Moscow's Domedodevo Airport, the crew began to put on their seat belts. Where, I wondered, was mine?

'Oh, your seat doesn't have one,' said the radio operator. So be it.

Three hours later I had fought my way out of the airport into a taxi and was standing at the reception desk of the Belgrade Hotel in the centre of Moscow. It had been almost twenty-four hours since I had been woken by Mr Nikitin in Nakhodka harbour and I was feeling tired, hungry and very irritable.

So was the receptionist who inspected my passport and scowled as only a Muscovite knows how.

'I see you entered the country on 10 June,' she said, 'and it is now 17 July. Where are your visa stamps for this period?'

Visa stamps? What was she talking about?

'You need a stamp in your visa from the police wherever you go in the Soviet Union,' she said with mounting impatience. 'Where have you been since 10 June?'

I explained that nobody had stamped my passport because during this period I had been on a ship between Murmansk and Vladivostock.

The receptionist's patience finally snapped.

'I asked you a serious question,' she said, 'and I did expect you to give me a serious answer.'

I repeated my explanation. The receptionist, exasperated, raised her eyes to the ceiling, left her desk and retreated into the office from where she made a phone call. There was another long silence before she emerged looking triumphant and venomous.

'It is,' she announced, 'impossible to travel by ship from Murmansk to Vladivostock.'

Appendix 1 Log of *Arktika* and *Igrim* from Murmansk to Nakhodka

Date	Time	North	East	Miles	miles /day	Avg. knots	Total miles	Remarks
13–June	12.00	69.00	33.02	0		0.0	0	Depart Murmansk
Thurs.	16.00	69.27	33.55	34.5		8.6	35	Open water
	20.00	69.02	36.51	68.7		17.2	103	Open water
	24.00	69.02	39.27	62.1	165.3	15.5	165	Open water
14–June	04.00	69.30	43.18	58.7		14.7	224	Open water
Fri.	08.00	69.40	44.45	60		15.0	284	Open water
	12.00	69.56	47.36	63		15.8	347	Open water
	16.00	69.53	50.37	63.3		15.8	410	Open water
	20.00	69.50	53.31	61.1		15.3	471	Open water
	24.00	69.55	56.11	50.5	356.6	12.6	522	10% thin ice
15–June	04.00	69.59	57.27	29		7.3	551	10% thin ice
Sat.	08.00	69.53	58.25	46.9		11.7	598	10% thin ice
	12.00	70.32	58.38	47		11.8	645	50% thin ice
	16.00	70.32	58.38	0		0.0	645	Stopped 16.00
	20.00	70.32	58.38	0		0.0	645	Stopped
	24.00	70.25	59.21	20.2	143.1	5.1	665	Under way 22.00
16–June	04.00	70.7	61.38	53.2		13.3	718	70% medium ice
Sun.	08.00	70.19	64.10	51.1		12.8	769	70% medium ice
	12.00	71.08	65.18	53		13.3	822	70% medium ice
	16.00	71.53	66.52	54.1		13.5	876	70% medium ice
	20.00	72.42	68.05	54		13.5	930	70% medium ice
	24.00	73.37	69.13	52.2	317.6	13.1	983	70% medium ice
17–June	04.00	73.52	71.55	52.5		13.1	1035	70% medium ice
Mon.	08.00	73.53	74.11	38.4		9.6	1074	70% medium ice
	12.00	73.47	76.46	41		10.3	1115	70% medium ice
	16.00	73.26	79.36	58.5		14.6	1173	70% medium ice
	20.00	73.40	79.47	49.7		12.4	1223	70% medium ice
	24.00	74.41	78.05	67.5	307.6	16.9	1290	70% medium ice
18–Jun	04.00	75.19	79.27	47		11.8	1337	80% medium ice

Date	Time	North	East	Miles	miles /day	Avg. knots	Total miles	Remarks
Tues.	08.00	75.58	81.03	49.5		12.4	1387	80% medium ice
	12.00	76.07	83.36	43		10.8	1430	80% medium ice
	16.00	76.16	86.17	41.6		10.4	1471	80% medium ice
	20.00	76.05	88.27	33.1		8.3	1504	80% medium ice
	24.00	76.15	89.10	35.2	249.4	8.8	1540	80% medium ice
19–Jun	04.00	76.14	89.37	6.7		1.7	1546	Fast ice (thick)
Wed.	08.00	76.14	90.11	9.8		2.5	1556	Fast ice (thick)
	12.00	76.14	90.45	6.5		1.6	1563	Fast ice (thick)
	16.00	76.16	91.11	6.8		1.7	1569	Fast ice (thick)
	20.00	76.13	91.31	6.5		1.6	1576	Fast ice (thick)
	24.00	76.09	91.57	6.2	42.5	1.6	1582	Fast ice (thick)
20–Jun	04.00	76.08	92.20	7.2		1.8	1589	Fast ice (thick)
Thurs.	08.00	76.10	92.54	8.6		2.2	1598	Fast ice (thick)
	12.00	76.10	93.34	9.2		2.3	1607	Fast ice (thick)
	16.00	76.16	94.36	16		4.0	1623	Fast ice (thick)
	20.00	76.20	95.16	8.4		2.1	1632	Fast ice (thick)
	24.00	76.23	95.55	9.5	58.9	2.4	1641	Fast ice (thick)
21–Jun	04.00	76.24	95.58	9		2.3	1650	Fast ice (thick)
Fri.	08.00	76.27	97.13	8.7		2.2	1659	Stopped at 07.30. Fast ice
	12.00	76.27	97.13	0		0.0	1659	Stopped to service engine
	16.00	76.27	97.13	0		0.0	1659	Stopped to service engine
	20.00	76.27	97.13	0		0.0	1659	Stopped to service engine
	24.00	76.24	97.21	3	20.7	0.8	1662	Fast ice
22–Jun	04.00	76.33	98.18	15		3.8	1677	Fast ice
Sat.	08.00	76.36	98.40	10.2		2.6	1687	Fast ice
	12.00	76.36	99.22	10.2		2.6	1697	Fast ice
	16.00	76.39	99.50	8.8		2.2	1706	Fast ice
	20.00	76.46	100.18	10.1		2.5	1716	Fast ice
	24.00	76.57	100.45	8.2	62.5	2.1	1724	Fast ice 2.2 m thick
23–Jun	04.00	76.59	100.50	7.7		1.9	1732	Fast ice 2.2 m thick
Sun.	08.00	77.07	101.03	8.3		2.1	1740	Fast ice 2.2 m thick
	12.00	77.16	101.26	10.5		2.6	1751	Fast ice 2.2 m thick
	16.00	77.26	101.56	10.8		2.7	1762	Fast ice. More puddles
	20.00	77.34	102.33	12.5		3.1	1774	Fast ice. More puddles
	24.00	77.41	104.30	4.5	54.3	1.1	1779	Stopped 2 hours
24–Jun	04.00	77.44	104.52	14.7		3.7	1793	Cape Chelyuskin 02.00
Mon.	08.00	77.44	106.13	17.5		4.4	1811	Fast ice 1.8 m thick
	12.00	77.41	106.30	4.5		1.1	1815	Stopped 09.40
	16.00	77.41	106.30	0		0.0	1815	Stopped. Service engines
	20.00	77.41	106.46	3.4		0.9	1819	Started 18.00. Fast ice
	24.00	77.11	110.07	55.3	95.4	13.8	1874	Open water at 20.50
25–Jun	04.00	76.25	113.58	72.1		18.0	1946	Some ice
Tues.	08.00	75.53	116.20	56.5		14.1	2003	80% ice 1.2 metres. Fog
	12.00	75.17	118.43	58		14.5	2061	80% ice 1.2 metres. Fog
	16.00	75.05	121.30	44.2		11.1	2105	80% ice 1.2 metres. Fog

Date	Time	North	East	Miles	miles/day	Avg. knots	Total miles	Remarks
	20.00	75.02	125.38	66.6		16.7	2171	Open water
	24.00	76.04	129.46	67.1	364.5	16.8	2238	10% ice
26–Jun	04.00	76.10	133.30	73.8		18.5	2312	Open water
Wed.	08.00	76.37	138.06	70		17.5	2382	Open water
	12.00	76.25	143.06	76		19.0	2458	Open water
	16.00	76.00	147.42	72.3		18.1	2531	Open water
	20.00	75.46	152.38	73.2		18.3	2604	10% ice
	24.00	74.55	155.34	72.5	437.8	18.1	2676	10% thin ice
27–Jun	04.00	74.76	156.12	42		10.5	2718	70% old Canadian pack
Thurs.	08.00	73.53	156.29	25		6.3	2743	70% old Canadian pack
	12.00	73.31	157.21	29.5		7.4	2773	70% old Canadian pack
	16.00	73.09	158.27	30.6		7.7	2803	70% old Canadian pack
	20.00	72.28	159.21	45		11.3	2848	70% old Canadian pack
	24.00	72.09	161.06	34	206.1	8.5	2882	70% old Canadian pack
28–Jun	04.00	71.57	162.48	34.9		8.7	2917	80% 2 year ice. 1 metre+
Fri.	08.00	71.38	164.22	35		8.8	2952	80% 2 year ice. 1 metre+
	12.00	71.24	165.28	25		6.3	2977	80% 2 year ice. 1 metre+
	16.00	71.08	167.26	42.6		10.7	3020	60% 2 year ice. 1 metre+
	20.00	70.29	169.45	63.3		15.8	3083	Open water
	24.00	70.01	170.34	23.5	224.3	5.9	3107	Drop anchor Pevek. 22.02
29–Jun	04.00	70.01	170.34	0		0.0	3107	Stationary
Sat.	08.00	70.15	169.09	30.07		7.5	3137	Sailed 05.50
	12.00	70.15	168.23	14.8		3.7	3151	Waiting for convoy 12.00
	16.00	70.15	168.23	0		0.0	3151	Stationary
	20.00	70.15	168.23	0		0.0	3151	Stationary
	24.00	70.15	168.23	0	44.87	0.0	3151	Stationary
30–Jun	04.00	69.58	167.31	21.8		5.5	3173	Sailed at 03.00
Sun.	08.00	69.41	165.54	41.8		10.5	3215	Fast 2nd yr ice 1.6m
	12.00	69.50	167.38	29		7.3	3244	Fast 2nd yr ice 1.6m
	16.00	69.51	163.26	38.4		9.6	3282	Escort completed 15.30
	20.00	69.57	164.03	0		0.0	3282	Stationary. Kolyma River
	24.00	69.57	164.03	0	131	0.0	3282	Stationary. Kolyma River
1–Jul	04.00	69.57	164.03	0		0.0	3282	Stationary. Kolyma River
Mon.	08.00	69.57	164.03	0		0.0	3282	Moved parking pl. 08.00
	12.00	69.57	164.14	7		1.8	3289	Stationary. Kolyma River
	16.00	69.57	164.14	0		0.0	3289	Stationary. Kolyma River
	20.00	69.57	164.14	0		0.0	3289	Stationary. Kolyma River
	24.00	69.57	164.14	0	7	0.0	3289	Stationary. Kolyma River
2–Jul	04.00	69.57	164.14	0		0.0	3289	Stationary. Kolyma River
Tues.	08.00	69.52	164.03	10.5		2.6	3300	Moved parking pl. 06.50
	12.00	69.52	164.03	0		0.0	3300	Stationary. Sailed 12.00
	16.00	69.41	166.02	45		11.3	3345	60% ice 1 metre deep
	20.00	70.06	168.02	51.1		12.8	3396	Open water
	24.00	70.00	170.28	59	165.6	14.8	3455	Anchor Pevek

Date	Time	North	East	Miles	miles /day	Avg. knots	Total miles	Remarks
3–Jul	04.00	70.00	170.28	0		0.0	3455	Stationary
Wed.	08.00	70.00	170.28	0		0.0	3455	Stationary
	12.00	69.54	170.19	15.4		3.9	3470	08.40 up anchor
	16.00	69.54	170.19	0		0.0	3470	Anchored 10.15
	20.00	69.54	170.19	0		0.0	3470	Stationary
	24.00	69.54	170.19	0	15.4	0.0	3470	Stationary
4–Jul	04.00	70.15	170.37	18.5		4.6	3489	Sailed 01.00
Thurs.	08.00	70.09	173.04	49.8		12.5	3539	Open water
	12.00	70.05	176.26	48.5		12.1	3587	Open water
	16.00	69.47	177.16	44.5		11.1	3632	20% ice
	20.00	69.36	178.39	30.9		7.7	3663	70% ice
	21.00	69.36	178.57	7.2		1.8	3670	20.41 *Arktika* stops
	24.00	69.34	179.20	20.2	201.1		3690	21.21 *Igrim* starts
5–Jul	04.00	69.25	179.25	17.8		4.5	3708	90% ice
		North	West					
Fri.	08.00	69.12	179.51	15.5		3.9	3723	90% ice
	12.00	68.53	179.04	29.6		7.4	3753	50% ice
	16.00	68.26	177.20	47.3		11.8	3800	10% ice
	20.00	68.02	176.30	44.6		11.2	3845	10% ice
	24.00	67.47	173.40	44.1	198.9	11.0	3889	*Arktika* departs 22.45
6–Jul	04.00	67.27	171.28	52.5		13.1	3941	Open water. Calm
Sat.	08.00	66.51	170.10	50.6		12.7	3992	Dead calm. Sunny
	12.00	66.05	169.30	53.7		13.4	4046	Pass Arctic Circle 09.35
	16.00	65.15	170.41	58		14.5	4104	Cape Dezhnev 12.05
	20.00	64.25	171.90	57.9		14.5	4162	Sunset 20.00. Bering Sea
	24.00	63.56	173.24	54	326.7	13.5	4216	Calm. Foggy
7–Jul	04.00	63.26	175.27	58		14.5	4274	Calm. Clear
Sun.	08.00	62.55	177.22	61		15.3	4335	Calm. Occasional fog
	12.00	62.26	179.11	58.1		14.5	4393	Fog
		North	East					
	16.00	61.59	179.04	57.8		14.5	4451	Cross 180 deg at 13.55
	20.00	61.29	177.23	57.1		14.3	4508	Fog
	24.00	61.58	175.35	61	353	15.3	4569	Fog
8–Jul	04.00	60.27	173.45	62.6		15.7	4631	Fog cleared 05.00
Mon.	08.00	59.56	172.04	59		14.8	4690	Fog
	12.00	59.23	170.31	61.3		15.3	4752	Fog. Slight swell
	16.00	58.47	168.57	61.3		15.3	4813	Clear. Some whitecaps
	20.00	58.18	167.09	60		15.0	4873	Slightly rougher. No fog
	24.00	57.31	166.02	59.6	363.8	14.9	4932	Medium swell
9–Jul	04.00	56.45	164.54	58.8		14.7	4991	Heavy swell. 3 m waves
Tues.	08.00	55.56	163.46	61.9		15.5	5053	Heavy swell. 3 m waves
	12.00	54.04	162.54	62.1		15.5	5115	Heavy swell. 3 m waves
	16.00	54.15	161.58	58.7		14.7	5174	Heavy swell. 3 m waves
	20.00	53.42	160.59	61		15.3	5235	Mod. swell. 2 m waves
	24.00	52.26	160.26	61.4	363.9	15.4	5296	Mod. swell. 2 m waves

Date	Time	North	East	Miles	miles /day	Avg. knots	Total miles	Remarks
10–Jul	04.00	51.41	159.28	64.2		16.1	5361	Slight swell. 1 m waves
Wed.	08.00	51.04	158.00	62.3		15.6	5423	Slight swell. 1 m waves
	12.00	50.24	156.46	62.5		15.6	5485	Slight swell. Fog
	16.00	49.49	155.30	63.3		15.8	5549	Calm. Fog
	20.00	50.50	154.03	66		16.5	5615	Kurile Straits. Calm. Fog
	24.00	49.42	152.34	60.3	378.6	15.1	5675	Sea of Okhotsk. Calm
11–Jul	04.00	49.11	151.17	60.6		15.2	5736	Calm
Thurs.	08.00	48.42	150.01	58.3		14.6	5794	Calm
	12.00	48.09	148.38	63		15.8	5857	Calm
	16.00	47.41	147.21	59.5		14.9	5916	Calm. Fog
	20.00	47.11	146.04	60		15.0	5976	Calm. Fog
	24.00	46.31	144.51	59	360.4	14.8	6035	Calm
12–Jul	04.00	46.06	143.40	61		15.3	6096	Calm
Fri.	08.00	45.50	142.13	62.5		15.6	6159	Laperouse Straits. Fog
	12.00	45.53	140.52	60		15.0	6219	Japan Sea. Fog
	16.00	45.25	139.34	59.6		14.9	6278	Sunny, calm
	20.00	44.15	138.19	61.3		15.3	6340	Calm
	24.00	44.23	137.08	61	365.4	15.2	6401	Calm
13–Jul	04.00	43.50	135.56	62.3		15.6	6463	Calm
Sat.	08.00	43.13	134.44	65		16.2	6528	Dead calm. Sunny
	12.00	42.54	133.21	62.7		15.6	6590	Calm
	16.00	42.46	133.51	44		11	6635	Alongside wharf 15.21
	20.00					0.0		
	24.00					0.0		

MILES FROM MURMANSK   6635

Appendix 2   Crew List

Ulitin, Grigorii	Master
Barinov, Alexander	2nd Master
Kulikof, Vladimir	1st Chief Mate
Sidorenko, Sergei	2nd Chief Mate
Shumilov, Maxim	2nd Mate
Cherepukhin, Andrei	4th Mate
Losef, Alexander	Fire Control Systems
Losef, Valerii	Hydrologist
Lushney, Stepan	Boatswain
Ignatev, Sergei	Chief Sailor
Popov, Nikolai	Chief Sailor
Lobinstev, Sergei	Sailor
Kolokolov, Valerii	Sailor
Shegera, Nikolai	Sailor
Simin, Vitaly	Sailor
Gorbulinsky, Gennadi	Sailor
Osipov, Nikolai	Sailor
Obrazov, Valerii	1st Diver
Zubov, Alexei	2nd Diver
Pavlov, Anatoly	3nd Diver
Korotkov, Vladimir	Chief Radio Officer
Zherebstov, Alexander	Radio Operator
Fishkin, Anatoly	Radio Operator
Shulepov, Leonid	Radio Operator
Rayushkin, Kharis	Naval Engineer
Kovalevsky, Vladimir	Archivist
Kapotov, Boris	Chief Cook
Myadelets, Alexander	1st Cook
Chernayavskaya, Evgenia	2nd Cook
Kokovin, Mikhail	3rd Cook
Kupriyanov, Alexander	3rd Cook
Burenko, Ludmilla	Baker
Amelin, Igor	Kitchen Assistant
Filatov, Viktor	Kitchen Assistant

284

Kosorukov, Andrei	Kitchen Assistant
Kolesnikov, Boris	Kitchen Assistant
Panenko, Tatiana	Waitress
Pushkar, Oxana	Waitress
Karabutina, Raisa	Waitress
Nepershina, Ludmilla	Cleaner
Vasina, Olga	Cleaner
Fedyanina, Elena	Cleaner
Salamatina, Olga	Cleaner
Rebrova, Tatiana	Cleaner
Burkova, Viktoria	Cleaner
Grushenko, Tatiana	Cleaner
Biryukova, Elena	Cleaner
Krasilnikova, Galina	Cleaner
Skrypleva, Ludmilla	Laundress
Golda, Svetlana	Laundress
Chernova ,Ludmilla	Secretary
Markin, Sergei	Senior Chief Engineer
Melikhov, Vyacheslav	Chief Engineer
Mansvetov, Valerii	Chief Engineer
Kaminsky, Boris	Physicist
Shepkin, Alexander	Chief Watch Engineer
Krekov, Alexander	2nd Engineer
Orlov, Yuri	3rd Engineer
Strakhovchuk, Sergei	4th Engineer
Mikhailov, Sergei	Operator NSP
Tomilin, Sergei	Operator NSP
Kozlov, Sergei	Operator NSP
Shoshokin, Valerii	Operator NSP
Kashka, Mustafa	Operator NSP
Mukhin, Vladimir	Operator NSP
Chepurov, Andrei	Chief Motorman
Garashenko, Viktor	Chief Motorman
Belayev, Alexander	Turner
Karpukhin, Viktor	Welder
Konovalov, Alexei	Motorman
Artamonov, Vyacheslav	Motorman
Melnikov, Mikhail	Motorman
Semenov, Ilya	Motorman
Klementev, Alexander	Motorman
Shishov, Valerii	Motorman
Burlachenko, Vladimir	Motorman
Bagaev, Viktor	Motorman
Strelnikov, Sergei	Motorman
Zaytsev, Vladimir	Motorman
Kovynev, Valentin	Motorman
Sokolov, Vyacheslav	Motorman
Zhelezny, Oleg	Motorman
Vankov, Alexander	Motorman
Kolyada, Evgeny	Chief Systems Engineer
Gorynin, Yuri	Systems Machinist

Susha, Alexander	Systems Machinist
Gridnev, Oleg	Systems Machinist
Tspelyaev, Viktor	Chief Machinist
Ponamorev, Igor	Chief Machinist
Nikolayev, Yuri	Chief Machinist
Rats, Pavel	Chief Machinist
Dubik, Sergei	Chief Machinist
Subbotin, Yuri	Chief Machinist
Silvestrov, Igor	Machinist
Musayev, Vugar	Machinist
Egoshin, Sergei	Machinist
Burkov, Andrei	Machinist
Skalozub, Boris	Machinist
Zhelebko, Alexander	Machinist
Yuzhakov, Sergei	Machinist
Kostelev, Andrei	Machinist
Diamentov, Yuri	Machinist
Svishev, Igor	Machinist
Dubinin, Vladimir	Machinist
Tinkov, Dimitri	Machinist
Grebenshikov, Andrei	Machinist
Popolitov, Oleg	Chief Electrical Engineer
Orlov, Vasily	Watch Electrical Engineer
Krupennikov, Nikolai	Watch Electrical Engineer
Trifonov, Sergei	Watch Electrical Engineer
Rusanov, Vadim	2nd Electrical Engineer
Filippov, Oleg	3rd Electrical Engineer
Nikitin, Dimitri	3rd Electrical Engineer
Petrov, Viktor	4th Electrical Engineer
Kopylov, Vladimir	Chief Electrician
Abdullin, Munir	Chief Electrician
Kobets, Alexander	Senior Electrician
Margiev, Levan	Senior Electrician
Golodayev, Evgeny	Senior Electrician
Malyshev, Igor	Senior Electrician
Stankevich, Boris	Electrician
Zhuravlev, Kirily	Electrician
Shkarubsky, Vladimir	Electrician
Svetukin, Sergei	Electrician
Sadov, Vitaly	Electrician
Kitaev, Boris	Electrician
Elisaev, Dimitri	Electrician
Golubevsky, Vladimir	Electrician
Sevostyanov, Yuri	Chief Control Systems
Serenkov, Dimitri	Control Systems Engineer
Shamarin, Alexander	Control Systems Engineer
Butorin, Alexander	Control Systems Engineer
Mukhin, Sergei	Control Systems Engineer
Grigorev, Gennadi	Senior Controller
Baranov, Vladimir	Senior Controller
Khabarov, Vladimir	Senior Controller

,Evgrafov, Vladislav	Senior Controller
Diduk, Mikhail	Senior Controller
Okhlopkov, Vladimir	Chief Nuclear Safety Engineer
Razumovsky, Leonid	Nuclear Safety Engineer
Kolchin, Andrei	Nuclear Safety Engineer
Vlasenko, Andrei	Nuclear Safety Engineer
Lazarev, Igor	Nuclear Safety Engineer
Debroshtan, Eduard	Nuclear Safety Engineer
Kokovin, Vladimir	Nuclear Safety Engineer
Nedilsky, Anatoly	Nuclear Safety Engineer
Nikolaychuk, Nikolai	Nuclear Safety Engineer
Kormilitsin, Dimitri	Nuclear Safety Engineer
Bulatof, Rafail	Nuclear Safety Engineer
Sabashvili, Vladimir	Doctor
Lazur, Andrei	Surgeon
Smirnova, Galina	Nurse
Albansky, Valentin	Senior Helicopter Pilot
Ivanov, Sergei	Helicopter Pilot
Varnavsky, Oleg	Helicopter Pilot
Shevelev, Alexander	Ground Crew
Mironov, Vladimir	Ground Crew

Index

Notes:
1. OW = Oliver Walson
2. Names of the ships are shown in italics

Billings, Joseph 238
birds *see under* animals
Biruli camp 111–12
Bona Confidentia 36
Bona Esperanza 36
books *see* literature
Boris Gleb border crossing 2, 3
Bowen, Emanuel 36
Bremen 26
Brezhnev, Leonid Ilyich 121, 265
British Naval Cemetery, Murmansk
   13
Burns, Robert 225
Buturlin, Judge Sergei
   Alexandrovich 75
Byron, Lord George 225

Cambridge 222–3
Cambridge Bay 151
Canada
   Cambridge Bay 151
   Carrot River xiii
   Ellesmere Island xviii
   Grise Ford xviii
   High Level xiv
   Inuvik xviii
   Prince Albert xiii
Cape Baranov 203
Cape Chelagsky Mountain 192
Captain Danilkin 47, 61, 62, 66
   appearance 48
   falling behind 71
   men lifted off 68
   offloads stores to *Sibir* 53, 55
   parts company with *Arktika* 71–2
Captain Khlebnikov 199, 201, 202,
   203, 207
Captain Sorokin 47, 61, 62, 72, 199
   design 48
   parts company with *Arktika* 72
   size 45
Carnegie, Dale 276
Carrot River xiii
Catherine the Great 73, 237–8, 261
Chancellor, Richard 36
Chaun Bay 151, 217, 218, 219, 221
   explored by Billings 238
Chaunskaya Guba *see* Chaun Bay
Chelyuskin 245
Chelyuskin, Cape 12, 99, 109, 110,
   115

contacted by Losef 140
described 147
discovery of 73–4
dogs sighted 146
Eyssen's journey 148
geography 146
Nordensköld anchored at 148
requests *Arktika's* identity 147
Chelyuskin, Semyon 73–4
Cherepukhin, Andrei 85, 168
Chernova, Ludmilla 187–8, 194,
   196–7, 209, 210
   family 210
   says goodbye to OW 227
   mentioned 219, 228, 251
Chukchi Peninsula 234, 238
Chukchi people 212, 219, 226, 248,
   250, 261
Chukchi Sea 182, 233, 234, 248
Chukotka Peninsula 238
Colmagro (later Archangel) 36
Columbia University 31
Communist Party Headquarters,
   Murmansk 13
Conquest, Robert 203, 256
Cook, Captain James 237
Copenhagen 26, 105
Coward, Noël 209
crew list 60, *see also* Appendix

Dali, Salvador 13
Dalstroy 256
Dalstroy (prison camp control
   organisation) 205
Defence, Ministry of, Moscow 12
Dextrase, Gene xiv, xvi
Dezhnev, Cape (formerly East Cape)
   111, 147, 238, 247, 248
   Bering's expedition 261
   Uelen 248
Dezhnev, Semyon 247, 248, 261
Dikson, Baron Oscar 110
Dikson Island 66, 67, 72, 73, 151
Diomede Islands 247, 248, 261
dogs 146, 152
Donegan, Lonnie 18
Dostoyevsky, Fyodor 153, 161, 208
Dragoy, Mr (fishmonger) 2, 9
Dudinka 66, 190, 246
Dzhurma 246, 256
   human cargo 246

291

Nordensköld Peninsula 110
Norilsk 66
North, Cape *see* Schmidt, Cape
North Cape xv
North East Passage
  atomic icebreakers in 108
  Cape Chelagsky Mountain 192
  completed 111
  completed by first Englishman
    249
  economics of ice breaker fleet in
    188, 189–90, 202, 204
  first English search for 36
  record voyage 11–12
  second navigation of 134
  sinking of *Chelyuskin* 245
  and tourism in 188–9
  Ulitin's story 214–15
North East Passage xviii–xix, 48,
  72, 96, 106
North Pole 33, 36
  and Amundsen 150
  on mural 32
  and Nordenskiöld 110
  and tourism 188–9
North Water (Greenland) 59
North West Passage 36, 75, 150
Northern Fleet naval base
  (Severomorsk) 28
Northern Ireland 35
Northern Sea Route *see* North East
  Passage
Norway
  Bekkarfjord xv
  Boris Gleb border crossing 2
  Longyearbyen xvii
  North Cape xv
  Storskoog border crossing 2
  Svalbard xvii, 2
  Tromso xv, xvii, xviii, 2, 7, 110
Novaya Zemlya 1, 40, 43, 58
Novgorod 157

Ob River 48, 58, 63
October Revolution 124
Okhlopkov, Vladimir 174
Okhlopkov, Volodya 209
Okhotsk 261
Okhotsk, Sea of 247, 256, 273
Omsk 116

'Owdoyoudo' (steersman) 44, 45,
  66, 92, 141
  appearance 29
  and 'fire' on the bridge 158
  weaving 69, 184, 191
  mentioned 202, 236
Oxford 223
oysters 165

Pacific Ocean 11, 111
Panenko, Tatiana 23, 137–8
Paris 122
Pasternak, Boris 160
Pestchany Island 157
Peter I ('The Great') 261
Petropavlovsk 168
Petropavlovsk 272, 273
Pevek 20, 108, 109, 205, 218
  Arktika leaves 221
  freighters trapped in ice 214–15
  geography 192–3, 215
  not allowed to visit 178
  power station 221
Pink Radiola *see* Golden Root plant
plantlife 115, 136, 152, 192, 196
  Golden Root 211–12, 254
Polyarni 28
Pomor people 157
Popolitov, Oleg 175
Port Arthur Bay (later Lushun) 168
Prince Albert xiii
Providenya 251
Prudhoe Bay xviii
ptichka (helicopter) *see under*
  aircraft
puffins 263
Pushkin, Alexander 234

Radiola Rozovaya *see* Golden Root
  plant
Razumovsky, Leonid 101
Red October formerly *Nadezhny*
  235
Redford, Robert 161
reindeer 95, 112
Resolution 237
Rhodostethia Rosea (pink gull) 75
Ross, Sir James Clark 75
Rossiya 16, 26, 123, 124
Ross's Gull 75
Rostov on Don 30